MW00721061

Vancouver's Society of

Italians

To cousin Catherine
— in celebration of our
families' contribution to
Vancouver's Society of
Italians.

Raymond

Vancouver's Society of Italians

Italians

Raymond Culos

with a foreword by Judge Dolores Holmes

HARBOUR PUBLISHING

Copyright © 1998 by Raymond Culos

No part of this publication may be reproduced, stored in a retrieval system or transmitted, in any form or by any means, without prior permission of the publisher or, in case of photocopying or other reprographic copying, a licence from CANCOPY (Canadian Reprography Collective), 214 King Street West, Toronto, Ontario, M5H 3S6.

Published by
Harbour Publishing
P.O. box 219
Madeira Park, BC Canada V0N 2H0

We acknowledge the financial support of the Government of Canada through the Book Publishing Industry Development Program and the Province of British Columbia through the British Columbia Arts Council for our publishing activities.
The B.C. Heritage Trust has provided financial assistance to this project to support conservation of our heritage resources, gain further knowledge and increase public understanding of the complete history of British Columbia.

Printed in Canada

Canadian Cataloguing in Publication Data

Culos, Raymond J., 1936–
  Vancouver's society of Italians

  Includes bibliographical references and index.
  ISBN 1-55017-188-7

  1. Italian Canadians—British Columbia—Vancouver—Societies, etc.—History.*   2. Italians—British Columbia—Vancouver—Societies, etc.—History.   3. Vancouver (B.C.)—Social conditions. I. Title.
  FC3847.9.I8C84 1998   305.8'51'071133   C98-910606-3
  V1089.7.I8C84 1998

THE CANADA COUNCIL | LE CONSEIL DES ARTS
FOR THE ARTS | DU CANADA
SINCE 1957 | DEPUIS 1957

Maureen, Daniel, Stephanie, Julia, Sophie:
May you embrace your Italian heritage and
enjoy its richness to the fullest.
—Nonno

The publisher and author of *Vancouver's Society of Italians* acknowledge with gratitude the support of their sponsors. The generosity of the following corporate sponsorships was a significant factor in making the dream of publishing this social history become a reality.

H.B. (Herb) Osen, President and C.E.O.
T O S Insurance Services Ltd.
3875 Henning Drive
Burnaby, British Columbia V5C 6N5

T.O.S. Insurance, founded in 1956, is ranked a major Western Canadian retail insurance operation in providing individualized insurance services throughout British Columbia. As a sponsor of this publication, Mr. Osen is proud to acknowledge his company's association with members of the Italian-Canadian community.

Ross McLeod, President
Great Canadian Casinos, Inc.
Corporate Office: #350—13775 Commerce Parkway
Richmond, British Columbia V6V 2V4

It is with a deep sense of pride of association that Mr. McLeod and Great Canadian Casinos, Inc. lend an assist in making this chronicle of Vancouver's pioneer Italians and their institutions available to the general public.

Contents

Foreword

$\mathcal{I}$ am delighted to write a foreword to Raymond's book about the early Italo-Canadians in the Lower Mainland area of British Columbia.

It is too often we forget the services performed by the earlier Italian families. We forget the services performed by our older people and relegate ourselves to our own generation peers, and in doing so, we lose and exclude lines of communication with our elders. This results, as we say today, in a "generation gap".

At the turn of the 20th century, immigrants came to this country from Italy primarily because of need, and the desire to provide a better living for their family. They came to a country which was, insofar as Western Canada was concerned, a practical wilderness which needed strong and healthy men and women to cope with the problems incidental to a sort of primitive society. Some of them actually came in the days of the covered wagon.

In addition to the proverbial problems involved, these people, in the major part, were poorly educated and came from various parts of Italy. They did not speak our language, and were strangers to our customs and to our country. Despite these very real difficulties, they remained—strong backs, strong characters, urged on by an unchanging desire to succeed. They came to adopt this country as their own because their native country was unable to give them a living. Being for the most part uneducated, after their arrival in Canada, they became engaged in every labouring type of enterprise.

They worked in the mines, they went to the woods, they worked in lumber camps throughout the province, they worked in sawmills and related industries such as pulp and paper. Many went into agriculture of all kinds and fishing, all basic industries of British Columbia; all became successful and became entrepreneurs.

In various areas of the Lower Mainland some lived in groups and for the main part spoke their native language and learned English very slowly and very poorly. This was attributed in part to the poor facilities for learning the language in the location in which they lived and other considerations. Today these difficulties no longer exist. As time went on many graduated from manual employment and went into basic industries and professions or business and became entrepreneurs.

When immigrants arrived in those days, there were no brass bands at the stations, and nothing in the way of immigration services such as we now have to assist newcomers.

Men and women of the community met the trains and the people and helped the new arrivals, gave them food and lodging, helped them to find work and helped them to get to wherever work was available in the province.

These men and women who immigrated to Canada were good, sturdy, strong Italians. The came to this strange land, and liked it. They remained here and became good, rugged citizens and to produce in that family a good harvest of young Canadians, now no longer Italians but Italo-Canadians. Because of this ethnic origin, they also preserved a good knowledge of the native land of their fathers, of great men, of its great cultural history and heritage, and consequently felt it their duty to preserve this knowledge in community affairs.

They personified the type, like my grandparents, who realized that although they were uneducated, they had a primary duty to educate their children so that their children might be prepared for a life that was beyond the reach of their parents when they arrived.

These children and succeeding ones went to school and graduated into various professions and occupations. This illustrates the fact that the opportunity was there and that Italo-Canadians succeeded. They earned and brought respect to this ethnic group.

With the generations so expanding into different occupations, the Italo-Canadians were gradually accepted into the great family of the Canadian nation. Italo-Canadian boys married Canadian girls or girls of other ethnic groups. Italo-Canadian girls did the same. Most Canadians of Italian origin have maintained the heritage of Italian culture and preserved it in order to enrich their lives. What a difference 50 or 75 years makes in the life of an ethnic group and in the life of a nation.

Around the time of the First World War, Vancouver was a relatively small town of thirty or forty thousand people which included about a thousand Italians. Now in the twilight of the 20th century, this city has become the third largest in Canada and has, in the

Greater Vancouver area, a population of well over one million people of whom forty or fifty thousand are Italo-Canadian.

This is a massive change in a comparatively short period of time; one cannot help wondering what the contributions of our children, as Italo-Canadians in the next century, will be.

I would hope that this book would help its readers to remember some of the names of the early Italian settlers in the mainland—names such as Philip Branca, John Galetti, John Crosetti, Angelo Calori, Tony Cianci, John Carrelli, Cirillo Braga, Peter Tosi, the familiar Minichiello, Benedetti, Brandolini, Stefani, Benetti, Canal, Girone, Gallia, Battistoni, Ruocco, Berardino, Caravetta, Nadalin, Rossi, Valente, Culos—to name only a few of the many.

These all were the pioneers who went to meet our immigrant forebears and to help them get jobs and settle, and who then went on to help write the wonderful factual history of the Italo-Canadians in this province which constitutes a true record of great achievement.

I think it is eminently fitting that such a chronicle of this wonderful period of history of the Italo-Canadians in the Lower Mainland has been written by Raymond—and that he is carrying on the tradition exemplified so strongly by his parents, Marino and Phyllis Culos, of service to our community.

Our families, the Minichiellos and Brancas stretched back to the 1920s—close friends, sometimes on different sides of the fence, but always with a sincere respect for that position, and always with a strong friendship that has successfully passed the test of time.

I take this opportunity to publicly thank Raymond for the many hours he has spent in compiling this history.

JUDGE DOLORES HOLMES

Preface

I subscribe to the view that our perceptions and actions are profoundly influenced by the people and events which went before us. And it is within this context that I take pride in presenting this historical account of Vancouver's pioneer Italians and their institutions. In memory of the many wonderful people who played a positive role in the progress of our Italian-Canadian community, circa 1904–1966, I dedicate this work. During the time I conducted my research, I was guided by a single criterion: to chronicle the documented contributions of the men and women closely associated with Vancouver's Italian mutual aid societies. I trust that I have fulfilled adequately this primary objective.

In researching this project, I obtained significant information from my father Marino's two publications, *Souvenirs "Ricordi"* and *Memorie Preziose*. In addition, I utilized his extensive collection of letters, photographs, diaries and original society minutes. I also benefited from my mother Phyllis's incredible memory for names, dates and events. Her assistance in contacting many of the 101 people interviewed proved invaluable. She continued to be a primary source of my research until the devastating effects of dementia denied her the ability to continue.

I have been blessed with many friends and colleagues who supported me throughout this endeavour. In particular, I am indebted to Marilyn Stusiak for providing a preliminary editing of the manuscript and for her unconditional encouragement. My sincere appreciation also is extended to Merrill Gordon, Joe Grosso and John Cervi for advice on business and financial matters. And I acknowledge with thanks the professional services of Beth Brooks, who uncovered vital information at the Dominion Archives in Ottawa. From the commencement of this undertaking, I have received special encouragement from my very good friends Nellie Cavell, Jimmy Ricci and Larry Politano for which I am truly appreciative.

I was privileged to have had unlimited access to the Pacific Press's library during the initial stages of the project. This unique benefit was extended upon my retirement from *The Vancouver Sun* and *The Province*. In addition, I enjoyed the full support and cooperation of Paul Whitney and staff in obtaining research information at Burnaby Public Library. The same level of professionalism was received at Vancouver Public Library, Simon Fraser University Library and the Vancouver Archives.

And to the scores of people who contributed their personal recollections to this exciting social history and to Her Honour Judge Dolores Holmes for providing the foreword, I offer my most sincere gratitude.

The author recognizes with special appreciation the contributions of the following interviewees (* indicates deceased):

Anita Adams, Lily Albo, John Alvaro, Meco Alvaro, Caesar Anderlini, Clara Arduini, Luigi Barone, Cyril Battistoni, Armida Beasley, Ray Benedetti, Violet Benedetti, John Benetti, Gina Benetti, Fiorenzo Benincasa, Robert Bevilacqua, Guido Bianchin, Gino Bosa, Gloria Bowe, Ermie Brandolini, Nick Brusesse, Elain Butz, Anita Campbell, Bill Canal*, Ines Cappon, Mario Caravetta, Dave Castricano*, Jodi Castricano, Noreen Castricano*, Nellie Cavell, Richard Cavell, Vito Cianci, Marino Culos*, Peter Culos, Phyllis Culos, Angelina Daminato, Sammy De Filippo*, Lucille Di Marco, Joe Di Palma, Rinda Dredge*, Rino Falcioni, Agnes Federici, Gerald Federici, Elsie Freeman, Alfonse Galetti, Graham Galette, Herman Ghislieri, Attilio L. Girardi, Bruno Girardi*, Dave Giuriato, Anita Godin, Josie Grdina, Edith Harris, Angelo Holmes, Judge Dolores Holmes, Gabriele Iacobucci*, Lina Iacobucci, Emma McMillan, Marguerite McPherson, Elio Maddalozzo, Ernie Maddalozzo, Emma Maffei, Antonietta Marino*, Agostino Martin, Mario Masi, Dave Mazzucco, Florence Mazzucco, Fred Minichiello, Louie Minichiello, Renzo Montagliani, Lu Moro, Mike Moscone, Elisa Negrin, Irma Pastro, Ella Pavich, Joe Penneway*, Carlo Pepe, Dolores Perovich, Mary Pettovello, Stella Pini, Iolanda Pitton, Charlene Politano, Norma Porter, Clara Preston*, Al Principe, Emma Ragona*, Vincent Jimmy Ricci, Peter David Ruocco, Silvio Ruocco, Edith Salfi, Midge Santaga, John Savio, Mary Stroppa, Lina Tesan, Mike Thomas, Angelo Tosi, Elmo Trasolini, Nita Tuan, Louie Valente, Elda Venturato, Ida Zilio.

RAYMOND CULOS

Marino Culos, a resident of Fellburn Hospital from 1988 to 1995, officiates at the opening of a new extended-care wing.

Farewell Marino

Addio Marino

They came to pay their respects to the man whose name had been synonymous with Vancouver's pioneer Italian community. To them, he was a leader, a foremost *amministratore,* and epitome of the glory-days of the former Sons of Italy Mutual Aid Society. Marino Culos, dead at 91, September 15, 1995.

Flanked by a fourteen-member honour guard from the Confratellanza Italo-Canadese Society and the Lega Femminile Italiana, Marino's coffin was guided to the front of Our Lady of Sorrows Church by familial pallbearers on September 18.[1]

Leading the entourage were the Italian societies' presidents and four former Confratellanza presidents including Angelo Holmes, scion of the Angelo Branca family.[2] Most mourners were descendants of Vancouver's pioneer Italian families who remembered Marino as the dynamic force behind many community initiatives spanning a 50-year period. He had always been a vibrant part of their ethnic milieu, and now it was sad to bid *"addio Marino".*

The words of Reverend Father John Bonelli and the eulogists confirmed that he had been a respected leader of Vancouver's Italian immigrants and Canadians whose family heritage is rooted in Italy. Peter Culos, Rocco Salituro and Armida Beasley praised Marino's contributions and accomplishments.[3] Collectively, they recalled lasting impressions of people and events connected with the Societa' di Mutuo Soccorso Figli d'Italia Inc. (Sons of Italy Mutual Aid Society, Inc.) between 1904 and 1966.

At the prayer service, the funeral mass, and at the Ocean View Cemetery mausoleum, scores of people nodded and smiled as they identified with the speakers' remarks. Among those with vivid memories of earlier days were Louie Minichiello, the last surviving participant of the Sons of Italy's 1927 six-mile marathon, Nell Dermody, the Veneta Society's 1937 queen contestant, and Pete Carotenuto, who was featured in one of Marino's *L'Eco Italo-Canadese* newspaper articles during the 1930s. Also present to say "*addio* Marino" were: Fiorenzo Benincasa, and Luigi Barone, past presidents of the Sons of Italy Society; Mario Caravetta, whose father was the Sons of Italy vice-president in 1945, when Marino was president; Gina Sanvido Benetti, former Italian language gold medalist; 83-year-old Al Principe, an organizer of the Vancouver Italian-Canadian Athletic Association in 1934; Lu Moro, the post-war advocate of sport and cultural activities for the society; and Iolanda Pitton, the energetic and vivacious *friulana* who had supported the Comitato Attivita' Italiane's plan for a *casa d'Italia* in the early 1960s.

The community's contemporary champion, Anna Terrana, MP for Vancouver-East, was present to pay her respects to a political colleague.

John Benetti, president in 1951 of the former Vancouver Italian-Canadian Society, offered personal condolences to the family on behalf of convalescents Rosina and Nino Sala, former restaurateurs prominent in the Vancouver Italian community. Also in hospital and unable to attend was Bruno Girardi, founder in 1936 of *L'Eco Italo-Canadese*, the Italian-language newspaper. His daughter conveyed words of sympathy for her father, who was an outstanding post-war president of the Sons of Italy. Sadly, Bruno Girardi died two days later on September 20.

Personal messages were received from Mario Masi, son of the Italian vice-consulate who was in office when Marino joined the Sons of Italy in 1926, and Alice D'Appolonia. During the Second World War, Marino helped Alice with business matters following her husband Santo Pasqualini's unjust internment under the Canada War Measures Act.

The social gathering that followed the funeral was reminiscent of the 1930s and 1940s. At the Culos home, the *confratelli* exchanged stories about some of the community's best known members: Angelo Calori, Giovanni Carrelli, Giovanni Galetti, Frank Rita, W.G. Ruocco, Luciano Zanon, Frank Comparelli, Mario Ghislieri, Tony and Rose Cianci, Mary Castricano, Enrichetta Benetti, Tosca Trasolini, Mary Balma and Angelo Branca. This would have delighted Marino as these people epitomized his first love: Vancouver's society of Italians.

Chapter 2

Liberty, Brotherhood, Equality

Libertà, Fratellanza, Uguaglianza

The Culos family set out by train for France from its home in San Giovanni di Casarsa, Italy in 1910. In Le Havre they boarded the *Provincial* which soon steamed across the Atlantic to America. The food available during the voyage was "different" and unappetizing. And their third-class passage accommodation left a great deal to be desired. On board ship, Marino slept in a hammock located next to the livestock in the vessel's steerage section. For sanitary reasons this area was hosed daily. On a moment's notice, unsuspecting passengers would be asked to grab their belongings and stand clear just before the hoses were turned on. It was meaningless to complain as no one understood Friulan, the Culos's northern Italian dialect. From New York they travelled by train to Montreal, then Vancouver. After an arduous month-long trip from the Friuli region of Italy, Marino Culos arrived in Vancouver with his mother, uncle and siblings a few days before Christmas 1910.

In Vancouver, dashing up the stairs from the imposing CPR station on Cordova Street, six-year-old Marino and his siblings saw their father for the first time in more than three and a half years. Pietro Culos embraced his wife Fiorina, shook hands with his brother-in-law Pietro Bozzetto, and briefly hugged his four children before whisking them into a Cadillac driven by Santo Brandolini.[4]

Castelgrandese provided strong leadership to the Sons of Italy.

Secondo and Vincenza Vagnini with their children Clara and Colombo
The widow Vagnini married Luigi Palazzini, a successful tile company owner and talented tenor.

As Brandolini propelled the Cadillac through Gastown, he repeatedly honked the hand-controlled horn located on the car's outside door panel. Once in front of 218 Carrall Street, however, the mood of the happy but weary travellers turned to guarded optimism as they contemplated their new circumstance.

The Klondike Hotel was owned by Giovanni Carrelli and his partner Severino Sanpietro, founding members of the Sons of Italy Society. It would be home to the Culos family until larger accommodation could be found. Living in overcrowded conditions was nothing new as they had lived in a two-house complex in Italy with 45 other Culos clan members for years.[5]

Marino's early orientation to the Sons of Italy Society was acquired through osmosis. He listened to his father and his friends discuss the society's activities. These conversations fascinated the young lad, especially when they abruptly turned into shouting matches as divergent views were expressed.

The fledgling society, founded by 59 immigrant men, was

Marino Culos stated that his grandfather had asked some of his children to leave the family home in Italy as the two-building complex no longer could accommodate the Culos clan, which in the early 1900s numbered fifty members. He also recalled the women cooking food in a caldron placed on an open fire—fogolar.

Antonio Cianci, left, and his cousin Felice Cianci (attending to a customer) at their Gastown barber shop, circa 1910.

incorporated in January, 1905. Its motto was *Liberta, Fratellanza, Uguaglianza*: liberty, brotherhood, equality. The membership included men representing a broad cross-section of Italy's geographic regions. Most of these immigrants had been drawn together through necessity in this new land. They recognized that in order to succeed they needed to assist one another.

Unifying this divergent group of nationals, however, was a major and often elusive challenge for the society's executive. The situation was protracted by the fact that Italians from regions north and south of the Mezzogiorno line in Italy often did not share the same rationale in resolving common problems.

As a mutual aid society, the Sons of Italy was constituted to provide members with services not readily available through other sources: sickness and death benefits, interpreter services, social and sport activities, plus cultural and linguistic programmes. Perhaps most importantly, the society provided a forum where the expression of ideas and concerns was encouraged.[6]

The impetus for the society's establishment came from Giovanni Carrelli, its first president. He understood the difficulties newcomers were experiencing. He enjoyed wide-spread popularity among Italians and had talked with many of them, including labourers who lodged at the Klondike Hotel. As a result Carrelli, an interpreter, knew what Italians faced when dealing with English-speaking employers, doctors and government agency representatives. Also providing services to their fellow countrymen were Giovanni Galetti, a notary public, and Angelo Calori, a successful businessman and owner of the Europe Hotel.[7]

Calori encouraged his colleagues and relatives to join Vancouver's first Italian mutual aid society. Among the founding members were: his stepson Giuseppe Martina, brother-in-law Davide Sanguinetti and Lorenzo Politano with whom Calori had a number of real estate deals. Politano, a swarthy Calabrese amputee, in awe of the exploits of Camillo Benzo Di Cavour, Giuseppe Mazzini, and Giuseppe Garibaldi, added a nationalistic flavour to the movement. His patriotic gestures included displaying an 1860s Italian flag, now an archival piece, at his store at 321 Cordova Street.

Between July and December 1904, a committee, chaired by Carrelli, worked to launch the new society. The committee's efforts were supported by *Cavaliere* Agostino Ferrera, Vancouver's first Royal Italian Agent (consul) and his 18-year-old nephew Cesare Anderlini.[8]

Others who contributed significantly to the fledgling movement were Giorgio Delasala who prepared a 30-page hand-written constitution and Antonio Cianci, barber and hotel proprietor. Cianci garnered support of fellow hotelmen including Francesco Marchese, owner of the West Hotel. Membership committee officer

D'Atillio and his sister Mary Castricano with her children Lily and Dave, circa 1912.

Judge Angelo Branca in his L'Eco d'Italia *column, "Branca's Corner," dated October 6, 1978, wrote, "There used to be a chap named Giovanni Carrelli. In the early days Carrelli operated a bar known as the Klondike Bar on Carrall Street and this was a gathering place for many of the Italians of the day. He served with distinction as an Italian interpreter at the courthouse for many, many years and he was very highly respected by the police department of this city, the lawyers, and everyone else who was connected with the administration of justice."*

"My father [Giovanni Galetti] arrived in Philadelphia in 1882. He was only 20 years old and eager to make his way in the new world. There was no work around there so they were 'riding the rods'. He slipped just as the train started up. His leg was caught underneath the car and severed. He made his own wooden leg. And that's the same leg as he died with."

—Alfonse Galetti.

Giovanni Maddalozzo, fourth from right, working with a sawmill crew circa 1923.

Achille Pini signed up several new members. He obtained applications from fellow Toscani including three of his six brothers. On December 14, the pro tem committee's recommendations were voted in place and Angelo Calori's proposal to name the organization the Figli d'Italia (Sons of Italy) was endorsed unanimously.[9]

Membership grew steadily and the dream of uniting the community was progressing nicely until a meeting in December 1910, when Filippo Branca quit the society.[10]

Rising on a matter of principle, Branca delivered an impassioned speech over the executive's handling of dance ticket reimbursements. He charged that a double standard existed regarding this question. When the table officers refused to acknowledge anomalies relative to their actions, Branca, the merchant from Milano, stormed out of the meeting. The meeting was chaired by Girolamo (Jimmy) Scatigno, the second of the society's seven presidents born in Castelgrande, Basilicatta, in southern Italy. Francesco Federici, a founding member was the first Castelgrandese president.[11]

Following his split with the Sons of Italy, the obstinate Branca established the Societa' Veneta di Mutuo Soccorso Inc. in February 1911. The Veneta Benevolent Society, made up primarily of northern Italian expatriates, was successful in attracting a significant number of followers including the influential Santo Brandolini and industrious Pietro Canal. Eight founding members of the Veneta, however,

Raffaele Caravetta, front row third from right, was a founding member of the Fernie Italian Society, circa 1900.

retained their membership in the Sons of Italy: Annibale Franceschini, Giovanni Campagnola, Sante Corra', Elio Baldo, Giuseppe Toffoletto, Augusto Corra', Giovanni Secco and Giuseppe Giardin.[12]

Born in Turbigo, a small town near Milan, Branca became a miner in Utah's salt mines in the early 1890s. He married Teresa Christopher who had travelled from her home on the Austrian-Italian border to be with him. Several years later they moved with their infant son Giuseppe to California. In pursuit of a more permanent job opportunity, they soon travelled to Vancouver Island. On the first day of spring, 1903, a second child was born near a mine site at Mount Sicker. The infant, Angelo Ernest Branca, was destined to become a future judge of the B.C. Supreme Court and B.C. Court of Appeal.

Filippo Branca befriended Giuseppe Crosetti, a fellow-miner living in Duncan. And shortly after their two families relocated on the mainland, they became partners in an Italian food importing business in the 500 block Main Street. Eventually, however, they went their separate ways with Crosetti, a member of the Sons of Italy, setting up the Europe Grocery Store a couple of blocks away in the 200 block east Georgia Street.[13]

A mandate of the Italian mutual aid societies was to raise funds to benefit members and to assist others in need. In 1905 and 1909 the Sons of Italy sent donations to victims of earthquakes in southern Italy. At the end of the Libyan Campaign, money was given through the offices of Nicola Masi, the Italian vice-consul, to aid wounded veterans. In this war with Turkey, Italy gained Libya and the Dodecanese Islands. Among the society members who fought in

Raffaella Trasolini, pictured with her husband Luigi and children, was president of the Lega for nine years, circa 1910.

Virginia and Pietro Canal at home on Atlantic Street. He was custodian of the Veneta's ceremonial flags.

The Politano family at their Cordova Street store.
Lorenzo and Angelina with sons Joe, Tony, Carl and Frank, circa 1915.

Giuditta and Giuseppe Crosetti.
Following their honeymoon in Italy the Crosettis returned to Cumberland (Union) on Vancouver Island, where Giovanni lost his leg in a mining accident, circa 1901.

this campaign before coming to Vancouver were Luigi Possagno and Giovanni Maddalozzo. Giovanni D'Appolonia had been a Canadian resident for four years prior to receiving an army call to report to his Bersagliere regiment in 1911. When his tour of duty ended in 1913, he returned to Canada.[14]

When Branca's 10-year-old son Giuseppe died in 1908, society president Tony Cianci, another Castelgrandese, sent a heartfelt personal letter of condolence to Filippo and flowers to Teresa Branca from the membership. After the funeral service, *confratelli* went to the Branca home to extend personal words of sympathy and support.

In the early 1920s, Vancouver's society of Italians attended another Branca funeral. This time it was Filippo Branca's daughter Anne Gatto. She died giving birth. While her death occurred at a time when automobiles were still considered a novelty, and only enjoyed by a few of the society members, the funeral motorcade comprised dozens of vehicles.

Sammy De Filippo, who drove the lead car, and Joe Peneway (Penneway), an attendee, remembered the funeral as the largest to date in the Italian community. A police escort and several musicians under the direction of Dominic "Manifico" Ricci preceded the funeral cortege. Its route led the procession past Branca's Main Street store before turning east on Union Street. It was at this point that scores of mourners fought to hold back tears as they witnessed the near emotional collapse of the deceased's brother Angelo. It was a sad day indeed in the history of the Italian community.[15]

As with all immigrant families, every member helped to support the family. As a youngster Marino Culos, along with his brother Tony and sisters Pina and Sunta, walked to the Klondike Hotel to do their chores before morning classes began at Strathcona School.

It was their responsibility to prepare the hotel's bar for the day's business. They cleaned spittoons along the length of the 60-foot bar and washed and stacked glasses. Fresh buns were sliced and trays filled with cheese and sandwich meat, all to be offered "free" to patrons ordering beer or whiskey.

Pietro Culos started to work at the Klondike following an accident sustained while working as a labourer on a railway gang in 1907. His injury, the result of being caught in a rock and gravel landslide, forced him to look for less strenuous work, so he took the innkeeper position at the hotel. One day he excitedly entered the manager's office to report that he had found a straight razor concealed under a bed pillow in one of the sleeping rooms. Carrelli literally jumped out of his chair shouting, "Don't you know what this means? It's a sign from la Mano Nera. This guy is a marked man. For God's sake, Pietro, put the razor back where you found it. And say nothing to nobody!"

The next night, from a doorway on the second floor, a *Napolitan*

Santo Brandolini, family head and hotel owner, supported the Sons of Italy and the Veneta societies.

Giovanni Galetti, second row, proposed to the widow Rossi, "If you take me with one leg missing, I'll take you with your two children." Circa 1907.

Gettulio Falcioni and Luigi Palazzini
Sons of Italy pioneer members hunted
near their homes in North Vancouver.

**Cesare and Rose Anderlini and
children Niva and Eva.**
Cesare, who remarried in the mid-1940s,
arrived in Vancouver in 1901 with his
uncle Agostino Ferrera.

was seen firing his revolver at the "marked man" as he scampered down the stairs four steps at a time. One bullet whizzed past his ear and lodged in the door jamb as he made a rather hasty exit. A few months later, the member of la Mano Nera or Black Hand, an organization similar to the Mafia, gave Pietro a pocket watch as a *ricordo* of the event. The Waltham timepiece has survived, but nothing more was ever heard of the fleeing tenant.[16]

On his daily walks to Gastown, young Marino Culos often became aware of an interesting event or happening. For example, on September 18, 1912, King George V's cousin, His Royal Highness the Duke of Connaught and Governor-General of Canada, arrived in Vancouver on an official visit during which he cut the ribbon to open the new Connaught Bridge, later called Cambie. Once the bridge was officially opened to traffic, Alberto Principe, a Sons of Italy Society member, became the first person to cross it in a horse-driven beer wagon.[17]

Along the Hastings Street parade route, the governor-general and his entourage passed under an arch designed and built by Vancouver Italians. At 64 feet in height, it was the tallest of the ethnic community arches especially constructed for the royal visit. The structure, of the Roman Corinthian order, represented the Arch of Constantine at Rome. It stretched the full width of Hastings Street at Homer Street. Across the top was inscribed, in both English and Italian, "Italian Colony, In Honour of His Royal Highness."[18]

The solid wood edifice had columns of plaster to imitate marble. The columns were described in the local press as being "exact replicas of the Corinthian caps, at Cori, Italy." The caps were engraved by a local sculptor, possibly Carlo Marega or Alemando Fabri.

Marega, a resident of the city since 1909, worked as a teacher at the Vancouver Art School.

Destined to gain immense popularity for his artistic creativity, Marega had been acclaimed as a local sculptor of promise for his bust of Vancouver's mayor David Oppenheimer unveiled at the Beach Avenue entrance to Stanley Park in December 1911.[19]

Fabri, a Sons of Italy Society member, arrived in Vancouver in 1911 from the Pittsburg Museum where he had served as resident professor. Born in Bangi di Lucca, Tuscany, Fabri had impressive credentials. He had studied in Italy, Germany and Russia under famous sculptors Vito Pardo of Rome and Tronbskoy of Moscow. A fiercely nationalistic Italian, Fabri, who had offices at 1248 Granville Street, is best remembered for his sculptured creations in the Marine Building foyer, at the Royal Bank's head office building, the Georgia Hotel, the old Medical Dental Building and the University of British Columbia.[20]

One block from Strathcona School stands the Ferrera Court, a

three-storey apartment block at the corner of Hastings and Jackson. Ferrera, a *cavaliere*, Knight of the Royal Italian government, believed Vancouver's business community would continue to grow east of Main Street. In 1912, he predicted that his enterprise soon would compete favourably with the Hotel Vancouver for the upscale business trade. His dreams unfulfilled, Ferrera eventually sold the hotel in the 1930s to establish a cheese factory in Chilliwack. The dairy venture was largely financed by his friend Frank Federici.[21]

Paul and Teresa Girone and children. He was a founding member of the Sons of Italy's Powell River Chapter in 1917. Mrs. Girone was president of the Lega in Vancouver circa 1930.

In a feature article in The Vancouver Daily Province, *dated July 26, 1947, reporter Ted Fairfax outlined Agostino Ferrera's early achievements, "The Maison de la Ville, owned and operated by A. G. Ferrera, which stood on what is now the site of the Rogers Building on [the 400 block] Granville Street. Mr. Ferrera cleaned the stumps from the site himself.*

"His first restaurant, constructed soon after he came to Vancouver in 1898, was the Savoy which was located on what is now the one hundred block Cordova.

"Other buildings which Mr. Ferrera built after the turn of the century were Ferrera Court on East Hastings Street and the Embassy Ballroom on Davie."

The Pietro Culos family, circa 1912.

Arch built in 1912 for the Royal Visit.
An Italian sculptor's creative archway, located at Homer and Hastings streets, was dedicated to the Duke of Connaught as a symbol of the Italian-Canadians' loyalty to the Crown.

When Ferrera stepped down as Royal Agent for Italy in 1915, he was replaced by Nicola Masi, another Castelgrandese [from Castelgrande, Italy].[22]

In May 1912, Sons of Italy president, John Galetti received two requests to convene special meetings. These were granted; the first, held at the London Hotel, May 12, was called to consider appointment of a delegation to visit Ladysmith on Vancouver Island for the purpose of meeting with representatives of the Felice Cavalotti Society. The intent was to encourage that group to affiliate with the Sons of Italy. Preliminary talks were conducted, but the objective was not achieved.[23]

The second petition was submitted by an influential group headed by Leone Brandolini, Giuseppe Battistoni, Luigi Battistoni, Giuseppe Crosetti and Giovanni Mazzocca. These members proposed that a cash donation be made in support of Joseph Ettor and Arthur Giovannitti who they said were "fellow countrymen who have been falsely imprisoned in the Lawrence, Mass., prison." Their proposal was accepted at a special meeting convened May 30 and a donation of $50 was sent to the American activists' defence fund.

The donation was acknowledged by secretary W.E. Trautmann

of the Defence Committee the following month. In his letter he stated, in part, that the "Penalty for Ettor and Giovannitti, if convicted, is death in the electric chair, for the others from five to 10 years in prison. The employing class is straining and using all their resources to get a jury to convict these men, and a judge to inflict the highest penalty possible, so that they will get their revenge on these fellow workers and comrades for having helped hundreds of thousands of wage workers in their battles for better wages and more rights."[24]

Sig. Angelo Calori
by Leo Tesan

Un gran pensiero a voi Calori,
Che foste il primo;
Ci legeste il nostro destino,
Cosi' la presentaste,
Ed il nome "Figli d'Italia"

Giovanni Galetti, with peg-leg, at his
Notary Public office, 207 Prior at Main,
circa 1913.

Gabriele Iacobucci worked for Nick Cosco in the late 1920s. Although physically short and slight of build, Iacobucci would regularly manually dig ditches seven feet in depth and occasionally would go down to a depth of 12 feet, removing rocks in the process, on construction sites. It had been prearranged for Iacobucci, as with most landed immigrants who arrived in the 1920s and 1930s, that he would work as a farm labourer for the first two years of residency in Canada. However, on his arrival to Vancouver, he stayed with his sister for a month and instead reported directly for work at a logging camp near Campbell River. "I laid wooden rail ties, a system used in transporting logs. I worked my guts out for two weeks but quit the job because the cook served us bear meat," recalled Iacobucci.

Murder!

Omicidio!

In later years, Marino Culos recalled hearing about Nick Cosco, the community's foremost building contractor. Cosco, who provided employment to many Italians over the years, including Marino's future fraternal colleague Gabriele Iacobucci, had a major contract in the construction of the Georgia Viaduct, circa 1913.[25] Upon completion of the project, Artemisia Minichiello (Marino's future mother-in-law) was among the onlookers who turned out for the ribbon-cutting ceremony. The bridge spanned a section of False Creek between Main and Beatty and was designed originally to accommodate street-car traffic through Little Italy to Campbell Avenue.[26]

Across the street from the viaduct at Main and Georgia streets, a tragedy occurred in the fall of 1914. The Italian community was shocked to learn that Angelo Teti (Tate) had been cut down in cold blood. Tate was a wealthy broker. He owned a major real estate portfolio which included the prestigious Sylvia Hotel on Beach Avenue, the Royal Hotel at 136 Water Street, an apartment building and a number of residential rental properties.

Just before noon on September 24, 1914, Tate was mortally wounded by his *paesano* and tenant, Mario Montenario, who coolly fired three shots at him at close range. Two bullets from his .38 calibre handgun entered Tate's body as he stood in the doorway of

McKinnon's Real Estate office in the 700 block Main Street, next door to Galetti's notary public office. Tate was felled by shots to the back and to his right side.[27]

According to Violet Benedetti (Benny), Mrs. Montenario, a temperamental redhead, supported her husband's decision to confront Tate before he could evict them from their house. Apparently, H. McKinnon & Co were endeavouring to collect an overdue mortgage which Tate held since loaning the mortgage money to Mrs. Montenario some years before. This effort was met by threatened reprisals and alleged threats on Tate's life. Montenario, who went down to the broker's office with the intent to seek out and kill Angelo Tate, put up no resistance when arrested at the scene. He was tried, convicted and sentenced to life imprisonment.

During the trial both Mrs. Tate and Mrs. Montenario were pregnant. "What happened was the trial came up—my mother was going to have another baby—and she's going to have one, too. And Montenario stood up, because when you're a *strega*, you can talk like a Philadelphia lawyer. She stood up in front of the judge and said, with her stomach sticking out like this, 'how have you got the heart to hang the father of this unborn child,'" Benedetti recalled. "Well, they put him in the B.C. Penitentiary in New Westminster but he escaped from jail," she continued. Benedetti is convinced that Montenario made good his escape by swimming along the banks of the Fraser River, later to settle in a remote mining town in Alaska.[28]

Tragedy was to plague the widowed Sabina Tate throughout her life. Seven months after her husband was murdered, her son Fio, serving with the 1st Canadian Division at the battle of Ypres, Belgium, was killed by shrapnel caused by an exploding shell during a German counterattack.[29]

Shortly afterward her teenaged daughter Nellie, spurning a suitor's proposal of marriage, was gravely wounded by a gunshot to the head. A family member suggests that Nellie was with the boarder when the handgun he was demonstrating accidentally went off. To save Nellie's life, the operating physician performed a new medical technique which, because of its success, was given prominence in a medical journal.

*"Shot in the Back by Former Friend,"
was the* Province's *story headline.
"Angelo Teti, Wealthy Italian Likely to
Die as a Result of Attack. Mario
Montenario Admits He Shot Man Who
Held Mortgage," were the sub-headings.
"Taking deliberate aim at the back of the
man whom he had repeatedly threatened
with death, Mario Montenario, an
Italian, shot and fatally wounded Angelo
Teti, a rich Italian contractor and broker,
as he stood in the office of H. Mackinnon
& Co. 748 Main Street just before noon
today," the story item continued.*

Angelo and Sabina Teti.
Tate was murdered by his paesano.

Chapter 4

Rose and Modesto Satti married in 1905.
He was a founding member of the Sons of Italy, circa 1920s.

Luigi and Rose Puccetti: second marriage, circa 1934.

A Pioneer Family of the Society
Una Famiglia Pioniera della Società

In 1913, Giuseppe Guasparri died. In the early 1880s he became the first Italian, with a future connection to Vancouver's Italian societies, to settle in the city's Hastings Mill area. He had left his Florentine home in 1856 for America in search of adventure and a regular pay cheque. Attracted by the promise of steady pay, he enlisted in the Union Army's Kentucky Cavalry. Soon, he was fighting in the American Civil War. While on active duty, he was forced to change his name by a pay-sergeant unable to pronounce "Guasparri" correctly. According to his granddaughter, Rinda Dredge, he was simply told, "From now on your name is John Lewis."

After America's worst carnage ended, John Lewis, the rugged, brazen but charming non-conformist, was lured to British Columbia by his lust for gold. Once in the Barkerville area, he parlayed his wages for some land. In the process, Lewis sold liquor to the Indians. Although he became rich, his shenanigans came to the notice of the provincial police.[30]

One step ahead of the law, Lewis boarded the CPR passenger train at Vancouver for Montreal. From Quebec he embarked on a steamer for safer havens in Italy. Finding refuge in Italy, however, did not satisfy his inner soul. He yearned to return to Canada.

In 1888, Lewis left Italy with his wife and infant children, Rose,

2, and Felix, 1, to settle permanently in Vancouver. Caterina Lewis, who was 25 years younger than her husband, died in 1948. In life she had attained the distinction of having been the second longest surviving spouse of a veteran of the American Civil War. She proudly displayed a certificate issued by the United States government in recognition of her unique status.

Lewis's daughter Rose became a prominent member of the Vancouver Italian community: society president, language instructor and community leader. Twice widowed, she married three pioneer members of the Sons of Italy Society. Rose first married Modesto Satti with whom she had four children. In 1934, she married Luigi Puccetti. Her third husband, Antonio Cianci, had been her first admirer.

(In 1904, it was rumoured that Antonio and Rose were romantically linked. Hearing of this situation, Vito Cianci came to Vancouver from Castelgrande, Basilicata, in an attempt to put an end to his son Antonio's infatuation with the "flirtatious" Rose Guasparri Lewis. His true motivation, however, was to convince Tony to return to his religious studies in Italy. Although the courtship soon ended, Tony refused to go back to the seminary. This decision devastated the elder Cianci who, in despair, returned to his home in Italy.)

Tony and Rose Cianci with Vito Cianci and Rinda Dredge, circa 1940s.
Twice widowed, Rose marries Tony, her first beau.

Gerolamo Scatigno, W.G. and Peter Ruocco
Three brothers, circa 1915. Gerolamo (Jimmy) is pictured in Canadian Medical Service uniform. A fourth brother, Angelo, served in the Italian Army during the Great War.

Chapter 5

For the Homeland!
Per La Patria!

When Italy entered the First World War on the side of England and France, its government immediately launched an appeal for the voluntary repatriation of all military-age Italian nationals living in Canada and elsewhere. These men were offered return-trip travel vouchers to *la patria* in exchange for military service.

The Sons of Italy Society, concerned over its sickness and death benefit obligations, issued a terse statement to members volunteering for active duty in the service of Canada and Italy. Those joining the military would be suspended from the society. They would, however, be eligible for reinstatement on their return to civilian life.[31]

Among those who enlisted in 1915 for active service in the Italian military were a group of Italians from Vancouver and the BC Interior. The volunteer brigade assembled at MacLean Park to begin drill exercises before officials completed arrangements for their passage to Italy. Young children, including Sammy De Filippo, watched in fascination as the recruits went through their exercises.

Bill Canal recalled his father, Pietro, mentioning that among the recruits were men formerly in the Italian Army who participated in the exercises. "A group of them formed something like a citizens' militia and would drill up on the MacLean Park playground. I remember my father saying that he and Filippo Branca were a part of it. My father had received some military training in Italy, you see. Neither one of them was called upon for anything, but it was an honest gesture on their part."

Jimmy Scatigno joined the Canadian Army Medical Corps. His brother Angelo Ruocco, still living in Castelgrande, served with Italy's crack Bersagliere Regiment. Although wounded in a gas attack, he was able to leave Italy after the war to join his brothers in Vancouver where he became a successful tailor and respected businessman.[32]

The Sons of Italy raised funds for the Italian Red Cross in 1917 and the Italian Wounded Veterans' Association in 1919. In 1920, the society received a Diploma of Merit for its donations to the National Association of the Wounded and Invalid Veterans of the Great War.[33]

There had been an economic recession in British Columbia around the time of the First World War and many families endured hardship. According to Rinda Dredge her father had become very resourceful in order to feed his family during this period. "It was around the end of the war when my father learned that Canadian soldiers were being bivouacked at the PNE grounds. We—and other Italian families—would go down to the temporary barracks at six in the morning in hope of getting some of the unused breakfast food. There were big tins of jam, bacon, bread—bread galore—and we would just run in there and stuff all the left-overs in our sacks. My dad got to know one of the cooks and would give him some wine made by my uncle Lu. I was the oldest, so I brought the wine because the cook would only let the kids come in to take away the left-over food items. One day my dad brought the cook a gallon of wine. As I was only 10 or 11, Dad had to give it to him because I couldn't carry the damn thing," concluded Rinda Dredge.

Sig. Giovanni Carrelli
by Leo Tesan

Per voi Carrelli
Vi giunge il nostro pensiero
Che per il destino presidente foste il
  primo,
E segueste il nostro cammino
Guidandolo sulla retta via

Chapter 6

Sacred Heart Church funeral service.
Photographs of deceased members often
were sent to relatives in Italy.

Remembering the Dead
Ricordate i Morti

Sons of Italy's first monument, circa 1921.
Members were buried in the Italian
section of Mountain View Cemetery.

In 1917, the society established a branch organization at Powell River, B.C. And in the following year another branch opened in Fernie in affiliation with the Grand Lodge of B.C.[34]

The Sons of Italy expansion programmes were achieved along with improved membership benefits. Acquisition of an exclusive burial site was proposed by Giovanni Penninbede (Penneway) who was instrumental in getting the Sons of Italy to purchase its first 18 cemetery plots in 1920. The plots, which cost $180, were located at Vancouver's Mountain View Cemetery, 33rd Avenue and Fraser Street. Founding member Ottavio Vanelli, who died in 1921, was the first person to be buried in the society's section.[35]

Funeral notices were mailed via overnight post to members following the death of a fraternal brother. These notices, sent by the correspondence secretary, would include a reminder to the member regarding his obligation to attend the funeral service. The majority of funerals were held at the Sacred Heart Church.

When a society member died, the sick committee literally handled all of the funeral arrangements for the bereaved family. It often provided pallbearers, contacted the priest, arranged for a band and, when applicable, a police escort.

The member's beneficiary received a death benefit of $125 to

$150. In addition, the family was offered assistance in making the funeral arrangements. The president or society orator, generally flanked by members wearing an around-the-neck *fascia* or sash, would deliver an eulogy at the graveside.[36] This service and other courtesies were a source of comfort to the member's family including *parenti* residing in Italy. Occasionally photographs of the deceased would be taken and forwarded to relatives in the old country.[37]

The Vancouver Italian-Canadian Society honours the memory of its deceased members.

"My father would visit members of the Veneta Society when they were sick. And when there was a death in the family, he would find out if there was enough money for a proper burial. If the people couldn't afford the cost of a funeral, the society would take up a collection to help the bereaved family. Dad would go around and collect contributions," stated Bill Canal.

On All Saints' Day, Vancouver's mutual aid societies would honour their deceased members. In the case of the Sons of Italy, its members would muster at the Silver Slipper Auditorium on the second Sunday of November, and in parade formation, would walk the three blocks to Sacred Heart Church. After the Mass, offered for the repose of the departed, the group would reassemble at Mountain View Cemetery.

At the cemetery, a band would play sombre tunes. It would precede the priest and the attendees in a march-past of the graves with-

Funeral service for Vincenzo Jimmy Fiorante attended by Civitanovese, circa 1927.

in the society's section. The priest, stopping periodically to recite prayers, would be joined by mourners putting flowers on the grave of a loved one. Speeches and a benediction would follow.[38]

"My dad is buried in the Vancouver Italian-Canadian Society section," recalled Irma Zamai Pastro. "I used to go to the cemetery every All Souls' Day because, you see, I was young and my dad had died when I was only 15, so my mother and I would always go.

"Dad died in 1941. He had been working in the mines and suffered from miner's consumption. They said his illness was minor, that he would get better within six months. He looked so good. As a matter of fact, when Mr. Luigi Giuriato—he was my mom's cousin—took dad to the hospital to be admitted, the nurse mistook Mr. Giuriato for the patient. He always had a kind of pasty look whereas dad had rosy cheeks. But they didn't have the antibiotics then that are available today. Just bad luck; it spread. I was going to King Ed High School, and they wouldn't let me see him because they said the disease was contagious. And for three years I never saw my dad, other than to wave to him from outside his hospital room. He died at 51."

Cemetery service at Mountain View. The first Sunday in November a special graveside memorial service was held.

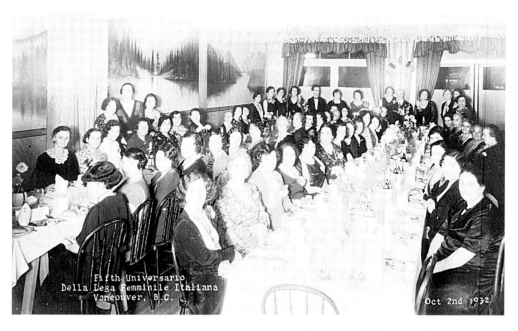

Chapter 7

The Lega's Fifth Annual Banquet: 1932.

The Italian Ladies' League

La Lega Femminile Italiana

On March 7, 1926, Marino Culos, 21, joined his father and brother as a member of the Sons of Italy Society. He was sponsored by Luigi Battistoni, a tailor operating a shop on the 500 block Union Street, directly in front of the Venice Bakery that was established by his brother Giovanni in 1909. The Battistonis were from Spillingbergo, a short distance from the Culos family's home town in the Friuli region of Italy. The two families often socialized, and were indeed good friends, and for these reasons Marino was extremely proud to be introduced to the fraternal organization by Mr. Battistoni.[39]

President Frank Pio Rita, a highly regarded member of the society, presided over the swearing-in ceremony. Rita, another Castelgrandese, was one of the society's most competent executive members. His knowledge of the society's constitution was unequalled and his effectiveness as a forceful and convincing speaker made him an outstanding president. He was to have a profound effect on Marino's decision to pursue a leading role in the affairs of the Italian community. At the end of his term as president in 1926, Rita was awarded a gold medal for his meritorious contributions to the society and made honorary president for life.[40]

The Veneta Benevolent Society, with the youthful drive of Branca's son Angelo, remained a viable alternative to the Sons of

Italy.[41] On July 1, 1926, the Veneta Society participated in Vancouver's Canada Jubilee Celebrations. It did so in spectacular fashion by entering a floral-crested float in the city-sponsored parade. Marching in front of the float was a contingent of society members lead by stalwart flag bearer Pietro Canal. Supervising the construction of the float, which typified the glorious and artistic art of Venice, was Cesare Durante, the society's president.

Concurrent with the parade entry, the Veneta held a queen contest that attracted many of the members' daughters as contestants. The contest created great interest and excitement throughout the Italian community. The attractive and talented Florence Toso sold the largest number of raffle tickets to win the title of Queen of Italy. Ermie Pulice, 17, the runner up, was crowned Miss Canada. These belles and fellow candidates Ines Falcioni and 14-year-old Angelina Graziano were featured on the parade float. Following the parade they were treated to a special dinner at the prestigious Ristorante Fior d'Italia in Gastown.[42]

The Fior d'Italia was owned and operated by Antonio Culos and Gaetano "Red" Papini. It was a premier Italian restaurant frequented by an established family trade and many visiting theatrical performers. One of its more famous patrons was Piero Orsatti, a popular tenor, artist and teacher. This native of Florence, who coached talented students such as Anita Panichelli at his Granville Street studio, performed at the grand opening of the Fior d'Italia restaurant.[43]

Italians wed at Powell River.
Paul Girone, wearing white gloves, established the town's first bakery, circa 1910.

The urbane tenor, who nurtured a penchant for fine wines, was a frequent visitor at the Paul Girone home. Margherita, the Girones' teenage daughter, loved to sing arias for her own personal enjoyment. Her parents were enamoured with her singing voice, however, and began to speculate as to whether or not their daughter should be considering a career in theatre. To gain a professional opinion, they invited Orsatti to dinner. With persistent encouragement from her mother, Margherita casually began to sing in the kitchen largely for the *maestro*'s benefit. Later that evening, Orsatti was to comment; "Good voice but not for opera."[44]

Ines Falcioni, Margherita's godmother, was among the brightest and most active people in the community. During her career she worked for the Italian Vice-Consul, the Italian Shipping Line and

Angelo Branca's law office. In addition, she accepted a leading role in the affairs of the Italian Ladies' League, the Sons of Italy's affiliate.

In 1998, Ines Falcioni Treselli, Phyllis Culos and Mary Pettovello are the sole surviving founding members of the Italian Ladies' League (Lega) which was established in October 1927. The impetus for the formation of the first Lega was provided by W.G. Ruocco during his inaugural term as president of the Sons of Italy. The mandate of the Lega was to present an independent voice for its members in the affairs of the Italian community. It also was encouraged to support the Sons of Italy and its social and cultural programmes. In 1926, Enedina Fabri was appointed interim president. Although she had been expected to become the Lega's first president six months later, Mrs. Fabri declined the nomination for maternity reasons. Instead a three-member provisional executive was appointed with Teresa Marchese serving as president until Oct. 2, when Angelo Calori's stepdaughter Rose Anderlini was officially elected *presidentessa*.[45]

Ruocco possessed an uncanny magnetism for attracting the community's best men and women to the ranks of the society and its affiliate. Scores of bright and energetic Italians and Canadian-Italians joined with him in developing programs designed to promote pride and understanding in their Italian cultural heritage. In 1927, he dubbed Marino Culos, Joe Politano, and John Crosetti the society's Three Musketeers. Marino, the idea man, became correspondence secretary in Ruocco's first term. Politano, the planner, soon won recognition and a gold medal for selling memberships, and Crosetti, the man of integrity, performed a myriad of tasks behind the scenes.[46]

Pitton family in Powell River.
Tony and Antonia with their daughters Nellie and Armida, circa 1928.

Italian Benevolent Society, Powell River
In 1924 Powell River's Italians established their own mutual aid society. It boasted 300 members and sponsored the very successful Labour Day Festival. Photo: Irene Zorzi, 1927 Labour Day Princess. Back row from left: August Fornari, Sam Statari, Giovanni Pavan, Albino Stradiotto, Camillio Raimondo, Giovanni Pellegrin, Luigi Castellarin, Isidoro Mantoani, Mario Venuti. Front row from left: Claudio Zorzi, Giovanni Brusadin, Giovanni Biazutti, Irene Zorzi, Nick Cimarosa, Luigi Cecconi, Ferdinando Bressanutti.

Chapter 8

Members of Vancouver's outstanding Young Canadian-Italian Athletic Club.

The Best in Sports
I Migliori Nello Sport

Peter Battistoni, placing second, successfully challenged adults in the Sons of Italy's first six-mile marathon in 1927.

In October of 1927, the Sons of Italy sponsored its first six-mile marathon as part of its Columbus Day Celebrations. Participating in the race were Peter Battistoni, Angelo Branca, Felice Cianci, Marino Culos, Gregorio Fuoco, Louie Minichiello, and Norman "Bananas" Trasolini. The course took the runners from MacLean Park (Georgia Park) west on Georgia to Main Street, south on Main to 12th Avenue, east on 12th to Commercial Drive, north to Venables and Vernon Drive, then west on Union Street back to the park at Jackson Avenue.[47]

Witnessing the exciting finish of the hotly contested race were an estimated 750 cheering fans. As Marino entered the park to complete the last lap of the race, he inadvertently veered from course. Duly warned by a spectator, he made the necessary correction, then lapped the park. As he flashed across the finish line, Marino felt the ribbon snap at his chest. Placing second was young Peter Battistoni who had been pressing Marino for the lead. Some distance behind was 14-year-old Louie Minichiello. Within a block of the park, he had ducked into his home at 567 Union Street for an unscheduled pit stop. Once relieved, Minichiello resumed the race to finish in third place. At the banquet and dance which took place that evening, mayor L.D. Taylor presented Marino with a handsome silver cup trophy.

Marino won again the following year and Gillie Brandolini, an outstanding all-round athlete, took top honours in 1930. During the race in which he placed first, Gillie slipped and fell. The resulting bruises were still very visible three nights later on Oct. 15, the day of his marriage to the vivacious and popular Ermie Pulice.[48]

The Italian community boasted a number of fine long-distance marathon runners, the best of whom was Giovanni Brait. The handsome Friulano and veteran of several Sons of Italy races, placed second in *The Vancouver Sun*'s 21-mile marathon in 1930.[49]

Tosca Trasolini, a truly brilliant athlete, captured local and provincial acclaim for her outstanding record of achievement in track and field, baseball, basketball and lacrosse. As the society's most consistent female super star, Tosca won the Silver Cup in the 100-metres (1929), half-mile (1930), and mile (1931) races. Nationally, she is recognized as having been a pilot and founding member of the famous Flying Seven.[50]

Commenting on his sister's exploits, Elmo Trasolini recalled his mother saying, "She should have been born a boy."

"Tosca would go out with the guys—drive motorcycles—and she would drive the motorcycle herself," he continued. "She used to take me flying before the war. I went up with her in a Taylor Cub; just a small Taylor Cub. I would sit behind her as she flew us around Richmond. It was pretty good. That's all she liked to do. In those days, what was it? It cost $5 an hour to learn; a lot of money in those days," concluded Trasolini.

Marino loved sports and enthusiastically participated in the organization of the Sons of Italy's Athletic Club in 1931. In its first year, the club fielded a softball team, formed a basketball team and placed several fighters in a boxing tournament. The year's activities concluded on December 16, with a highly successful Snowball Frolic and Dance at the Majestic Hall.

However, the club that truly captured the hearts of the community's sports fans was the Young Canadian Italian Athletic Association. Its softball team, organized by Sammy De Filippo, co-owner of Service Taxi, was managed by Marino for a year or so. As the society's sports organization evolved into the YCIAA, the Italian athletes took the Pacific Softball League senior championship in 1932. In 1933, De Filippo's team captured the Senior "A" championship without suffering a single loss. The Young Canadian Italian Athletic Association had triumphed with a record of 25 straight wins.[51]

The YCIAA obtained the use of the gymnasium at the Silver Slipper Hall in which they constructed a boxing ring. The arrangement with the Veneta was amicable enough when the Young Italians had a membership of 100. However, by July 1933, membership was down to 20. This prompted president Johnny Berrutti to write to the Veneta about the amount owing on the rent.

Tosca Trasolini and John Brait were two of the Italian community's outstanding athletes, circa 1929.

Chuck Davis writing in The Province, *July 19, 1991, publicized the 55th anniversary of the Flying Seven Club. His column included, "Tosca Trasolini snaps on her flying helmet, climbs into the cockpit of the Fairchild, shouts, 'Contact!' and rolls down the runway and up into the mist.*

"Canada's first all-woman dawn-to-dusk patrol has begun."

Angelo Branca, the boxing barrister, became Canadian amateur middleweight champion in 1934.

Canadian-Italians were crowned the 1932 Pacific Softball League Champions.

In his letter to John Branca he stated, "The YCIAA has done much to advertise Italian ability, especially in athletics, but it is gradually finding out that without steady financial cooperation, it is a very hard job. Please keep this in mind when you do not receive payments as soon as you would wish and as soon as we would like to make them. But we promise that your account will be taken care of in the best possible manner."[52]

In December the Young Canadian Italian Athletic Association obtained a benefactor. The cost to operate its football club, starring such notables as Gillie Brandolini, Cecil Cima, Ernie Magliocco, Armando Minichiello and Bob Peroni, was underwritten by Charlie Peneway and Joe Nadalin, co-owners of the Columbia Hotel.[53]

Al Principe, in commenting on YCIAA, stated, "When we formed the Young Canadian Italian Athletic Club—which we did to prove to Canada that we were loyal—we got the gym going under the wing of the Veneta. We had boxing matches there. I was the boxing promoter. George Paris came down to coach. He trained Angelo Branca, who became middleweight champion of Canada, at the gym in the city police station. To make money, we used the Veneta Society's beer permit to sponsor fund-raising drives in order to buy uniforms, shoes and balls. The Sons of Italy put a squawk in and they torpedoed us. Then we didn't have any more funds. They were just being jealous bastards."[54]

The Vancouver Sun ran a boxing news item with a photo of Angelo Branca Oct. 4, 1934, "Angelo Branca. Better known around Vancouver as one of our leading barristers, will forget all about law books tomorrow night when he dons the gloves to meet Jack Henderson, former B.C. amateur middleweight title holder, in one

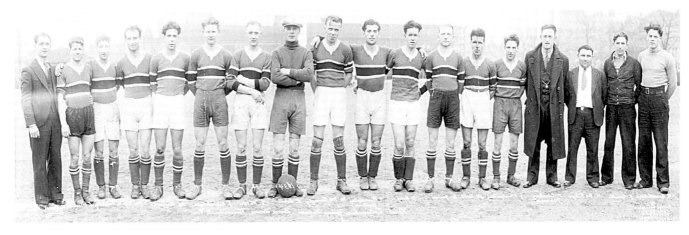

of the bouts on the big benefit program to be staged by the Hastings Community Association at the Exhibition Forum, starting at 8 o'clock."

Branca K.O.'d Henderson in the second round to take the Canadian championship title.

Bill Canal was one of the boxers who recalled the days of the YICAA. "I boxed at the Silver Slipper when George Paris was the coach. I remember I had a fight—it was a smoker—with Joe Ferari (or Ferario) with whom I had sparred before. I guess I got lucky. I hit him a good one, then after the fourth hit, he went over to the side of the ring and threw up. That was one of my last boxing matches."

Other Canadian-Italians associated with the ring at the Silver Slipper were pro-fighters Felice DiPalma alias Phil Palmer and Tom Paonessa. Among the amateur boxers who fought on Phil Palmer's Amateur Show card as members of the East End Athletic Club at the Hastings Auditorium in 1948 and 1949 were Phil's brother Patsy DiPalma, Albert and Tony Perry, Larry and John "Peewee" Creanza and "Killer" Roy Callegeri, pride of the East End.

"All the guys that used to fight at the Hastings Auditorium during the '40s did their ring training at Dave De Camillis's Western Cartage 'gym' at 803 Keefer Street," recalled Joey DiPalma. "Roy Callegeri was a killer in the ring and out. He was tough. He could take a real beating. And he knew how to dish it out too. I've seen him pulverize a fighter like nobody else. Like the time he beat Tony Churskay. Boy, Roy was an awesome fighter, no kidding. He was the only fighter I ever knew who knocked his opponent

Coached by Sammy DeFilippo (third from right), the Young Canadian-Italian Athletic Association fields a championship-class soccer team in 1934.

Canadian Hall of Fame member Lu Moro, centre front, with Trail lacrosse champions, 1938.

Girardi Brothers Soccer Champs: 1944–45
Front from left, Midge Santaga, Dukey Adams, Elso Genovese, Fred Brisco, George Bogdanovich, Red Matthewson, Elmer Cheng. Back from left, Bruno Girardi (manager), Ray Benny, Chuck McFaddin, Guido Stefanni (coach), Ray Girardi, Don Faoro, Marino Crema, Attilio Girardi (sponsor).

Sacred Heart Softball Champs: 1954–55
Front from left, Roy Albo, Larry Crema, Father Joseph, Pete Brunato, Gaynard Hales. 2nd row, Elso Genovese (manager), Lionel Wallace, Don Robertson, Ernie Maddalozzo, Renato Zanatta. Back row, Danny Rosenbund, Douglas Currie, Ricci Genovese.

down, then kicked him. He should have been disqualified but the referee never called it.

"But in the lightweight division the boxer that had the greatest potential was Larry Creanza. Larry could have beaten the best. But that wasn't to be," stated DiPalma.

Larry's brother, "Peewee" Creanza, at 22, was a brilliant and determined featherweight. Coached by Art Hodgkisson at the Junior G-Men's Club in Vancouver's East End, the younger Creanza fine-tuned his skills at the Western Sports Club. In 1956, Creanza captured the Golden Gloves title by defeating the Canadian champion in a first round knock-out at the PNE Gardens.

Tommy Paonessa, 90 when interviewed in 1997, started his amateur boxing career in 1920, becoming Canadian amateur bantamweight champion in 1923. He then turned pro as a feather-weight, thrilling hundreds of fight-fans by answering the bell in 45 matches. "I fought pro for seven years, sometimes fighting three times a week and winning most of them by decision. After that I did a lot of refereeing. As a matter of fact, I refereed a few of Peewee's matches in the late '40s," declared Paonessa.

On the west side of town, aspiring boxers trained at Jimmy Philliponi's Eagle-Time Athletic Club. Fred Minichiello recalls frequenting the gym, located at street level in the Penthouse Cabaret building on Seymour. "My favourite amateur boxer of the late '30s was Wally 'Blondie' Wallace, the exciting middleweight fighter, who lived in the Giuseppe Maida family home in Vancouver East," stated Minichiello.

Born Felice (Felix) DiPalma in Civitanova, Italy in 1922, Phil Palmer excited Vancouver's Italian community like no other Italo-Canadian boxer. Jimmy Ricci followed his career from the PNE Gardens to New York's Madison Square Garden. "I remember how he got into the boxing game and why he had to change his name," reminisced Ricci.

"He was an altar boy at Sacred Heart Church when he was a young teenager. In those days, the church door was always unlocked. A guy went in and stole the chalice from the altar. Phil saw this guy take off and gave chase. He caught up with him and started to fight with him, pushing, shoving, pummelling all the way down the Keefer Street hill. Beat the crap out of the guy and returned the chalice to the church. An onlooker said, 'You're good with your fists. Why don't you become a fighter?' When they realized at the Jr. G-Man Club that he had great natural ability and skill, the trainer asked Phil to let him put his name on that week's fight card. Phil

Phil Palmer with Tom Paonessa, trainer.
Felice Di Palma was featured at New York's Madison Square Garden in 1944.

Marino Victor Culos proudly displays his father's trophies, circa 1935.

Muhammad Ali with Mario Caravetta. Caravetta was a Royal Canadian Navy boxing division fighter during World War II.

John "Peewee" Creanza, Golden Gloves Champion, 1956.

replied that if his mother ever found out he was boxing, she would kill him. 'Then let's change your name to Phil Palmer,' suggested the trainer. And that's how it happened," concluded a smiling Jimmy Ricci.

"By August 1946, my brother Phil had fought 41 professional fights at Madison Square Garden. His record was 34 wins, 12 by knock-out, and seven losses," recalled Joey DiPalma. They just pushed him too fast: 41 fights in two years. Besides, he was matched with welterweights the likes of Robert Garcia, Joey Peralta and Johnny (Honey Boy) Bratton a bit too soon. Then Phil lost his first fight to Garcia. The first loss in 25 bouts. I don't know if Ronnie Beaudin was his trainer at the time but whoever it was he made a big mistake in matching Phil with some of the big pros too early in his career. This was especially true about Bratton who eventually became world welterweight champion. If they had just taken it easy with him, who knows?" surmised DiPalma nostalgically.

Chapter 9

The Grape Merchants

I Commercianti d'Uva

Augosto Bosa (seated) and nephew Vincenzo Aballini at Food Fair, circa 1960s.
The much respected Bosa was a leading grape merchant in the 1960s.

Dan Minichiello, Frieda and Afonse Donati, Artemisia Minichiello making arrangements in California to ship grapes to Vancouver, 1929.

ince the 1920s Vancouver Italians have been pressing California grapes every September in their basement *cantini*. These expert wine makers are renowned for capturing the taste and bouquet of the red and white wines similar in flavour to those enjoyed in Italy. More recently through the energy and expertise of the "Cap" Capozzi family, grapes from the Okanagan have added a zestful variety of wine-grape from which to add to their drinking pleasure. Vancouver's major importers of grapes were Filippo Branca, Peter Tosi, Sam and Donato Minichiello and Augusto Bosa while Errigo Spagnol was the main source of California grapes in New Westminster.

During his peak selling years, Donato (Dan) Minichiello imported 24 box-car loads (480 tons) of California grapes in a single season. These grapes would be sold by the box, each weighing approximately 33 pounds. The average Italian bought his grapes for family consumption only and wouldn't consider selling wine for a profit. Members of the pioneer Iaci family topped the customer list by purchasing two or three tons of Zinfandel with a single order. In the early years, the grapes would be shipped via rail from the Fresno Valley. After the war, they arrived by freight trucks, the distribution of which was organized largely by Minichiello's capable daughter Rose DiPalma.[55]

Scores of Italian families sold small amounts of home-made wine to their friends and lodgers, especially during the Depression years. But the purveyors of major liquor sales were in a category unto themselves.The real bootleggers were strictly in the delivery end of the business. Their customers were the clubs, high rollers, and sophisticated members of Vancouver's elite. The big four booze baron families lived on Seymour, Prior, Union, and Georgia Streets. During the decades of the 1920s and 1930s in particular, they each made small fortunes selling "unsealed" whiskey and quality beer to speak-easies, unlicensed clubs and high-profile citizens including mayor L.D. Taylor.

"I used to deliver a lot of booze to Taylor. He used to party. Oh, I remember the old Gladstone Cabaret on Kingsway. They called it the Gladstone. He phoned me up because he trusted, me, see. He says, this is so-and-so. Oh, yeah. 'You bring me something good, you know.' I says, okay; two or three bottles, you know. Gave me a tip, you know. Oh, yeah, he was a good customer of mine," stated a former bootlegger who requested anonymity.

"I worked for Savario; he was at it a long time. What a life, eh? God, he used to get those headaches, fierce headaches, you know. Drive him crazy. You go to bed and you got the phone right beside you. What do you expect? I would be out on a call—out on a delivery—I come back to the house and lift the telephone. I would ask the operator to ring the line and Savario would have the next order ready for me."

The liquor laws in B.C. during this era were quite different from the ones in force today. It was easier to operate in a clandestine manner in the mid-1920s as one could buy liquor wholesale from a distiller such as Kennedy & Son and Nasdillers.

However, it usually took a little ingenuity and skulduggery on the part of the booze barons to qualify as "exporters" of liquor and thus get their whiskey at wholesale prices.

The front men would falsify Canadian export forms on which they stated that the purchase of whiskey was for resale abroad. This "unsealed" product could be purchased at discounted or wholesale prices to net the bootleggers huge profits when sold at bootleg prices.

"We would go to Nasdillers on Richards Street around 6 o'clock in the morning two or three times a week to load up. The whiskey came in sacks; 12 bottles with straws attached. We would have phony papers made out for going across the border.

"We'd take up to 50 cases per time. Instead of travelling back to the East side, we would head south and go across the old Cambie Bridge in case the cops were watching. Once across the bridge we would turn left in the direction of Main Street. I would be driving the Hudson with a full load. Once back at our premises on Union

"I used to lock the doors when we were ready to—you know—I used to work a lot of bloody hours. From Sunday from 2 o'clock in the afternoon to Monday at 7 in the morning. I was doing it for $25 a week. And the rest of the week, it was like going to work around 6:30 to 7 p.m. till 7 o'clock the next morning. That was steady; seven days a week. We would lock the doors, say about 3 o'clock in the morning, put all that money on the kitchen table. My pockets were full, you know. And count it all, and check up. So much for this one, so much for the next one. The money was all on the kitchen table.

"But I sure learned a good lesson; I got acquainted with a lot of police. They liked me and I got along good with them. No problem. I used to go to their affairs. I had invitations; I was the only bootlegger they invited."

—Anonymous bootlegger

Street, we would stash the booze in two areas; the biggest cache in the wood pile. And that was a dandy. Jesus, we could load a lot of stuff in there," the former bootlegger continued.

Vancouver's police were a constant nemesis to the Italian booze barons and many raids were conducted and numerous liquor offence tickets doled out. Dry-squad members Bill Copeland and Gordon Ward were partners. It is alleged Copeland would enter a bootlegger's home or warehouse and break the walls looking for the booze. His partner Ward, who lived on Williams near Victoria Drive, was considered a good man but Copeland was regarded as a SOB by the bootleggers.

It wasn't only the police who raided the bootleggers, but also thieves intent on stealing booze for resale to unsuspecting bootleggers. However, because of the excellent relationship that existed among the prominent families, few heists were successful.

"Somebody hijacked my dad. At the time there was only one kind of liquor he sold: Dunbar Scotch Whisky. I'll never forget it. The hijacker then sold the liquor to a 'fence', you know a guy in between. The fence was never told that the liquor had been stolen from my father. And they went to various bootleggers in an attempt to sell the stuff. The Prior Street bootlegger was approached but he refused to deal with them because he figured the shipment belonged to his counterpart on Union Street," stated the bootlegger's son.

Once it was determined that the liquor had been stolen from the bootlegger on Georgia, the booze barons set a plan in motion. The unsuspecting middlemen were directed to Georgia Street where they were told the liquor could be sold.

"My father called him—you know because they worked together—and do you know, he said, 'What kind of booze was it?' He said, 'Dunbar'. He said, 'Son-of-a-bitch. Keep them there as much as you can. No, better still—they don't even know it's your booze—tell them to go back to your place and sell it to you.'

"'Come in, son, just back the truck right in.'—I don't know if you remember that big garage we had in the back—but I'll bet those two guys wished they never left England or wherever they came from...they gave those guys a good licking. They hit them with champagne bottles," concluded the bootlegger's son.

It was the Depression era that spawned the joke about the Brancas in which the phrase "keeping it in the family" was coined. "Filippo sells the grapes and the wine is made. His son John, the dry-squad detective, pinches the bootlegger who then retains Angelo to beat the charges in court."

Cyril Battistoni at the Union (Street) Grocery Store, circa 1926.

Various associations including the Italian Veterans group held their feste at the Silver Slipper Hall (Hastings Auditorium).

The First Italian Hall
La Prima Casa d'Italia

Alberto Principe (right) was a dedicated executive member of the Christopher Columbus Society.

*A*lthough the Sons of Italy had a significantly larger following, having sold its 500th membership in December 1928, the Veneta won the race in establishing a community centre.[56]

Buoyed by their society's popularity as a benevolent society, the Brancas commenced a fund-raising program to construct Vancouver's first Casa d'Italia. Shares were sold to Veneta members and other interested parties. The Silver Slipper Hall, later known as the Hastings Auditorium, was built in 1928 on the 800 block East Hastings Street in the centre of Little Italy. The facility boasted the finest sprung ballroom dance floors east of Granville Street and became a great source of pride to its members and individual shareholders.

Once its games room became operational several boxing matches, smokers, and other youth-oriented events were organized and sponsored at the hall. During this year of major achievement, the Veneta voted Filippo Branca honorary grand president for life.

The rival societies continued to go their separate ways. On September 12, 1929, the Sons of Italy signed a lease to operate the top floor of the Traders Building located at the southeast corner of Hastings and Homer Streets. Signatories for the 12-month agreement that would cost $1,500 were Joe Politano, Luigi Battistoni,

W.G. Ruocco, Felice Cianci, Lino Gallazin and Cesare Anderlini. The rental property, also known as the Majestic Hall, improved the society's cash flow at a time when monthly dues were $1 and the fine for missing a meeting without cause was 50 cents. Attendance at the general meetings also increased during this period. The society's clients for meeting rooms and the banquet hall included the *fascio* (Partito Nazionale Fascista) which booked monthly meetings through its secretary Dr. Eugenio Zito.[57] Ruocco, the brilliant innovator, knew what would appeal to his constituents. In 1929, he struck a school committee with the objective of establishing an Italian Language School. The committee comprised the Italian vice-consul Nicola Masi, the society's physician, Dr. Zito, Felice Cianci, its secretary, Marino Culos and Frank Pio Rita. Mrs. Teresa Girone, president of the Lega, also sat as a member of the committee. Among other things, she encouraged the women to send their children to Italian language classes. As president, Ruocco automatically served as ex-officio member.[58]

Classes commenced in February, 1929, at the Sacred Heart School which then was located in the 900 block East Pender Street.

Nicola Masi and Dr. E. Zito

Vancouver's Consular Corps, including an Italian delegation, at the Orpheum Theatre, circa 1930.

Masi arranged to obtain the textbooks from Italy, and the teachers including Rose Puccetti and Anita Ghini were enlisted from society members. For his extraordinary efforts as a director of the Italian school during its first year of operation, Masi was awarded special recognition and a citation.[59]

Following one of the school committee meetings, Marino agreed to buy Zito's Essex automobile. Soon after the sale, however, Marino was involved in an accident with the car—lucky to escape with his life. With collision expenses to pay, he resigned from the school committee to take a good paying job at Port Alice.[60]

Dr. Zito was a Fascist with connections to Rome. As secretary of the Circolo Giulio Giordano, he sold memberships to the *fascio* organization. To qualify for membership, applicants swore allegiance to Italy and stated that they were ready to die for Mussolini if necessary.

Zito approached Marino about joining the Giordani. Although Marino spurned his offer, several members of the local Italian "intelligentsia" and a number of the Ex-Combattenti, the Italian War Veterans' Association, became members of the pro-fascist club.[61]

Meanwhile, the Italian language classes were proving very popular. Emma Green, daughter of Giuseppe Crosetti, was one of the original students to enroll. She attended class every Friday at Sacred

Giulio Giordani members and friends at Bowen Island picnic site, 1939.

Heart School. Once she became pregnant, however, she dropped out. Emma and Jack Green's son became an excellent athlete. Young Jackie's talent, however, was never fully realized due to his untimely death during a hunting trip in the early 1950s.[62]

The Crosetti family was very active in the Sons of Italy. Emma's brother Johnny, like his father, worked with much energy and determination for the society. The Crosetti siblings supported all of the social functions, including the annual masquerade ball. Attending their first masquerade ball in February 1927, Emma and Johnny placed second in the "best costume" category.[63]

Johnny was a member of the Feste Committee and enjoyed decorating the Majestic Hall before a major event. He did this in particularly good fashion for the society's 25th anniversary banquet held in January 1930. The silver anniversary program began with a toast by Italian consul Nicola Masi to the Patria Lontana and one by Ennio Fabri to the Patria Adottiva. Members remember with pride the recital by musicians Felix and Alfonse Galetti, soprano Rose Anderlini and the scintillating singing of tenor Luigi Palazzini. The guests were also treated to a classical piano concerto solo by Norma Gallia. Closing the programme's entertainment line-up was tenor Antonio Villa, a founding member of the Sons of Italy Society. He sang rousing Italian favourites under the direction of Piero Orsatti.

Midge Santaga played lacrosse with Jackie Green and was devastated by the news of Green's untimely death at age 23.

"We were playing for the Kimount team when we captured the 1952 B.C. championship. We won the cup mostly because of Jack. He was that good. I would say he had the potential of becoming a future inductee to B.C.'s Hall of Fame. Burrard's Walt Lee was a phenomenal goalie. On approaching retirement he stated, 'I'll retire when I see the kid who is ready to take my place.' Well, it was Jack Green who replaced Lee. I saw Green perform in the play-offs against the Adanacs. He was unbelievable and responsible for the team winning the series. God, I miss him," concluded Santaga.

Masquerade Ball participants, 1927.
Award winners John Crosetti and sister Emma, seated fifth and sixth from left.

Masquerade winner: Annie Tate, 1929.

Prior to the dance band playing its first selection, president W.G. Ruocco introduced founding members: Cesare Anderlini, Angelo Calori, Gettulio Falcioni, Giuseppe Martina, Lorenzo Politano, Michele Rosa, Pietro Tamburro and Achille Pini. He presented them with silver anniversary diplomas.[64]

By this time, Achille was the only Pini brother active in the society. His brothers Adolfo and Marco were occupied with their gold mine in Atlin. Brother Raffaele's daughter Clara Preston recalls, "Marco and Adolfo had this mine and it was paying good but tragedy soon struck. They would go to town with a wad of money. And of course they used to drink and carouse. One night uncle Adolfo, after one of these binges, was attacked and killed by a bear as he staggered back to the mine site.

"Some American mining speculators—the way I heard it—got Marco to sell. He just made an 'X' and when he was sober, he realized what he had done."[65]

The second youngest of the Pini brothers was Giuseppe. His son Tony was the first to have a dine-and-dance facility in Vancouver, according to Stella Pini, Tony's wife and a daughter of Sabina Tate. "It was the Lido located under Pini's Restaurant. My husband looked after his grandmother Cristina Pini in the living quarters of the same building. He attended to her and bathed her when she became an invalid. She died in September 1926.

"My husband and his brother Paul went to the mine site in Atlin, B.C. in 1932. It was [the] Depression and Tony didn't have work. People had no money, so they were not going out to night clubs. So, they went ahead and I followed, accompanied by Philip

Mancuso who also worked at the Lido. I had to take the boat to Prince Rupert, fly to Carcross in the Yukon and take the train before taking a second boat to cross Lake Atlin into the town of Atlin. My daughter Dolores was born there May 6, 1933," Stella recalled.

"I lived in a tent to start. It had a pot belly stove and the wind—this is no lie—the wind was so strong, me and Paul and Tony couldn't shut the front door. And I had Dolores in a basket right up against the stove. And I had the stove red hot. The wind blew against the stove and fanned the flames singeing the baby's blankets. We later found out that it was the coldest winter in 40 years. I'll never forget that," she shuddered.

"When we left, everybody at Carcross already knew that somebody was coming out in the cold with this baby, one of the very few white children to be born in the area at that time. We had to break through the ice on Atlin Lake coming through on the boat. It was September. That was the summer boat. You slept outside where the rooms are located. When I awoke in the morning, my face was stuck to the pillow. I had a difficult time getting it off. As we were about to depart from Skagway by boat, there was a big storm brewing. Soon after, the captain announced that we were pulling back. He said he was doing this because there had been a similar storm the night the *Sophia* went down with all passengers," she concluded.

Violet and Fonse Benedetti, winners of the 1929 masquerade ball best costume award.

The Sons of Italy's silver anniversary banquet.
John Crosetti decorated the society-managed Majestic Hall for this event in 1930.

Italian Young Girls' Club members
aboard MV Cellina with Pietro
Colbertaldo and W. G. Ruocco, 1935.

Chapter 11

The Italian Girls' Club
Il Circolo Giovani Italiane

One of the Sons of Italy's popular orators was Antonio Pitton. He very much believed in the Italian Language School and encouraged his three daughters to learn Italian. Nellie, his eldest, recalls her father saying, "Furlan is not the language to learn. It's Italian. The real Italian is what you need." Nellie Pitton, the outstanding student in the class of 1931, excelled in the study of Italian, achieving top marks in the advanced class.[66]

Because of the enthusiastic acceptance given to the three-year-old Italian Ladies' League, Ruocco suggested to Mary Castricano that she help to organize a club for younger Italians. As one of the Lega's most popular members, Castricano responded with enthusiasm. Her efforts resulted in the establishment of Club Delle Giovani Italiane, the Italian Young Girls' Club, in 1930. The club attracted young women between the ages of 15 and mid-20s, most of whom had parents involved in the men's and women's societies. Soon, this lively group was organizing outings, dances and sewing bees. They made beautiful Italian peasant costumes under the skilled supervision of Mary Castricano, described as a "spitfire" by her daughter Lily, one of the club's early presidents.[67]

The girls' club membership steadily grew, peaking during the mid-1930s. Two of the club's popular members, Ermie Brandolini and Rosina Signori, worked for Mrs. Castricano at her up-scale fashion store, The Marie Gown Shoppe, located across from Oreste Notte's Bon Ton pastry shop on Granville Street. Brandolini became president in 1933 and under her administration the Club Delle Giovani Italiane introduced excursions to Bowen Island, Nanaimo, Victoria and Cultus Lake.[68]

One of the club's outings was planned by Mary Juliani whose brother Jimmy was an enlisted sailor stationed at Esquimalt. Mary, with friends including Lily Castricano and Rinda Satti, organized a club excursion to Vancouver Island during which they visited with Jimmy.[69]

Members delighted in wearing their Italian regional costumes on special occasions. And on Sunday, May 5, 1935, approximately 20 IYGC members joined more than 100 other Vancouver Italians on aboard the MV *Cellina*. The young women had been invited by the Italian consul through his secretary Ines Falcioni. It was a beautiful day and an air of festivity permeated the 17,000-ton merchant ship in Vancouver with a load of consumer products for the city's Italian merchants. Local Italians, along with Monsignor Antoniolli, Benedictine abbot from Sacred Heart Church and members of various organizations, were there to provide a family atmosphere for the visiting crew members.[70]

Cavaliere Carmine Marino, a member of the Circolo Giulio Giordani and longtime resident of Vancouver, was a special guest. Mussolini had recently honoured Carmine by making him a *cavaliere*, knight of the Fascist government. *The Vancouver Sun,* reporting

Cavaliere Carmine Marino, knight of the Fascist Italian government, wearing his prized medal, circa 1935.

Italian Language School, 1931.
Directors and students (Nellie Pitton Cavell, second row seventh from left).

Il fascio Littorio.

È il segno dell'Italia fascista.

Le verghe riunite e strette insieme significano concordia, unione, amore.

La scure significa coraggio, forza.

Sotto questo segno gli italiani disciplinati e concordi lavorano per la grandezza della Patria.

82

IL DVCE

Tutti i bimbi italiani amano Mussolini, il Duce che guida la nuova Italia e che senza riposo lavora per il bene della Patria.

Il volto austero del Duce si illumina di dolcezza quando Egli guarda i bambini.

Sanno i bimbi italiani perchè il Duce li ama tanto ?

Li ama perchè i bimbi sono le più belle speranze d'Italia, perchè se essi cresceranno forti, laboriosi, buoni, l'Italia anche sarà forte, potente, felice.

83

First Reader containing Fascist symbols and propaganda, circa 1930.

"You know, Eugene De Paola started an Italian school; an Italian language school. At the time, I was attending Vancouver Technical School in the early 1930s. It was down at the old wooden church, Campbell and Keefer. And I became an instructor as I could speak Italian, although it was dialect. He would correct me—gave me a few lessons—and then I started teaching the younger groups."
—Bill Canal

on the festive event, said that the honour had been bestowed upon Carmine, "because he represents, according to Italian residents, all that is finest in the worker's character."

Not everyone, however, shared this view about the self-professed Fascist. "Some *paesano* was real jealous because he have this. They ask, 'What for he have this medal?'," stated Antonietta Marino. The *cavaliere*'s daughter-in-law recalled that it was Dr. Zito who presented the medal to him. "Dr. Zito come to my place. Nice young man. He said to my father-in-law, 'Mr. Marino, I have to give you something nice from Italy.' I don't know where this come from, if it come from the king or Mussolini. I can't tell you," Mrs. Marino confided.

In a whimsical tone, Mrs. Marino confessed to having thrown out her 70-year-old father-in-law's coveted decoration with the garbage. "I said, my husband have to go away [to the internment camp] and I have to look after this guy. I was mad. Twenty-two months," she explained.[71]

After the official ceremony, a dinner party was hosted on board the *Cellina* by Captain Rodolfo Muntian. Emma Lussin was among those who attended the festivities. "I remember going to this party, and I remember Mr. Colbertaldo taking me to a dinner on board the ship—pretty fantastic food, I had never seen anything like it before.

Then one of the officers came up to me and spoke softly about something I didn't quite understand. I asked Mr. Colbertaldo, what is this man trying to say to me? Apparently, I was being invited to a shipboard Pirate's Party. Although I was reluctant at first, I did go with him and I had a wonderful time. The officer who had spoken softly to me in Italian had said, 'Don't you think you would have a better time over here with us than associating with the older people on board?' Things don't change much, huh?" concluded Emma Lussin Maffei.[72]

Ines Falcioni (centre) and friends at a Giovani Club sponsored outing, circa 1930.

Bruno Girardi, in a moment of reflection, pined, "You know in the 1930s, when the ships landed in Vancouver—a line of 10 ships—the first one would be flying the Italian flag. After the war, if an Italian ship came in at all, it would be number 11 in the line."

The guests aboard the *Cellina* sang songs, spoke Italian, and witnessed the ship's crew receive their colours as they became initiated into the Dopolavoro Club, the Afterwork organization. It had been initiated by Mussolini, and was designed "to bring all ranks of workers together during leisure hours for cultural recreation." It also served to provide fascist indoctrination to nationals living abroad.[73]

The young women's club members simply were not involved in

Lega Members' Diploma, 1932.

any political discussions. They were there, however, to provide a tasteful Italian family atmosphere to crew members who had been away from home for several weeks. These programs were so successful, Mary Castricano often would invite a number of the crew along with a few of the girls from the club back to her home for coffee and biscuits. These impromptu coffee parties offered the seamen an opportunity to experience a touch of "home-away-from-home" hospitality.

"I know that quite a few of them came to our place. It was one of the ways mother fulfilled her role as a community leader," Lily later recalled.[74]

Lega's Giovani members Emma Dalfo, Lina Gazzola and Nellie Pitton.

Shipboard welcome for visiting Cellina crew featuring the Lega's Giovani Club.
Vancouver Italians at Dopolavoro Dedication, 1935.

Chapter 12

The Vancouver Italian-Canadian Society

La Societa' Italo-Canadese di Vancouver

Tony Venturato weds Elda Battistoni.
The Venturatos were active members of the Vancouver Italian-Canadian Society and Lega, circa 1930s.

The establishment of Vancouver's third Italian mutual aid society took place on April 16, 1934. Marino suspected the idea for the new society came from Veneta members seeking leadership roles not readily available to them in Filippo Branca's organization. Others have noted that the formation of the Vancouver Italian-Canadian Mutual Aid Society Inc. coincided with the Veneta's sale of the Hastings Auditorium. Founding member Cirillo Braga was voted first president of the VICS. A hotel waiter and resident of the city since 1919, Braga previously had served as president of the Veneta Society. He now held current memberships in all three societies. Another prominent member of the VICS was Nicola Di Tomaso, a former vice-president of the Veneta. *Compare* Nick, as Di Tomaso was called by his close friends, became vice-president of the new society in 1935.[75]

Cesare Primo Durante served as the Veneta's president in 1927. He too joined the Vancouver Italian-Canadian Society quickly establishing himself as one of its most influential founding members. Durante's reputation as a major organizer within the Italian community was acknowledged during his tenure as president of the New Westminster Italian Mutual Aid Society. The membership of the

Anita Zanon married Dukey Adams in 1950.
She is pictured with her parents, her sisters Ella, Lucille and Gina and her grandmother on her wedding day.

New Westminster-based organization presented him with a gold medal for his outstanding contributions in 1931.[76]

The Veneta's Italian Ladies' League, founded in 1928, became the Vancouver Italian-Canadian Society's affiliate in 1935. The Lega had a talented executive led by Enrichetta Agnolin (Benetti), its president. The table officers included Antonietta Corra', vice-president, and Clorinda Piccolo, correspondence secretary. Each held the important distinction of being a member of the Italian societies' executive committe, Il Grande Comitato. A leading director of the Lega in the 1930s and 1940s was Elda Venturato, whose parents operated the Venice Bakery. The treasurer was Cecilia Zanon, who in private life assisted her husband in operating the popular Montreal Bakery.[77]

Luciano Zanon was a member of the Veneta, serving with distinction as president for a term. He was recognized as a foremost speaker and had the ability to stimulate and captivate an audience with his oratory. As a businessman, he showed great promise. In 1934 he moved his bakery operation across the street to new facilities at the corner of Keefer Street and Hawkes Avenue. With this move, he added a fleet of new delivery vans.

"In the early years, there was no such thing as the Montreal Bakery," stated Cyril Battistoni. "Luciano began in the business working for my father at the Venice Bakery when we operated next to Sam Minichiello's house. In fact, he lived upstairs where I slept. Yes, Luciano Zanon lived in our place. He was a number one baker. A good one. He built up a pretty good business on Hawkes Avenue. And he was a good baker. All by hand. Jesus, that Luciano worked with my dad like a horse too. Only trouble was he had bad eyes," recalled Battistoni.[78]

The Vancouver Italian-Canadian Society's most dynamic pre-war president was Mario Ghislieri. He arrived in Vancouver in 1935 with impressive credentials. A former officer in the Italian army, Ghislieri had been born to a family of noble and aristocratic lineage in Alessandria di Sale, Piedmont. His family genealogy included truly illustrious members: Giacomo Filippo Marquis Ghislieri of Santo Stefano and Pope Pius V.[79]

In 1925 the Ghislieri and Rossini families combined their substantial resources in Italy to purchase a vast track of fertile land near Alessandria. To consolidate the venture, Mario sold his holdings and lucrative furniture factory business and his brother-in-law, Roberto Rossini, put up equal equity in cash. Their new venture included a dairy section with 100 purebred Holstein cows, which supplied milk to local hospitals. A stable of horses and its 100 workers came under the supervision of Ghislieri. This large parcel of fertile land was irrigated by the Ganaro and Po rivers. In the spring of 1926, flood waters resulting from torrential rains caused the dikes to burst in several locations. Within three weeks the area's choicest producing land was under a 15-foot sea of water. Everything was lost. Both families declared bankruptcy. These very rich and privileged families now were all but paupers.

A family connection in Canada led the Ghislieris to leave Italy in July 1927, to homestead in Saskatchewan. They stayed with a cousin who farmed an area 30 miles south of Moose Jaw along Johnston Lake. Soon they were working their own land. During the first two years Mario made excellent progress and soon had enough money to expand his wheat producing enterprise to include 3,000 acres. Then the wrath of the Depression descended upon the Prairies. Crop failures due to a lack of rain, early frosts, and devastating hail storms brought financial ruin to the Ghislieris for the second time in eight years.[80]

A short time after arriving in Vancouver, Ghislieri joined the Vancouver Italian-Canadian Society. It wasn't long before the executive realized the potential of their new member. Mario's education and natural ability, coupled with his expertise as an orator who spoke perfect Italian, quickly projected him into a leadership role.

In addition to his VICS directorship, he became a director, organizer and leading spokesperson for the VICS's

Mario Ghislieri, World War I veteran.
Mario Ghislieri served with distinction as an officer in the Italian army.

Society's Feste Committee.
Fantino Durante, fourth from left.

"A certain Ghislieri came from Constantinople to Bologna with St. Petronio in the year 430 thus establishing the family's roots in Italy. In 1445, Filippo or Lippo, son of Tomaso, chief of the Guelfs, was expelled from Bologna and settled at Bosco, now Bosco Marengo, in the province of Alessandria, Piedmont. This branch of the family includes a Ghislieri who became Pope Saint Pius V. The son of Paolo and Domenica Angeri, he was born at Bosco, Jan. 17, 1504 and died in Rome, May 1, 1572.

"Two popes of the same name: S. Pius V was a Ghislieri and Pius VIII, the son of a Ghislieri. Napoleon was a guest at the Ghislieri house on May 4, 1796 and again in 1800. King Vittorio Emanuele, in the autumn of 1853, stopped overnight."

—Herman Ghislieri

youth organization, the Circolo Giovanile, the Associazione Combattenti (Italian Veterans' Association), the Circolo Giulio Giordani and its ladies' affiliate, Circolo Roma.[81]

Ruocco, working with Ghislieri, registered a major coup in 1935. He successfully brought together executive members of the mutual aid societies and women's organizations under the auspices of Il Grande Comitato Esecutivo Delle Associazione Italiane Di Mutuo Soccorso. The Grand Committee, as it was commonly called, did much to promote union within Vancouver's Italian community. It established communications among the societies, especially with respect to the scheduling of social events and cultural activities.[82] However, Eugene De Paola was not invited to participate by chairman Ruocco, a fellow Castelgrandese, because Ruocco did not regard De Paola's Christopher Columbus Society as being in the same league with the mutual aid societies.[83]

De Paola, a notary public, had been responsible for promoting Columbus Day celebrations since 1913. And with a small band of loyal associates, including Alberto Principe, organized banquets and dances to commemorate the epic voyage of Christopher Columbus. During the 1930s, all of the Italian organizations were competing for the community's support of this celebration. De Paola, aided by a handful of executive members including Paul Girone, honorary president, and Tony Mazzucco, the association's publicist, formalized his mandate in 1935 by founding the Societa' Cristoforo Colombo Inc.[84]

Without question, 1935 was a banner year for Vancouver's Italian community. The year was capped by the distribution in November of *Souvenirs, 'Ricordi' of the Progress and Activities of the Members of the Italian Colony of Vancouver, 1935*. The booklet, print-

Armistice Day banquet, circa 1930s.
Italian war veterans meet to remember.

ed in Italian and English, was edited and published by Marino Culos. This significant documented social history highlighted the achievements of the societies and their leaders. In particular, it emphasized the progress made by the Sons of Italy Society during its 30-year history.[85]

During the six months it took to research his project, Marino interviewed scores of people and wrote most of the featured articles. In addition, he sold advertisements for Cliff Hayes, whom he had hired to coordinate the publication's advertising content. Phyllis Culos typed all of her husband's notes, correspondence, copy and invoices. The Italian translation consultant for the project was Count Joseph U. Montalban Troya, editor of *Italian Life*, the official newsletter of the Italian Business Co-operative Association.[86]

The 31-year-old Marino enjoyed interviewing people. He contacted scores of people including Italo Rader, manager of Catelli Macaroni, with whom he discussed copy for articles featuring the academic careers of three of his children: Louis, Italo Jr. and Dr. A.F. Rader.[87]

Rader Sr. had immigrated to Canada in 1900. He made his decision to do so after viewing a CPR display at the World's Fair in Paris, which advertised Canada as "The Land of Opportunity." Once discharged from the Italian army, Rader travelled to Alberta with only $37 in his pocket. His astute business acumen enabled him to establish a macaroni business in Lethbridge in 1915. Through the implementation of timely marketing strategies, Rader sold thousands of tons of macaroni to the British army and navy. In 1928, he sold his thriving business to Catelli Macaroni Company for a reported $80,000. Two years later he opened the company's Vancouver office.[88]

In pursuing interviews with prominent Italians, Marino next approached Isobel Campbell, Norma Gallia's music instructor. Campbell was able to provide detailed information about the brilliant local pianist. Gallia, well known to society members, had passed her Licentiate Solo Performer's examination of the Associated Board of Royal Schools with the highest marks ever awarded in Vancouver. And she favoured Vancouver's Italians by performing at many of the society's functions.

"I think I played at every concert they ever held at the Majestic Hall," recalled Norma Gallia Porter.[89]

Grande Ballo Coloniale

CHE SI TERRA' SOTTO GLI AUSPICI DELLA

SOCIETA' ITALIANA CRISTOFORO COLOMBO INCORPORATA
LUNEDI OTTOBRE 12, 1936
NEL MOOSE HALL, 638 Burrard St.

DALLE ORE 8 P. M. ALLE ORE 1 A. M.

CONCERTO MUSICALE, BALLO, DISCORSI COMMEMORATIVI DA PROMINENTE PERSONALITA' ITALIANE E CANADESE

ITALIANI IN ALTO I CUORI
E RICORDATEVI

CHE LA PRIMA INIZIATIVA DI FONDARE LA CELEBRAZIONE COLOMBIANA IN VANCOUVER, BRITISH COLUMBIA, FU STATA FATTA DAL NOSTRO ENERGICO CONNAZIONALE SIGNOR EUGENE DE PAOLA, IL GIORNO 12 OTTOBRE 1913 – ED HA EGLI SPETTANO I MERITI, E NON GIA' A POCHI CHE NON HANNO FATTO MAI NULLA, E NULLA SAPRANNO FARE, MA SANNO FARE SOLO CHE.

ATTEGGIARSI A PALADINI???

TUTTI GLI ITALIANI DI VANCOUVER, E D'INTORNI, SONO IN-TELLIGENTI ABBASTANZA, PER MEMORARE IL PASSATO, E CON CUORE S'INVITA TUTTA LA COLONIA ITALIANA D'INTERVE-NIRE NUMEROSI ED UNANIMI ALLA VERA FESTA E CELEBRA-ZIONE COLOMBIANA, CHE SI TERRA':

NEL MOOSE HALL, 638 BURRARD STREET
OTTOBRE 12 1936 - ORE 8 P. M. TO 1 A. M.
BOLOGNA ORCHESTRA   RINFRESHI
Ammissione: Signore o Signori 25c

PER IL COMITATO ESECUTIVO
COLONIA ITALIANA E
SOCIETA' ITALIANA CRISTOFORO COLOMBO
(TUTTI SONO CORDIALMENTE INVITATI)
DIO SALVI IL RE

Christopher Columbus Society Notice.
De Paola reminds Italians that it was he who initiated the Columbus Day celebrations in Vancouver.

Minichiello, Di Tomaso and Ricci families.
With friends in Stanley Park, circa 1918. Sam Minichiello, family head and hotel owner, is third from left.

Hollow Tree, Stanley Park

Angelo Calori, patriarch of Vancouver's
Italian community, circa 1905.

Alberto and Assunta Principe. A fine
horseman, "Prince Albert" often rode his
trotter in Stanley Park, circa 1907.

Agostino Ferrera, at front left, Tony
Cianci, top right, and friends, circa 1910.

In 1933, Gallia won a scholarship to study in Italy under Herr Artur Schnabel. Accompanied by her mother, she was in Italy only a short while when notified of the sudden death of her father, Delfino. The need to return immediately to Vancouver signalled an end to her special training. Unfortunately, Gallia was forced to set aside her career in favour of assisting her mother with the running of the St. Alice Hotel in North Vancouver. The grand hotel, built by her uncle Antonio Gallia, a founding member of the Sons of Italy, had been named for her aunt Alice. Eventually Gallia resumed her study of music and in the 1990s continued to be a successful and well-respected piano instructor.[90]

Raffaele and Marcella Cervi, Palmira and Santo Brandolini, and Fantino Durante.

La Locondiera (The Inn Keeper).
From left, Ines Falcioni, Bruno Girardi, Nino Sala, Emma Maffei, Armando Biscaro, Marino Fraresso, Mary Pettovello. Seated in front, Pietro Colbertaldo (consul), Emma Dalfo and Cleofe Forti (director), 1937.

In its May 22, 1936 issue, The Vancouver Sun headed a news item, "Vancouver's Loyal Italian Wives Donate Their Gold Wedding Rings to Il Duce." According to the article, 150 women exchanged their golden wedding rings— blessed by Father Antoniolli—for steel ones at a ceremony conducted by Colbertaldo on board Italian MS Rialto at her berth at Great Northern Docks. "The rings were donated to the Italian Red Cross and the steel rings given in return were engraved with the date of Nov. 18, 1935 together with the words 'anno 14,' meaning the 14th year of the Fascist regime."

Political Polemics
Le Polemiche Politiche

As the year 1935 came to an end, many of Vancouver's Italians started to seriously question the actions of their country of birth. Mussolini's invasion of Ethiopia had earned him the condemnation of the League of Nations. Fascist Italy was being viewed by Britain and other western nations as a major potential adversary. A backlash of Canadian resentment toward Italians in Canada was becoming evident. And within the Italian community a growing resentment toward Mussolini's aggressive acts was being voiced. The local newspaper quoted Francis Federici, proprietor of the Hotel Vancouver Barber Shop, and one of Vancouver's best known Italians as declaring, "'I am most sad,'" over the Ethiopian dispute. "Mr. Federici said that not only have Italians always had a high admiration for the British, but they feel more at home under the British flag than under other flags."[91]

This antagonism toward Italians in general was apparent to Elmo Trasolini who felt put upon when he was a student of Florence Nightingale School. "In those days, I have to admit we were kind of shy—we had to be careful—when old Mussolini went to Ethiopia. I took a lot of flack over that at school. If I could get that teacher today, I would kill the son-of-a-bitch. We were studying history and we were getting onto the subjects of dictators and stuff like that and he would point to me and say, 'Who is the dictator of Italy?' And I had to get up and answer. Then you know, 'Mussolini-Trasolini'. Boy, to this day, I am telling you," recalled an agitated Trasolini.

Prior to the outbreak of the Ethiopian campaign, Marino had accepted an invitation, extended by his old friend Montalban Troya, the First World War Italian fighter pilot, to represent *The Voice of Italy*. This Italian-English-language weekly newspaper, which was being published in New York, had 30 general agents in the U.S. but only one in Western Canada. As its circulation distribution agent, Marino promoted the sale of the newspaper and periodically submitted articles for publication. His fascination with this fiercely pro-fascist newspaper, however, did not last long.[92]

On Oct. 23, 1935, Marino wrote to Igino A. Manecchia, editor of *The Voice of Italy*. He advised him that subscription sales had fallen off because the majority of prominent Vancouver Italians were very concerned over the direction the newspaper was taking with regard to the grave problems currently existing between Italy and England. Supported by Mrs. Montalban, the newspaper's former Vancouver representative, Marino suggested that the newspaper include articles of greater appeal to its Vancouver readers. Manecchia, whose mandate it was to "defend and spread the spirit of Mussolini's Fascist Italy," wasn't listening.[93]

Ten days after the end of the Italian conquest of Ethiopia, Marino again wrote to Manecchia. He reminded the editor that a copy of the *Souvenirs 'Ricordi'* booklet had been sent to the newspaper the previous December for review in *The Voice of Italy*. Because there had been no reply, Marino asked Manecchia to respond with his comments on the subject.

In what appeared to be an uncharacteristic move to gain critical acclaim at any cost, Marino appealed to the editor's fascist sympathies. He did this by stating that he knew the secretary of the *fascio* in Vancouver, and that he was a member of the Italian consul's organizing committee charged with arranging for a grand banquet to commemorate the victorious conquest of Ethiopia. Moreover, Marino reminded Manecchia that he was the newspaper's Vancouver subscription sales agent and, as such, was available to assist him should there be something the editor might want him to do. The editor still wasn't listening. The only acknowledgement was from Peter Celiberti, the newspaper's subscription manager regarding subscription payments.[94]

The changing attitude toward Italians culminated with demonstrations at the Italian consulate's office in Vancouver. Emma Lussin, Vice-Consul Pietro Colbertaldo's secretary in 1935, was in the consular office at the Dominion Bank Building, 207 West Hastings Street, when anti-war demonstrators took up positions at the front entrance to the building. The picketers carried placards and shouted

Sons of Italy calendar, 1935.

On a section front in The Vancouver Sun, Oct. 3, 1935, a news item ran, entitled "Italians Here Volunteer." Pietro Colbertaldo, Royal Italian vice-consul, commenting on those wanting to fight for Italy in Ethiopia was quoted as stating, "About 15 men have so far requested me to take their names as volunteers. It is not the practice of Italy to call to the colours reservists resident in foreign lands. But they can volunteer.

"Included in the list so far are three brothers, Italians, but B.C.-born. I have had requests from Canadians who were born in England."

In the following day's edition, a Vancouver Sun reporter talked to a dozen or so young Italians just after newspapers had heralded word that Italian troops had invaded Ethiopia and the war was on. He concluded that Vancouver's young Italians were not getting excited about the war and that there would be no great rush from Canada to join Mussolini's forces in Africa.

**Sons of Italy and Italian Ladies'
League members, 1936.**
(Mario Caravetta is the youngster in
front.)

anti-Italian slogans in protest of Italy's invasion of Ethiopia. Lussin, taken aback by this demonstration, began to use the rear door to enter and leave the building.

One day, a large parcel arrived by post at the Italian consulate's office. It had no visible markings and looked very suspect. Since the picketing incident, the staff was instructed to be wary of unmarked packages.

Lussin requested Colbertaldo examine the suspicious-looking package. As beads of perspiration formed on his forehead, the clerks drew back from the counter. While gingerly and painstakingly removing the brown wrapping paper, he slit open the carton to reveal its contents. He paused, drew a breath, and uttered a nervous laugh. As the tension mounted, Pietro Colbertaldo slowly searched out the contents of the carton with his hands. With a sudden jerking

D'ITALIA INC.
LE ITALIANA

B.C. PHOTO SERVICE
DEC. 6TH 1936

motion, he turned to reveal four bottles of wine, a gift from a friend in the Okanagan. "I damn near collapsed," Lussin declared.[95]

During Italy's Fascist regime, all government correspondence included Roman numerals after the date. This was done to signify the number of years the Fascists had been in power since their march on Rome in 1922. This usage appeared to have had a carry-over effect to the Lega when Ines Falcioni became recording secretary in 1931. An examination of a few pieces of correspondence from the Italian Ladies' League file reveals the sporadic use of the Italian model over a period of several years, i.e., "4 dicembre 1937/XV."[96]

Three and a half years after his appointment as Royal Italian Vice-Consul for British Columbia, the affable Pietro Colbertaldo was replaced in May 1937 by the dynamic *Cavaliere* Dr. Giuseppe Brancucci. The handsome career diplomat, with the rank of lieu-

Gina Benetti's scholastic medals, Cenerentola doll and Italian school textbook.

Cenerentola.
Italian language school students star in a stage production of Cinderella at the Strathcona auditorium, circa 1937.

tenant in the Italian army, was from Potenza, Basilicata near Castelgrande.[97]

A special dinner for Colbertaldo prior to his leaving to take up a new post in Winnipeg was held at the Hotel Vancouver's Italian Room. Attending the formal banquet were some of the Italian community's most influential 'inner-circle' citizens.

Italo Rader, the cultured businessman, served as chairman. Speaking in Italian in loud staccato tones was Aristodemo Marin, a huge figure of a man with an acute hearing problem. He was followed by Ennio Victor Fabri, a young lawyer with a high-pitched voice. He delivered his remarks in English. Cleofe Forti, an Italian national, offered words of farewell to her employer on behalf of the Italian women of Vancouver.

Colbertaldo responded to the accolades of the partisan audience by delivering a valedictory, generous of kudos and political rhetoric. He thanked in particular W.G. Ruocco, president of the Sons of Italy, Cirillo Braga, first president of the Vancouver Italian-Canadian Society, Mrs. Enrichetta Agnolin (Benetti), president of the VICS affiliate Italian Ladies' League. He also recognized representatives of the Sons of Italy: Ines Falcioni, president of the Italian Ladies' League, Mrs. Mary Castricano, director of the Italian Young Girls' Club and her daughter, Lily Castricano, president of the Italian Young Girls' Club, for their unfailing cooperation in support of activities presented for the good of the Italians of Vancouver. He lauded the successes of Cleofe Forti, especially with regard to the Italian Language School and the live theatre production of *La Locandiera*. He concluded by applauding the Royal Italian government for making it possible for the popular *direttrice* to teach in Vancouver.[98]

The stage production to which he referred was Carlo Goldoni's brilliant three-act comedy *La Locandiera*, (The Inn Keeper). It had

been presented four weeks prior to Colbertaldo's special evening by the Italian School Board under the enthusiastic direction of Cleofe Forti. It was performed to a capacity house in the Strathcona School auditorium. Starring in the smash hit were society members Nino Sala, Bruno Girardi, Armando Biscaro, Marino Fraresso, Emma Lussin, Ines Falcioni, Emma Dalfo and Mary Minichiello.[99]

The board's second successful theatrical venture involved a troupe of younger performers. The participants, students enrolled in Forti's language classes, were featured in the Italian language production of *Cinderella*. In the lead role was Ada Trevisan, who was supported by a group of 50 young teens smartly dressed in authentic costumes. They acted, danced and sang to the delight of their parents, friends and members of Vancouver's society of Italians.[100]

The text of Colbertaldo's speech was reproduced in *L'Eco Italo-Canadese*: "And finally, guided by the genius of the *Duce*, with the cooperation of fascism and with all its good and courageous people, Italy has conquered those lands before denied but which by destiny were to be part of the new Italian Empire of which we celebrated the first glorious anniversary on the 9th of May. In the conquest of the Empire, you, together with other Italian people of this Province, have done your part too, by donating money, gold, and even by volunteering [for active military service during the Ethiopian campaign]."[101]

The gold to which Colbertaldo referred related to Italy's call to expatriates around the world to make a personal contribution to Italy's Ethiopian war effort. Specifically, women of the Empire were asked to follow Queen Elena's example and donate their gold wedding rings to the cause. In Vancouver, Ines Falcioni contacted a number of women's society members and asked for their support in this endeavour with a modicum of success.[102] Among those who traded their gold rings for steel replicas were Mary Castricano, Artemisia Minichiello and Raffaella Trasolini. According to her son, Elmo, Mrs. Trasolini's gold rings had been melted down but for some inexplicable reason never handed to Falcioni. Today, the nugget is worn as a necklace ornament by Elmo's wife.[103]

Colbertaldo then asked his guests to raise their glasses and join with him in a toast: "Let us toast to our beloved King Emperor Vittorio Emanuele III, and to Imperial Rome." The attendees responded with a chorus of "Viva Italia" which, like the sound of a clarion, reverberated throughout the banquet hall.[104]

"Bruno Girardi, I think, spiked the Coke at one of the dress rehearsals. We became a little tipsy and laughed and giggled throughout the scene during which Armando Biscaro wore his wig back to front. Armando also caused us all to laugh on stage when he had trouble unsheathing his sword."
—Emma Maffei.

Victor Emanuele III, King-Emperor.
Drawing by Silvio Ruocco, a talented artist and sculptor.

Veneta banquet: 25th anniversary, 1936.
Head table (centre), Filippo, Teresa, Angelo and Vi Branca.

The Veneta's Twenty-fifth Anniversary

Il Venticinquesimo Anniversario della Societa' Veneta

A spectacular and memorable event took place Wednesday, Feb. 12, 1936, in the Sala Veneta at the Silver Slipper Hall. As the honorary grand-chairman of the Societa' Veneta approached the podium, the screech of wooden chair legs preceded an enthusiastic standing ovation by a jubilant constituent audience. It was a proud moment indeed for Filippo Branca, flanked by his wife and youthful son, Angelo, on the occasion of the silver anniversary of the founding of the Societa' Veneta in 1911. The merchant of Milano was in his element as he acknowledged, with a twist of his somewhat ostentatious mustache, the admiring glances of personal friends. Filippo Branca appeared at the very pinnacle of his success as he prepared to address the comparatively small but intimate partisan audience in the Italian community hall which had been his crowning contribution to Vancouver's society of Italians. Although relishing in the adulation, the titular head understood the applause to be for contributions past. The real credit for the successes in administrating the direction of the Societa' Veneta now was in the capable hands of his sons, Angelo, president, and John and Joe, directors.

"*Membri, signori e signore*. Members. Ladies and gentlemen," he began in a raised voice. (translation) "It is indeed a great privilege for me to be here tonight in the company of such a distinguished group of Italo-Canadians. I am deeply touched by your generous reception. After 25 years of providing social services and benefits to our membership, our society can be justly proud of its achievements. Our programs have reduced the anxieties related to our efforts in establishing ourselves in our adopted country while encouraging all to become good citizens [of Canada].

"My sincerest wish is that our future events and programmes will continue to foster beneficial results and that they might encourage personal prosperity, health and happiness for our members and all Italians in general," he continued.

"And to this end, I ask that you make every effort to ensure that the praiseworthy principles upon which this organization was founded: brotherhood, fidelity and charity, continue to motivate your actions on behalf of Italians living and prospering in this country," Branca concluded.

The Societa' Veneta's executive members and directors, which included Carlo Stefani, Nicola Rizzo, Pietro Canal, Angelo and Carlo Franceschini, Carlo Casorzo, Rinaldo Masi, Bortolo Barichello, Egidio Sturam, Giovanni Piccolo, Giuseppe Toffoletto, Luigi Noal, Giovanni Gagno, Beniamino Giraudo, Salvatore Seminara, Pietro Tosi and founding member Massimo Costantini, rose in unison to lead the assembly in applauding their *capo presidente*.

Teresa and Filippo Branca.

Chapter 15

The successful L'Eco Italo-Canadese became a weekly publication circa 1937.

Founding the Italian Newspaper

Il Giornale Italiano e' Nato

Joe Philliponi, a well-known sports booster, was a foremost supporter of The Vancouver Sun's *walking marathons of the late 1930s and early 1940s. In 1939, he put up the prize for the women's division, loaned an Eagle Time Delivery truck for use in the marathon races and acted as one of the starters. That was the year that Mario Caravetta placed second in the A Class, boys under-17 group. In 1941, Mario came in first overall in the 11-mile Sun Walkathon for the second consecutive year. This achievement prompted the Sons of Italy to recognize Mario's successes in a special announcement at its general meeting and to send him a letter of congratulation. It read in part, (translation) "Therefore, the society is honoured to have one of its junior members active in sports, the accomplishment of which not only provides a sense of pride to us [in the Italian community] but also to our beautiful city of Vancouver and the province of B.C."*

The content in the May 26, 1937 issue of the *L'Eco Italo-Canadese* presented an interesting dichotomy. On the political right was Bruno Girardi's feature story on Colbertaldo's farewell party and Gregorio Fuoco's nationalistic appeal to Italy's veterans of the First World War.

In his commentary, Fuoco, section president of the Italian Veterans' Association, asked fellow veterans to observe the May 24 anniversary of Italy's entry into the First World War. He credited Italy's decisive action for making possible the Allied victory and the resurgence of Imperial Rome. Then Fuoco asked his fellow veterans to remember the mother country and be guided by the sage advice offered by their *Duce*. In conclusion, he offered greetings and best wishes for a long and successful stay to "our Royal Vice-Consul, Mr. Brancucci."

The political centre was taken up by Angelo Branca. In his lead article, covering four full columns, Branca counselled his readers to vote Liberal in the forthcoming June 1, B.C. provincial election. His partisan remarks, which may have been an attempt to 'deliver' the Italian vote, were complemented by a double-page advertising feature profiling Liberal candidates including Gordon S. Wismer, K.C., one of Branca's professional colleagues.[105]

In the same newspaper were advertisements welcoming

Brancucci to Vancouver. A two-column by nine-inch ad announced, "Best wishes for a long and successful stay to Dottor Giuseppe Brancucci, R. Vice-Consul of Italy in Vancouver [from] Angelo E. Branca, A.G. Marin, P. Tosi & Co., J. Bordignon & Son, Italo Rader, Angelo B. Calori, Venice Cafe, Ennio V. Fabri and Marie Gown Shoppe, Maria Castricano, Manager."

Finally, Girardi, the newspaper's editor, added his patronizing touch to the Brancucci fascination. In his column *"Gira La Ronda,"* he wrote (translation), "Countrymen—we are lucky that in our country of origin, in our beautiful Italy, we have a flowering government, we have a supreme leader who leads us, we have a faultless system. Italians do not need to fight against the system governing them because they could never ask for a better one."[106]

L'Eco Italo-Canadese was still a novelty to its Vancouver audience. It had been founded by Bruno Girardi in Oct., 1936. His collaborators, in the bi-monthly newspaper, were Leo Cecarini, Louis Marino and John Trevisiol, who first named the publication *L'Eco Italiana.*

Now a vibrant and folksy publication, the newspaper's columns contained a generous amount of non-partisan local news. Editorially, however, it was unabashedly pro-Italy. Front-page treatment of Mussolini dictates were a regular feature. On its first anniversary, *L'Eco Italo-Canadese* went weekly and began with a series of select stories in English.

Girardi and Cecarini co-edited the publication and were responsible for the editorial policy and international news content. In addition, they each wrote a weekly column: Girardi, *"Gira La Ronda,"* and Cecarini, "Town Crier." Joseph Montalban covered financial news while Marino Culos wrote "Sidelines," a column detailing the activities and progress of Vancouver's Italian societies. Although Tosca Trasolini's column "Flight" appeared infre-

L'Eco Italiana: first edition.
Bruno Girardi and colleagues launch Vancouver's Italian language newspaper, circa 1936.

5c L'ECO ITALIANA 5c

Vol. 1. FRIDAY, OCTOBER 9, 1936 Number 1

CELEBRAZIONE COLOMBIANA

C. Piccolo Eletta Isabella con 64,925 voti
P. Pulice: 53,250 voti, M. Canal: 22,225 voti

Il 444.mo anniversario della scoperta dell'America verra' celebrato nella Silver Slipper Hall, 828 Hastings li 11 e 12 del corr. mese. Le societa' italiane si sono quest'anno unite per commemorare Quel Grande che definitivamente apri' la via per il Nuovo Mondo. E' la celebrazione d'una opera importante, frutto del genio, della tenacia e del ardire di un nostro connazionale. E' nostro dovere commemorare C. Colombo, esponente alle vette alle quali puo' arrivare la nostra razza.

Nessuna occasione e' piu' bella per unirsi in gran numero e onorare Il Grande.

PROGRAMMA

Domenica 11 Ottobre alle ore 8 p.m. ci sara' il Gran Concerto (nella Silver Slipper Hall) ove sentirete i migliori artisti locali. Ammissione Gratis. Contribuzione alla porta.

CONCERTO

Berettoni	Orchestra
Frankie Petroni	Accordeon Solo
Leo Petroni	Tap Dance
Patricia Pulice and Betty Dowman....	
	Songs and Tap Dance
Victor and Lawrence Cavalli ...Accordeon	
	and Clarinet
Frank Iaci	Song
Dominic Raino	Banjo
Maria Rathorne	Soprano
Frank Bologna	Violin Solo
Fratelli Berettoni ... Accordeon and Violin
Mrs. Allen Egan	Soprano
Victor Rinci .... Song and Accordeon
N. Proctor	Tenor
Theresa Principi	Soprano
Signora Elfie Boccini	Pianoforte
Rose Jackson .... Coloratura Soprano
Una Sorpresa	

Banchetto—Lunedi 12 Ott. alle 6 p.m. Biglietto $1.50, incluso il ballo.

Gran Ballo—Dalle ore 9 p.m. in poi. Estrazione dei grandi premi a mezza notte. Il primo premio e' un viaggio andata e ritorno in Italia oppure un valore in contante di $300.00, e molti altri premi saranno estratti, tutti dovrebbero acquistare dei biglietti. Orchestra—Charles Berrettoni and His Melody Kings.

Il comitato esecutivo e' composto di:

Presidente Onorario—Il Signor Pietro Colbertaldo, Regio Vice Console d'Italia. Direttore—Signor Mario Ghislieri, assistito dai due Presidenti Sig. W. G. Ruocco e Sig. Angelo Branca e le Presse Signore Raffaela Trasolini e Enrichetta Agnolin. Segretario di Corr.—Sig. Gregorio Pocco, assistito dalle Signe Emma Lussin e Clotilda Piccolo. Seg. di Finanza—Sig. Felice Cianci. Tesoriere—Sig. Filippo Branca. Comitato Stampa per Inglese—Avvocato Angelo Branca.

Continua nella Pag. 2

MARY CANAL, S.V.M.S.

L'ITALIA SVALUTA LA LIRA

Tariffe Tagliate Sulla Merce Esportata

ROMA.—Il Cabinetto Italiano ha votato di svalutare la lira, mettendo la rata a 90 lire per sterlina inglese e 19 lire per dollaro americano.

La decisione monetaria fu annunziata in un bullettino ufficiale, nel quale fu anche dichiarato che il Cabinetto agira' in modo da prevenire un incresento in prezzi. Fra l'altro il bullettino leggeva: il Duce ha esaminato la dichiarazione Anglo-Francese-Americana che segui' l'aggiustamento del franco francese e ha dichiarato che il ricovero economico del mondo e' una cosa necessaria in modo che le nazioni, che vogliono pace, possano collaborare.

Inoltre il Duce ha messo in rilievo l'eventuali ripercussioni che la svalutazione puo' portare. Il Cabinetto ha specialmente dichiarato che per almeno due anni non ci sia alcuna crescita nella pigione di appartamenti, uffici ed altri edifici, ne' alcuna crescita nelle rate per elettricita', gas ed altri servizi pubblici. Il governo, fu inoltre autorizzato di cambiare le dogane e tariffe a rispetto del nuovo sistema monetario.

Un prestito nazionale che il governo ha avuto dai proprietari verra' pagato in 25 anni. Le dogane di tutte le merci esportate furono generalmente tagliate di piu' del 50%. Il Cabinetto ha valutato la lira a circa 5.2 soldi americani in contrasto della quota di sabato che la valutava a 7.6 soldi americani.

Un allevamento di buoi di Cesena ad Addis Abeba

ROMA.—Il Ministro delle Colonie, on. Alessandro Lessona, si e' recato oggi a Cesena ed ha affidato ad un gruppo di agricoltori una concessione agricola, presso Addis Abeba.

Nella concessione verra' istituito un vasto allevamento di bovini della pregiata razza che viene ora allevato nel territorio di Cesena.

Gli agricoltori cui e' stata assegnata la importante concessione partiranno subito alla volta dell'Africa Orientale.

Il Domerat Celebrato nell'Etiopia

Con grandi feste gli Abissini hanno celebrato la fine delle pioggie. Circa 50,000 persone hanno celebrato il Domerat, rito che chiude le feste del Mascal.

Ad Addis Abeba si trovavano presenti il Vicere', Maresciallo Rodolfo Graziani, il Duca di Ancona, le autorita' civili e militari della citta' e i rappresentanti di tutti i centri dell'Etiopia.

Era pure presente l'Abuna Circillo col vescovo di avorio e il parasole regalatogli da Graziani. Il capo della chiesa etiopica, in suo nome e in quello dell'intera popolazione, ha rinnovato il solenne atto di fedelta' verso l'Italia.

L'ECO ITALIANA

Essendo la Colonia Italiana di Vancouver ancor priva di qualsiasi periodico locale italiano, viveva in me, ed in parecchi amici, l'orgoglio di poter dare a questa un piccolo giornale che nel suo contenuto potesse tener piu compatta ed unita la fratellanza italiana.

Non avendo nessun soggetto politico da trattare, questo giornaletto avra' l'aspetto di pura neutralita.' Il suo principale scopo sara' di tener informata la Colonia Italiana di piccoli avvenimenti di natura sociale e sportiva ed altre novita' che solo possono interessare un italiano.

Sembra gia' che questa idea abbia colto l'entusiasmo di parecchi principali membri della nostra colonia. Tutto questo certo serve ancor ad innalzare lo spirito iniziativo del nostro giornale. Voglio ringraziare di cuore quelle persone che con saggi consigli di iniziativa vogliano innoltrarci per diritta e sicura via.

Ognuno conosce a quale umigliazione sia oggetto, ogni qualtanto, l'emmigrante, a causa di preguidizi e supestizioni. Vogliamo quindi eliminare cio che fra di noi e' supestizioso e tutti uniti innalzarci in qual pedestallo che e' conforme alla razza Italiana.

L'aiuto di ogni Italiano certo servera' al progresso di questo giornale, quindi ognuno di questi e pregato di accettarlo nella propia famiglia come simbolo d'italianita' e di causa italiana.

La prima copia verra' distribuita gratuitamente; dopo di questa il prezzo sara' minimo, cosicche' ogni famiglia italiana possa ottenerlo.

—EDITORE

C. PICCOLO, V.I.C.M.A.S. e S.F.

P. PULICE, S.M.S.F.I. e L.F.I.

Antonio Pitton, Italian World War I veteran.
Italian consul Dr. Brancucci berated Pitton for anti-fascist remarks.

The Voice of Italy: a pro-fascist newspaper published in New York.
"A newspaper of American-Italian opinion."

quently, a number of regular volunteer stringers provided the newspaper's regional coverage: Colombo Vagnini, "North Vancouver," Onofrio Fiorito, "*Di Qua e di La'*," Fred Tenisci, "*Da* Trail, B.C.," Toni Simoi, "*La Cronica da Michel e Natal*, B.C.," and Andy A. Ercolini, "Alberni."[107]

The enterprising Montalban also promoted the establishment of a taxi service business with a fleet of new 1934 Oldsmobiles equipped with sealed meters. Shares in Star Cabs were sold to a group of Italians including Dave De Camillis, Louis Giuriato and his brother-in-law Alfonse Benedetti (Benny). Unfortunately, the enterprise soon faltered with heavy losses being incurred by the rather naive investors.[108]

L'Eco Italo-Canadese's editorial content was very much influenced by the Italian consul who supplied a steady stream of propaganda material including newspaper clippings which Girardi often plagiarized. Brancucci, in particular, realized the value of a pro-Italian press in publicizing his pet projects. The dashing diplomat had no qualms whatsoever in 'requesting' the newspaper's cooperation. This he did repeatedly in order to gain news publicity for enterprises such as the Italian Language School and its theatrical productions.[109]

Brancucci, with misplaced dogmatism, would reproach liberal-minded Italian-Canadians who dared criticize Italy's Fascist regime. The Monday following a meeting of the local chapter of the Italian War Veterans' Association at which Tony Pitton proffered anti-fascist sentiments, the respected orator was summoned to Lieutenant Brancucci's offices at the Marine Building. Ushered into the vice-consul's office by his embarrassed daughter Nellie, who was employed as Brancucci's secretary, Pitton was greeted with an emotional tirade that left him aghast. Brancucci, however, failed in his bid to intimidate his fellow *ex-combattente* who continued to feel free to express his views as he saw fit.

In the Sept. 4, 1937 issue of *L'Eco Italo-Canadese*, Marino departed from his normal "Sidelines" column format. Instead, he devoted more than 12 column-inches to the Marconi memorial service held in Vancouver. Writing in English, Marino scribed, "Marching with the Italian and British flags and banners draped with black crepe ribbon, members of the Sons of Italy Society Inc. and affiliated Ladies' League; members of the Vancouver Italian-Canadian Mutual Aid Society Inc. and Ladies' League Inc.; members of the Veneta Benevolent Society Inc.; members of the Fascist Party and of the Returned Men (Ex-Combattenti), entered by the turret doorway to the church which bore the mourning crepe, and the message, 'In Memorium [sic], S.E. *Senatore* Guglielmo Marconi.'" Marino continued, "Men and women from all stages of life were there, side by side, with saddened faces. It was the first time in the history of the Colony that such a gathering of organizations responded in one unit to the call of the Italian Vice-Consul, Dr. G. Brancucci."

In a front-page lead story, Girardi reported the details of the late Senator Marchese Guglielmo Marconi's memorial service, held at the Hastings Auditorium and Sacred Heart Church. In part he stated, "Two Italian war veterans, Gregorio Fuoco, president of the Ex-Combattenti Section, and Secondo Faoro with two Fascists, Nino Sala and [eulogist] Erminio Ghislieri, stood on guard at the Catafalque."[110]

The naive and somewhat egotistical Marino Culos continued to respond to Brancucci's overtures. A month after the Marconi feature, he was asked to write an article comparing Italy's Balilla with the Boy Scouts of Canada. In researching this item, Marino interviewed *il giovanotto* Pete, a teenager and former *capo squadra* of the Balilla, who had recently arrived from Italy with his mother and sister to live in Vancouver. Based on this and other sources, Marino wrote that the Balilla, in which membership was compulsory, had saved many Italian boys between the ages of eight and 14 from a life of depravation in the streets. "The paramilitary movement had been formed at a time when most nations were in a chaotic state. This condition spawned harsher and more disciplined ideals, justifying the training of the Balilla in the use of small weapons.

"Although the Boy Scouts were a semi-military training program, its members were not trained in the use of the rifle because when the organization was founded in 1910 the world was largely at peace," opined Marino.[111]

In July 1938, Alberto Boccini, the newspaper's co-editor, and Marino Culos bought *L'Eco Italo-Canadese* from Girardi. A business agreement was signed recognizing Boccini as being responsible for the editorial and news content. He would work full time and be paid a salary. Marino would maintain the financial records and continue to write his column. His compensation, however, would be limited to a share of the profits. Included in the terms was provision for a third part-

Alberto Boccini, Elisa Martini and Onofrio Fiorito returning to the Italian newspaper office, circa 1940.

Herman Ghislieri, on the pyramid, was a member of the Balilla in Italy.
He acted as gymnastics instructor for the VICS's Circolo Giovanile.

ner. If one was deemed necessary, correspondent Onofrio Fiorito would be their choice.[112]

The Boccini-Culos partnership arrangement lasted but a few weeks. They disagreed frequently over a number of issues, but clashed irrevocably over Marino's demand for a key to the office in order to audit at will the financial documents. Angelo Branca represented Boccini whereas Marino acted as his own counsel.[113]

An argument between the partners ensued at the newspaper's 12th-floor office in the Dominion Bank Building. Verbal abuse escalated to push and shove. The men struggled toward an open window. With Marino pressing his thumbs against his adversary's throat, Boccini fell backward onto the window sill. Draped precariously on the outside ledge, Boccini barely managed to save himself from falling to the street below. Fortunately, both men came to their senses in time to avert a certain tragedy.[114]

The 'partnership' dissolved with Boccini in full control of B.C.'s only Italian newspaper. Boccini stepped up his pro-fascist editorials, praising Mussolini's government's every move and added a front page ear-lug which proudly proclaimed, "Don't forget you are Italian."[115]

La Voce Degli Italo Canadesi, was one of the few Italian-language newspapers available in Canada which offered an anti-fascist opinion. It was published from offices at 441 Queen St. West, Toronto. In a page 2 article, Dec. 16, 1939, the newspaper stated, "It is reported that a number of prominent people in our community on the pretext of 'professional reasons' require the membership lists of the various societies for the purpose of distributing the fascist word and to communicate instructions which they receive from fascist propaganda sources."

The news item said, in effect, that the newspaper was against the activities of these individuals because "prominent Fascists in our community [Toronto] bring dishonour to the liberal and democratic traditions of the Italian people."[116]

After the split, Marino discontinued writing his column. However, he regularly submitted copy which was reproduced without the usual by-line. In the Feb. 12, 1940 issue, Marino detailed the progress of the leadership of the Italian societies. Then, in the March 23 issue, he coordinated a special two-page advertorial feature on the occasion of the Sons of Italy's 35th anniversary. It is surprising to note that this wartime pro-Italy newspaper carried several large advertisements placed by the Liberal Party of Canada. The copy, written in Italian, had a clear message, "Vote Mackenzie King for prime minister...who has demonstrated his determination to vigorously lead Canada against the war against dictatorship."[117]

In 1943, *La Vittoria* (Victory) claimed it was the only Italian-language newspaper published in Canada. Its masthead read,

La Voce.
This anti-fascist publication from Toronto was Italo-Canadians' voice of freedom and democracy.

Venice Bakery: French bread. The taste was heavenly...
From left, Rudy Zazinovitch, Armando Battistoni, Tino Francilia, and Peter Battistoni.

National Bakery: delicious pastry a specialty.
Tony and Pina (Lussin) Grdina owners.

Montreal Bakery: famous rye breads and buns.
Luciano Zanon with his fleet of delivery trucks, circa 1935. Zanon's bakery products were served to the King and Queen on the Royal Train in 1939.

P. Tosi Imported Foods product label, circa 1930s.

"Organ of the Italian-Canadian Unity Committee for Victory of the United Nations. Girolamo Malisani, President. Ennio Gnudi, Managing Editor."

When Antonio Pitton died on March 6, 1943, Marino submitted a news release to the Toronto-based *La Vittoria* which published his obituary in its March 27 issue.

Two grand ladies also died in 1943: Letizia Battistoni and Angelina Politano.

Mrs. Battistoni, the mother of seven children, had been operating the Venice Bakery with her sons Peter, Armando and Dario since her husband Giovanni died in 1931. Two of her other sons, Leandro and Alberto, who were normally the operators of the bakery's delivery vans, were serving in the Canadian Forces at the time of her death. Ciro was a partner in the Service Taxi while Elda Venturato, the only daughter, was active in the Lega affiliated with the Vancouver Italian-Canadian Society. The incredibly good-tasting bread products—especially the French bread loaf—solidified the continued popularity of this family bakery for the three decades of Peter Battistoni's tenure as master baker.[118]

On Aug. 5, 1943, Joe Politano was devastated by the news that his loving mother Angelina had died at St. Paul's Hospital. He and his wife had been caring for her since the death of his father the previous year. He asked his friend and society colleague Marino Culos

C. Marinaro Wholesale Italian Grocery located in the 500 block of East Hastings Street.

Delivery driver Norman Pressacco and Mr. Ogilvi near entrance to Paris Bakery.
Santo Pasqualini, a former partner of Luciano Zanon, established a solid hotel and restaurant business prior to being arrested as an Enemy Alien in 1940.

to officiate at her funeral service. As duly reported by the Canadian-Italian press, Marino spoke eloquently and from his heart about Mrs. Politano, her husband Lorenzo, and their children and grandson Larry. Angelina Politano had been revered by the Italian community and in particular by her friends in the Lega, the ladies group of which she was a founding member.

Chapter 16

Veneta sponsored queen contestants and society executive, 1926.
Back row from left, Primo Durante, Carlo Franceschini, Lungo Marchi, Filippo Branca, Carlo Stefani, Ida Giulani, Santo Corra'. Second row from left, Ines Falcioni, Elsie Stefani, Florence Toso (Queen of Italy, 1926), Ermie Pulice, Angelina Grazziano. Front row from left, John Branca, Angelo Branca, Attilio Brandolini.

Italian Celebrations
Le Feste Italiane

The societies' history of *feste* [celebrations] included Christopher Columbus Day which had been enthusiastically featured in *L'Eco Italo-Canadese* since 1936. Eugenio De Paolo is credited with being the first person in Vancouver to promote and to commemorate the discovery of America by the famous navigator from Genoa. His society's celebrations, however, were conducted independently of the other societies.[119]

In the early 1930s, Amelia (Pat) Minichiello, a talented, and attractive young stenographer, who worked for De Paolo at his Italian Club (West Coast Cultural Club) on Main Street, agreed to serve as hostess at the 1933 Columbus banquet. Beautifully turned out in a stylish gown, Minichiello mingled with the guests and danced a featured waltz with De Paola's protégé son Tommy. This innovation became the forerunner of the popularity and queen contests introduced the following year.[120]

A popularity contest staged for the Sons of Italy in conjunction with the Young Canadian Italian Athletic Association, the Italian Ladies' League, and the Italian Young Girls' Club, was coordinated by Marino Culos in early 1934.[121]

First to receive the Most Popular Member distinction within the Italian community was the vivacious 19-year-old Lily Castricano. She was a belle: attractive, bright and very resourceful.

—FOR—

Miss Fulvia Patricia Trasolini

_____
Name

·

_____

10 Votes for 10c   10 Votes for 10c

These Votes Will Boost the Leadership of
Miss Fulvia Patricia Trasolini
(Favorite Selection of the Giovine Italiane)
in the
POPULARITY CONTEST
Sponsored by the Sons of Italy Society, Inc. for Mutual Benefits

Contest closes on FEBRUARY 12, 1934, at 6 P.M. Results will
be announced at the MASQUERADE BALL, to be held Feb. 13th
at the Silver Slipper Hall.

10 Votes for 10c   10 Votes for 10c

Fulvia Trasolini's personalized raffle tickets.
The contestant who sold the highest number of raffle ticket books was declared winner and queen.

"Nobody knew who had won until we got there. They ushered us into the dressing room at the Silver Slipper Auditorium. Then they came running in, yelling, 'Lily, you've won!'" she recalled.

The committee members presented Lily with a bouquet of flowers as attendants pinned a *tre colore* sash on her beautiful gown made by her mother especially for this occasion. Then just before the start of the evening's masquerade dance, Italian consul Pietro Colbertaldo called Lily to the podium to present her with a gold medal and $25.

"I remember feeling like a queen," she said.[122]

The Canadian-Italian Athletic Association—Ladies' Branch— entered its president Teresa Turone in the popularity competition. Fulvia Trasolini was also a candidate. She, like the others, gained votes by selling raffle tickets in aid of her group's special projects. In what might have been a tongue-in-cheek gesture, Lina Gasperdoni, a valued Lega member, entered her mother-in-law as a contestant in this popularity contest. Teresa Sciarini, at 80, was one of the oldest members of the Italian Ladies' League (affiliated with the Sons of Italy) and a Vancouver pioneer. She placed third.[123]

Eight months later, two separate Christopher Columbus Day queen contests ran simultaneously. As on previous occasions, the

Ines Giuriato represented the Vancouver Italian-Canadian Society on the Canadian Folk Society parade float entry, circa 1950.

North Vancouver's Italian band.
Signor C. d'Alession, maestro. Circa 1913.

Mary Grippo, queen contestant.
Queen contests highlighted Columbus Celebration Days during the 1930s.

Maple Leaf Band from Trail.
The marching band performed at Italian Days at Vancouver's Cambie Street Grounds, circa 1938.

candidate selling the greatest number of raffle tickets was declared the winner.

On Oct. 12, 1934, 700 people witnessed mayor Louis Taylor crown the effervescent Betty Alvaro Mansueto, Queen Isabella, at the Moose Hall. Betty, representing the Christopher Columbus Society, competed with contestants from Vancouver and New Westminster.[124] At the Queen Isabella dinner, she was presented with diamond earrings and necklace by mayor Taylor and society president Eugenio De Paola.

Across town at the Silver Slipper Hall, Caroline Tonelli, sponsored by the Lega Femminile Italiane, was also being honoured. The vibrant Tonelli, crowned Columbus Day Queen, was awarded a diamond ring. Doing double duty that evening, the mayor officiated at both ceremonies.[125]

The mayor, famous for his red bow ties, participated at a number of these coronations in the 1930s including the one at which Frances Crude was crowned Queen Isabella at the Town Hall Ballroom, 1027 West Pender. At her coronation, Queen Isabella's throne was festooned by a royal entourage that included Iolanda

Dominatti, Mary Cardillo, Mary Grippo, Lillian Giuliani, Clara Moropito, Amelia Menini and Ines Visentin.

In 1935, Corrine Paula Bland, representing the Christopher Columbus Society, was crowned queen. The following year, Clorinda Piccolo captured the coveted award. Piccolo's candidacy had been sponsored by the Vancouver Italian-Canadian Society and its Lega affiliate.[126]

During Vancouver's 50th anniversary celebration, Aug. 26, 1936, Rosina Signori made her debut as a regal representative of the Italian community in the city's Parade of Progress festivities. Gracing the Italian community's specially constructed float, she and her attendants, Clorinda Piccolo and Lina Gazzola, wore elegant gowns. To complement the contingent of belles, members of her honour

Sig. W.G. Ruocco
by Leo Tesan

Dodici anni della tua vita
Come presidente tu l'hai servita;
Sul petto la medaglia d'oro portaste
Per le tante cose che tu organizzaste;
La tua filosofia
Stata quella una buona via;
La Lega Femminile che tu fondaste
Fui il sogno che tu sognaste,
L'hai fatto per l'unico scopo—
"In alto il nome di W.G. Ruocco."

Clorinda Piccolo, with attendants, poses as Queen Isabella, 1936.

entourage Nellie Marchi, Emma Dalfo, Mary Barazzuol and Mary Pettovello wore traditional Italian costumes.[127]

The consultant for the Parade of Progress entry was sculptor Carlo Marega. It was he who suggested Marino Culos take responsibility for the Italian community's participation in the event.

With a draft design in hand, Marino turned to his friend Mario Ghislieri for support. Ghislieri, a skilled contractor, built the parade float in Sam Minichiello's car barn. Rosina Signori and her royal entourage readily agreed to ride aboard the float in the city's parade.[128]

In 1936, Ruocco's Il Grande Comitato succeeded in sponsoring a Christopher Columbus program with the full cooperation of the Sons of Italy, Veneta, Vancouver Italian-Canadian societies, and Italian Ladies' League affiliates. The two-day celebration began with a concert at the Silver Slipper Hall. The following night a sold-out

"Queen" Betty Mansuetto was presented with jewellery at her Moose Hall coronation, 1934.

Betty Mansuetto vividly remembered her coronation. "I was dressed in robes which were the exact replica of the Spanish Queen's court gown. Mayor Taylor presented me with the diadem."

The Vancouver Sun carried a photo of Alvaro in her Queen Isabella gown on its front page, Oct. 12, 1934. The lead story read, "Italian Queen For Tonight. Miss Betty Alvaro chosen from a large field to reign over the Columbus celebration in Moose Hall this evening, celebrating the anniversary of his discovery of America.

"A court of nine pretty Italian girls will attend her.

"Mayor Taylor will perform the crowning ceremony after she has been presented by Eugene de Paola, chairman of the general committee in charge of arrangements. The affair is sponsored by the local Italian colony and is a gala occasion.

"Delegations will be present from New Westminster, Revelstoke, Victoria, Bellingham, Seattle and Fraser Valley points.

"Mr. de Paola will deliver the official celebration speech, and Angelo E. Branca will also speak."

crowd turned out for the banquet and dance at which Clorinda Piccolo, the VICS's candidate, was proclaimed queen. The vote-counting placed Patricia Pulice second and Mary Canal third. During the same evening, the Christopher Columbus Society hosted a Columbus Day dance at the Moose Hall.[129]

Eugene De Paola was a maverick and self-publicist who, according to Marino Culos, would not be denied his place in the sun. On Aug. 8, 1936, he sponsored a week-long 'Grand Spectacular' event at the Cambie Street Grounds, a park located directly across the street from the present site of the Queen Elizabeth Theatre. In this endeavour he arranged for the construction of Roman columns on the site and brought in the 60-member Maple Leaf Band from Trail, B.C. to provide music. The mutual aid societies, however, showed no interest in officially supporting this Italian Days exhibition which sadly turned out to be less than successful.[130] Elda Venturato witnessed the event and recalls that the site was smartly decorated but that it attracted very few people from the community. "There was jealousy. Nobody supported him," she stated.

An outstanding cultural success for Vancouver's Italians was the recital of the famous Italian soprano Amelita Galli-Curci at the Denman Auditorium, Oct. 8, 1937. *L'Eco Italo-Canadese* pronounced it the major social event of the year and quoted Galli-Curci as saying, (translation) "I have a lot of faith in our *Duce* and believe him to be the greatest man in the world." A week later, however, the community became witness to a far less glamorous cultural event during the promotion of the queen contest and its candidates.[131]

A major incident involving the distribution of raffle tickets caused a temporary split among executive members of the leading societies. The three 'queen' candidates, Nellie Santamaria, Emma Lussin and Rosina Signori each had a maximum of $1,000 worth of raffle tickets to sell. Unbeknownst to the contestants, some of the Veneta Society's unsold contest books had been given to the Vancouver Italian-Canadian Society. This redistribution of raffle tickets, it was alleged, had the potential of affecting the final vote tally.

Earlier in the contest, the VICS had sent 25 raffle books to its out-of-town supporters. However, neither book stubs nor unsold raffle tickets had been returned. Knowing that its candidate likely would not sell all of her tickets, the Veneta Society gave 25 of its raffle books to the Vancouver Italian-Canadian Society to make up for the shortfall.

During the official ballot-counting process, Lussin, who had sold over $900 in raffle tickets, noticed that some of the Vancouver Italian-Canadian Society's tickets bore the "Societa' Veneta" stamp. As a result, she called for an enquiry on the matter.[132]

Although Rosina Signori was declared the winner, the actual number of books transferred to the VICS campaign was not known to Lussin. Consequently, Marino, as Lussin's campaign manager, immediately lodged a formal protest. In a statement referred to as "The Acid Test" and read to the executive members of the societies involved, Marino chastised Angelo Branca, grand committee chairman of the Columbus Celebrations, for not dealing effectively with the "irregularity". Moreover, Marino demanded that either the anomaly be dealt with or the contest results be declared invalid.[133]

Branca replied to Marino's allegations in a Letter to the Editor. *L'Eco Italo-Canadese* reproduced his letter under the heading, "Explanation of the Festival," in which Branca shot back at Marino for insinuating deception had marred the balloting procedure. This public admonition caused Marino to also use *L'Eco Italo-Canadese* as a vehicle to convey his sense of indignation.[134]

Notwithstanding the animosity which prevailed, the Sons of Italy and the Veneta Society held their banquet as scheduled at the Hastings Auditorium. However, instead of acknowledging the winner of the queen contest, four-year-old Anita Satti presented beautiful baskets of flowers to mayor George Miller and his wife, and to Emma Lussin and Nellie Santamaria. According to *L'Eco Italo-Canadese*, "The contestants were delighted with this act of hospitality that they admiringly kissed the little flower girl." Although duly honoured by the Vancouver Italian-Canadian Society, no mention was made of Rosina Signori, queen-elect, in the newspaper article.

The Christopher Columbus Society queen contest fared much better. As in past years, its pageant was held at the Moose Hall where Eugene De Paola began his speech predictably with *Silenzio, Silenzio*. And after offering his emotional spiel on the life of Columbus, he concluded with the equally predictable words, '*Viva* Canada! *Viva* Vancouver! *Viva Italia!*'

As the band played the "Italian National March", mayor Miller rose to place a golden crown on the head of queen-elect, Josephine Romano. Congratulating the regal beauty were Romano's maids of honour: Yolanda Costanzo, Nancy Sardone and Edith Minichiello.[135]

The Italian community's social calendar for 1938 proved positive and rewarding. A grand Columbus Day celebration was initiated by the Sons of Italy, Lega, and Giovani Italiane, and the Veneta. The *festa*, held at the Hastings Auditorium, featured a grand concert organized by Piero Orsatti and the talented pianist Elfie Boccini. The participants included Ray Benny, Armida Pitton, Amelia Minichiello and the Cavalli brothers. Also on the program were singers Patricia Pulice, Dalton Eason, Lina Coello and Bettie Andrun. Fred Minichiello provided the musical accompaniment. Leading the singers and musicians were community favourites Vic Ricci and the brother-sister team of Osvaldo and Anita (Nellie) Panichelli. The tal-

Louise Culos, Daughters of Italy member
Queen contestant from Powell River.

COLONIA ITALIANA

CARRO ALLEGORICO ITALIANO
"PARADE OF PROGRESS"
VANCOUVER, B.C. AGOSTO 26, 1936.

Italian community's parade entry, 1936.
From left, "Queen" Rosina Signori,
Clorinda Piccolo, Lina Gazzola, Nellie
Marchi, Mary Barazzuol, Mary Minichiello.

ented Panichellis also performed dance numbers as did Ada and Nita Trevisan.[136]

The Christopher Columbus Society sponsored a spectacular province-wide queen contest in 1938—the last of its kind to be held prior to the outbreak of the Second World War. It was highlighted by 10 superbly qualified contestants: Betty Alvaro, North Vancouver; Jene Di Giustini, Vancouver; Vivian Favetta, Nanaimo; Lena Gatto, North Vancouver; Dora Giardin, Vancouver; Margherita Girone, Vancouver; Evelyn Manzini, Nanaimo; Elma Menini, Vancouver; Louise Principe, Vancouver; and Louise Culos, the Native Daughters of Italy representative from Powell River. Eighteen-year-old Margherita Girone, with 30,500 votes, was declared the winner. The vivacious debutante modestly credited her father's popularity for her success in selling a record number of raffle tickets, which were converted into contest votes.

Chapter 17

The Italian Language School
La Scuola Italiana

Italian language student graduates received decorative diplomas, circa 1938.

Setting aside past differences, Branca and Marino again worked together successfully. They were members of the Sacred Heart Rectory fund-raising committee in 1938, and now became associates as members of the Italian School Board. The board also comprised Rosa Visentin, vice-president; Rose Puccetti, treasurer; Nellie Pitton, secretary; plus Gregorio Fuoco, Mario Ghislieri, Angelina Brandalise and Nicola Di Tomaso. As executive vice-president of the board in 1939, Branca reported to board president Dr. Giuseppe Brancucci.[137]

The school reached its pinnacle under the direction of Cleofe Forti. Its popularity led to classes being established in North Vancouver and New Westminster.[138] The North Van outlet had been promoted by a committee which included Colombo Vagnini.[139]

The combined graduating classes of 1939, from Vancouver, North Vancouver and New Westminster, comprised 145 students, each of whom was promoted at a ceremony held at Strathcona School on June 23.

Forti, however, appeared a paradox as she was both a free spirit and a fascist adherent. But she accomplished much on behalf of the Vancouver Italian community during her tenure and is remembered fondly by former students. Many of these students were given special tutoring and treated to warm hospitality at her Cardero Street

"My sister Marchy and I attended classes in North Vancouver. The school was located upstairs in the I.O.O.F. Hall and Anita Ghini was our teacher. She was young and pretty. She had control of her class but wasn't a slave driver. She never taught us any of the propaganda that was in the reader. She didn't believe in it as this was Canada that we lived in and told us what was propaganda."
—Dorina Boscariol Honey, a silver medalist.

Lino Giuriato, a brilliant academic, is pictured with his Italian language school honour-grade gold medals.

"My brothers were cheeky in an acceptable way. The boys would climb the huge folding doors which would make a rattling sound as they opened onto the classroom. The boys would come in one by one and each time call out, 'Buon giorno signorina.' Then bang goes the door. Then two seconds later Elso [Genovese] would come in. Same thing. They drove her up the wall.

"When Ines Giuriato and I, along with another friend Albina, were in Rome in 1951 we met Miss Forti. We went into a little cafe and chatted. She remembered a lot of her former students and certainly had fond memories of having been in Vancouver,"
—Lina Tesan

apartment. In spite of this close relationship, it is clear that the young students were oblivious of any overt political objective that might have formed part of the Italian government's plan to fund the Patronato Scolastico Italiano.

The government in Rome had sent Forti, age 47, to Vancouver in 1937 as part of Mussolini's newly placed emphasis on supporting Italian language schools abroad.[140] The popular instructor served as teacher and director of the school board's cultural programmes. This development effectively shifted control of the linguistic programmes from the Sons of Italy to the Italian vice-consul.[141]

An excellent teacher, Forti left an indelible mark on the Italian community. Although very stern, she was loved and respected by her students, and did much to create an awareness of Italian cultural activities. Because of her dedicated efforts, scores of Canadian-Italian youths learned to speak and write well in Italian.

"As a result of attending Miss Forti's classes I was able to write letters in Italian for my mother to relatives in Italy," recalled Irma Pastro.

Topping the list of students who excelled under Forti's tutelage were gold medalists Gina Sanvido (Benetti) and Lino Giuriato. Sanvido, who subsequently chose a career in teaching, was awarded three gold medals for scholastic achievement.[142]

"I was fortunate—you know, we were all fortunate—to have had Miss Forti. She was so good; an exceptionally good language teacher," recollected Gina.

Bronze medalist, Al Maddalozzo remembers that it wasn't all work and no play at the school. "Miss Forti was very strict but I did learn, *'io sono, tu sei, egli e', noi siamo,'*...I loved learning Italian. It was quite different than what we had been used to with the Trevisani dialect at home," recalled Maddalozzo. His brother Ernie remembered having a bit of fun when paying the monthly dues by deliberately speaking in the familiar broken Italian, *"Signorina Forti, questi sono i miei 50 cents per questo month."*[143]

Also teasing the no-nonsense Italian teacher was Alexander Lussin. "My brother Alex, the Faoro boy and Bruno Carniello were practising their verbs aloud while Forti was writing on the board. She could hear them talking in the back of the classroom. They were actually singing their verbs, *'Io ho, tu hai, lei ha.'* She called on my brother to give an example of the verbs to which he responded, *'Noi abbiamo una bella maestra'.* [We have a beautiful teacher.] She just got red in the face and said, *'Oh, si' Alessandro'.* He was quite diplomatic, especially when he was in trouble," chuckled Emma Maffei.

Jimmy Ricci vividly recalls his experiences at the Italian school. "The classes were held at the old Sacred Heart School on the 900 block Pender. My dad encouraged Tony and me to attend. I did well—and after two years Tony asked to quit—because I was speaking Italian at home. My mom and dad wanted to know why it was that I could read and write and Tony couldn't even speak Italian. What they didn't know was that Tony, with his friends Ray and Louie, were playing hookey."[144]

Wearing her cultural quasi-political hat, Forti would recommend a list of students to Brancucci for the free trips to Italy. According to one newspaper account, between 1934 and 1939 more than 500 young people left Canada to partake of Mussolinian hospitality in Fascist camps, to meet with Fascist youth leaders, and to become involved with the "glory" of fascism. The children were expected to become enthusiastic propagandists for Italy upon their return to Canada.

The maximum number of free trips allocated to Vancouver in 1937 was set at five. The young women who were selected to go that summer were the Grippo sisters, Mary and Florence, and their cousin Maria Grippo plus Rosa Berardino and Eda Giorgi. Their chaperon was Rina Bidin.[145]

Travelling via CPR, some with employee passes provided by their fathers, the quintet embarked from Montreal with all of the other Canadian-Italian students aboard Cunard's B.F. *Ascania* to Le Havre and then by rail to Italy. During their visit to France, they attended the World's Fair in Paris. In Italy they stayed in a convent at Anzio after which they were free to visit family for a month.

On their return home, they were interviewed by *The Vancouver Sun*. A news item headed, "Mussolini is Grand, That's the verdict of Vancouver Girls who went to Italy," appeared Sept. 11, 1937.

"Enthusiastic over Italy and specially pleased with *Il Duce*, whose guests they were, three Vancouver girls of Italian parentage returned home this morning. 'Mussolini is grand,' the girls declare." A photo with the article pictured Rose Bernardino [sic], Edith George, and Rina Bidin. And Miss Bidin was quoted as stating, "Italy is just wonderful. The people are so busy and contented; there is such progress everywhere; the cities are so modern from what we had expected. It's all beyond description."[146]

Mary Stroppa later recalled, "My dad accompanied my sister and me by train from Vancouver

The Vancouver Sun *ran an article with photo, Sept. 13, 1937, headed "Home From Italy." It read as follows, "Guests of Il Duce's government for the past two months, the young ladies above are members of 80 Canadian Italians who returned to Vancouver Saturday after visiting parents [sic] [relatives] in Italy." The photo pictured Rose Berardino, Edith George and Rina Bidin who arrived ahead of the three Grippo girls. "'So happy and undisturbed, that you'd never know they are on a verge of war,' said Rose."*

"'It's a really modern country; I thought Vancouver was modern till I saw Rome,' Rina exclaimed."

"'But we didn't see Mussolini!', was Edith's regret."[146]

Italian language school students en route to Italy via B.F. Ascania.

Ship antics on board B.F. Ascania.
Rina Bidin chaperoned Vancouver students.

Sacred Heart Rectory Building Committee.
From left: Luigi Giuriato, Frank Comparelli, Father G. Bortignon, Angelo Branca, Aristodemo Marin, Father Leonard Della Badia, Ennio Victor Fabri and Marino Culos. Mario Ghislieri, contractor (in background wearing tie), with four carpenters. The project became the home to the Sister of the Immaculate Conception: teacher-instructors of Sacred Heart School, circa 1938.

Cleofe Forti and Emmy Ragona.
At the World's Fair, San Francisco, 1939.

to Winnipeg where we were met by Pietro Colbertaldo. We, along with students from Manitoba, went to Montreal, at our own expense, to join others from Sydney, Nova Scotia and North Bay, Ontario. We were billeted in Montreal.

"We sailed via Cunard Lines to England and Le Havre. In France we had a little trouble because the French didn't like the fact that the Italian government had sponsored our trip. We were asked not to let them know the trip was sponsored by the Italian government. We took a train to Switzerland then to Italy with a stop in Milan then Rome. We were taken to Anzio and stayed at a luxurious mansion and ate in the beautiful gardens overlooking the sea. It was marvellous!

"One of our chaperons in Italy was William De Bonis whose brother Vito lived in Vancouver. He accompanied us to Pietra Galla, Potenza, where another brother ran a hospital. De Bonis took us all

over including Anzio and the Amalfi coast. We were given time away from the guided tour for visits to areas were we had relatives. I spent a lot of time with family, especially cousins.

"In Anzio the Italians didn't like us too well because we were Canadians and sanctions had been imposed against Italy [during the Ethiopian crisis]. But it was one of the happiest trips of our lives," stated Stroppa.[147]

There seemed no end to the energy and degree of commitment with which Forti pursued her professional objectives. Although she relished the time she spent in the company of special friends such as Emmy Ragona and Rosa Puccetti, Forti readily responded to any assignment given to her by the Italian vice-consul.[148]

When Brancucci encouraged her to support the activities of the Circolo Giovanile, the youth organization of the Vancouver Italian-Canadian Society, she accepted with her usual enthusiasm. This association must have given her particular pleasure as most of the *giovanile* were children who attended her Italian classes.

Although the inspiration for the new club, the first of its kind in Canada, came from its founding director, Mario Ghislieri, his son Herman suggests Brancucci was the instigator. The movement was modelled after a youth organization that existed in Italy.

At its inaugural meeting, March 21, 1937, Ghislieri addressed a large group of people including youths between the ages of 10 and 16. Directing his remarks to the children, he stated that there were two loves they should always remember: love for their parents, and love of the club. In a single chorus, the youngsters repeated his words as a pledge.

In addition to Mario Ghislieri, the elected board members included his three children: Erminio, gymnastic instructor; Federico, secretary; and Gabriela Ghislieri, undersecretary, a position she shared with Remo Visentin. Nellie Santamaria was the auditor, and Mary Barazzuol, Emma D'Andrea and Annie Toffoletto served as instructors.[149]

The children were treated to picnics, free ice cream, and day trips at which they often sang patriotic Italian songs. Jimmy Ricci, Ray Benny, Ines Cappon and Irma Pastro remember contemporary patriotic songs being taught and a type of uniform: cap, scarf, and shirt or blouse being worn.

"We had a uniform with a yellow tie and a hat which we wore. I wore the uniform on Sundays when they used to take us by bus to the Roma Hall in Queensborough," recalled Ricci.

A couple of years later, some of these uniforms were destroyed by anxious parents at the onset of hostilities with Italy.[150]

In an atmosphere of rising political tension, Ghislieri continued his close association with the Italian Veterans' Association. He

VICS Circolo Giovanile 2nd Anniversary, 1938.
Children of Vancouver's society of Italians join in the fun and festivities.

"We had the cap, the blue shirt, and the dark blue or black tie. We went on—I remember this like it was yesterday—we went on a bus ride. They took us on a picnic and I think we went somewhere, possibly Strawberry Hill or Langley. We had a whole bus load and right after that the war broke out. And that's when they rounded everybody up."

—Ray Benedetti.

was elected president in 1940, an office he held until the organization was forced to disband a few months later by the RCMP.[151]

Gabriela (Ella) Ghislieri also was a spirited organizer. In December 1936, she was a founding member and first secretary of the Associazione Figlie di Maria. The Children of Mary Association, a spiritual group, was closely linked to Sacred Heart Parish. "We would meet for spiritual and social reasons," recalled Monica Heath Mulvihill. "At the time, I was a student at Sacred Heart School as was Joe, my future husband. The girls—about 40 of us—would be given direction by the priest as to who we might assist through prayer. For example, we might pray for the poor and disadvantaged children of the world," concluded Mulvihill.[152]

Picnics and banquets had been the mainstay of the Italian mutual aid societies' social activities for 35 years. Hundreds, including entire families, were lured to the annual picnics by the sweet smell of the home-cooked *salsa per la pasta* (sauce), warm friendships and wholesome family fun.

The day-long outings, which followed Sunday Mass, were held at idyllic settings on the North Shore—the Lynn Valley Flats at the beginning, then over to Seymour and Swedish parks with occasional

Galetti, Marchese, Gerolin picnic group. Italian picnic, Lynn Valley, North Vancouver circa 1920s.

forays to Belcarra and Bowen Island. It was a day off from a rigorous lifestyle; a time to relax with friends. The men talked politics and business. Some played *bocce*, which is similar to lawn bowling, and *la mora*, a type of scissors and rock game involving predicting the number of fingers one's opponent will hold up. The women caught up on news and matchmakers among them scrutinized the new prospects. In addition, the teens met and fraternized under conditions acceptable to their parents. Kids ran in races, ate mountains of hot dogs and devoured gallons of ice cream and pop. The brave entered the greasy-pole and spaghetti-eating contests. Everybody enjoyed the picnics.

"Oh, yes, those were real picnics over at Lynn Valley and Seymour Park. Families would bring roast chicken, a little wine," recalled Bill Canal. His wife Norma's memories are of the rides to the picnic grounds with her friends. "I remember when Mose'

Zanatta had trucks to transport wood and coal from their lumber yard on the 600 Prior Street. A good many people didn't have cars in those days and Zanatta would bring his flat-deck truck. And we would all pile on the truck and head over to North Vancouver for the Italian picnic."

Non-car owners would take a Number 14 streetcar and travel east along Hastings to Cassiar. There they would be met by Sammy De Filippo or Cyril Battistoni, co-owners of Service Taxi which provided a shuttle service to the picnic grounds via the old Second Narrows Bridge. In the 1950s, this service was provided by Patsy Valente, whose Empress Taxi charged 35 cents per person—"when the taxi has five passengers"—with no bridge tolls to pay.[153]

For a decade and more the famous picnic pasta sauce was prepared by the Pitton family. Antonia Pitton made the *sugo* in quantities sufficient to serve up to a thousand people.[154] She would keep the sauce secured in her home under lock and key until the morning it was to be transported by Ottavio Bevilacqua to the care of volunteer cooks. Once in safe hands, Tony Culos, Santo Pasqualini or Nino Sala would work their magic with the menu. The steady flow of the wondrous spaghetti and meatballs was served under the direction of Iolanda Pitton and Teresa Pettovello. Each society had its incredibly efficient work committee members. The Veneta/VICS Lega picnic and banquet committee included Maria and Antonietta Faoro, America Bianco, Enrichetta Benetti, Antonietta Corra', Nell Dermody, Giuditta Facchin, Rosa Visentin and Cecilia Zanon. However, for the Lega affiliated with the Sons of Italy, Pettovello was perhaps the hardest working woman of the picnic

Bocce played at Italian picnics.
The game of bocce as played on a North Vancouver picnic grounds court.

Italian picnic celebrants at Seymour Park, North Vancouver.
Maria Pressacco, Primo Mazzocca with Angelina, Luigi Palazzini, Cio Fabbro and two children and adult (wearing hat) unidentified.

Pini and Satti families with friends.
Children and entertainment integral part of Italian pioneer picnic scene, 1919. Third row, 3rd and 4th person: Mr. and Mrs. Carrari (she with arm on her husband's shoulder. Second row, Annie and Lazaro Stefanini, unidentified, Modesto and Rose Satti (he with arm around his wife), Raaffaele (with Josie) and Maria Pini, Rizieri and Genoeffa Stefanini and children Joe and Aldo. Children in front from right Christie, Clara, Bessie and Rinda.

Backyard bocce: secco!

committee: her prowess made her a culinary legend.[155]

And there was more. Activities included foot races, singing, tug-of-war, softball games and *bocce* competitions and the incredible greasy-pole climb. The latter event was dominated by young men in search of the cash prize tied atop a grease-slicked 20-foot pole. One year, their hopes literally slipped from grasp when Tosca Trasolini won the event, proving she could do anything a man could do, only often better.[156]

After dinner while friends sipped home-made red wine, the songs of Italy would be sung. Beautiful voices, including those of Antonia Pitton, Alice Pasqualini and Antonietta Pistor, in harmony with the music of guitar and mandolin players, spoke eloquently of the richness of the Italian legacy. There would be dancing too. Musicians like Dave Giuriato, Fred Minichiello, Ralph Ricci and Bruno Della Porta would excite the younger generation with their spirited renditions of current jive and Latin hits. As many as 1,200 people attended one or all three of the mutual aid societies' annual picnics. With post-war prosperity came an admission charge to the picnic grounds of 25 cents per adult. On a hot day, the amount of gate receipts was exceeded only by unlicensed sales of beer and wine at Little Joe's concession secluded in the shallow basement of the Seymour Park pavilion.[157]

During the weeks and months leading to Italy's entry into the Second World War some of these festivities, especially those sponsored by the pro-Italy groups, often came under surveillance by the RCMP.

For example, the Circolo Giulio Giordani and its ladies' auxiliary, the Circolo Roma, held its 1939 summer *festa compestre* at Bowen Island. To the majority in attendance, no obvious political propaganda points were being made by the organizers. The picnic, attended by many women and children, simply was a fun-filled outing. However, several of the family men including *Cav.* Carmine Marino, conspicuous in his black shirt, were known to be fascist sympathizers. The politically naive were to suffer by this association.[158]

On Sept. 27, 1939, Mrs. Angelina Brandalise, president of the Lega sent a note to the members of the Italian Ladies' League and Italian Young Girls' Club (Josie Battistoni, president) stating in part,

"During the last three weeks, the situation in the world has changed dramatically. Because of this and after careful consideration at a special meeting of the society, we have decided that, 'This year we will not be celebrating the feast of Columbus but we will continue to sell tickets for the raffle.'"[159]

In late April 1940, the Circolo Giulio Giordani held a Natale Di Roma banquet at the Hotel Vancouver. Its chairman, Mario Ghislieri, and committee members C. Braga, G. Caldato, C. Casorzo, R. DeRico. A. Dotto, O. Facchin, O. Marino, E. Pavan, and S. Pasqualin [sic] organized the affair. The evening's featured speakers were Rosa Puccetti, Gregorio Fuoco, Dr. G. Brancucci and Prof. G. Bovio.[160]

Marino and Phyllis Culos had been invited to attend the special dinner but Marino refused to go. His decision not to attend was based on two factors. Firstly, a military accord between Germany and Italy had been reached. The 'Pact of Steel', soon to be ratified by signatories Von Ribbentrop and Ciano, would irreversibly seal Italy's fate as a member of the Axis. This suggested to Marino that war with Italy was imminent. Secondly, he was aware that Angelo Branca would soon be presenting a significant pact of his own. Although minor in comparison, it had the potential of dividing the Vancouver Italo-Canadian community into two diametrically opposed political camps. Already a party to the Branca manifesto, Marino did not deign to be hypocritical. Neither did Angelo Branca.

Phyllis on the other hand, intent on attending one of the community's principal social functions, went along to the Hotel Vancouver with the Antonio Cianci party. Later she learned that RCMP officers posed as waiters at the banquet. They had surreptitiously made copious notes regarding what they had witnessed. Within a few weeks, the entire membership of the banquet committee would be arrested under the provisions of the Canada War Measures Act.[161]

Five months prior to the Giordani banquet, Marino had been elected 14th president of the Sons of Italy Society. In his inaugural speech in Jan., 1939, he credited past administrations for fulfilling the society's mandate regarding member's benefits. Over $50,000 had been paid out to members and survivors since 1905. Marino also outlined a full schedule of activities and immediately introduced his *raison d'etre*: closer ties among Vancouver's

Backyard bocce played in Little Italy.
Alec Savian at a court on East Georgia gets ready to play bocce.

Giordani autographed banquet menu.
RCMP agents were among the banquet waiters. The Club's directors were interned within a few months of Natale di Roma, 1940.

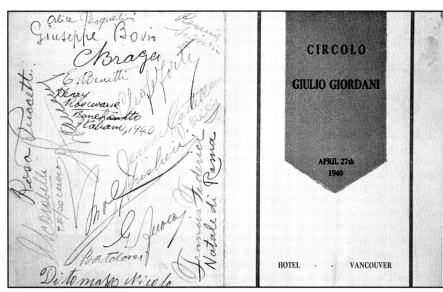

Bruno Della Porta Orchestra.
Della Porta and his Latin music
entertained society's 1953 dance.

**Fred Minichiello, band leader, played at
Italian picnics, banquets and
weddings, 1930s–1950s.**

society of Italians. In this regard, he had a major ally in Nicola Di Tomaso, who recently had been elected president of the Vancouver Italian-Canadian Society.[162]

An early opportunity presented itself in which Marino was able to advance the cause of unity among the Italian organizations—the British Royal visit to Vancouver in May 1939.

An executive committee comprising 26 members of three societies was established. Officers were appointed, including Eugenio De Paola as president and Marino Culos as correspondence secretary and member of the decorating committee.[163] The group's mandate was to coordinate events designed to celebrate the visit of King George VI and Queen Elizabeth. The committee, however, did not include an official representative from the Veneta. This may well have been due to the death on April 26 of Filippo Branca, its founder and honorary grand president.

The plan to coordinate the Italian community's entertainment programme got off to a late start and sputtered terribly midway through its mandate. Various ideas and proposals were presented among which was a fund-raising dance. It was organized and launched in one week. Apparently in the process, De Paola took executive licence in facilitating the committee's agenda. At its May 22 meeting, there was a display of such polemic confusion that Marino wrote the chairman the following day to say he was withdrawing his support of the committee's actions and any future decisions which might be taken.[164]

De Paola, determined to achieve his goal, advanced the construction cost of a viewing stand on the west side of Main Street across from the Canadian National Railway terminal. "It was noticed [the viewing stand and members from the Italian societies who occupied it] by everyone along the parade route and we had an excellent opportunity to see the King and Queen," stated Elisa Negrin who was on the viewing stand with other prominent members of the Italian community.[165] Included in the parade was a contingent of Italians led by flag bearer, Antonio Lussin.[166]

Italian society officials on the review stand erected for the Royal Visit, 1939. Fourth from left, Virginia Canal, Elisa Martini, Giuditta Facchin, Eugene DePaola, Angelina Brandalise. Raffaele Caravetta has his arms folded.

In cooperation with the Vancouver Folk Festival Society, representatives of the Italian community assembled in Stanley Park to make presentations to the Queen. "I was selected to give a bouquet to the Queen and she pinned a commemorative medallion on me. I was so proud. Flora Culos, whose mother Rosina made her regional Italian costume, also gave the Queen flowers," recalled Anita Panichelli.[167]

Publicly, Marino courted all Italian organizations, including the members of the pro-Italy groups. In its Aug. 3, 1939 issue, *L'Eco Italo-Canadese* reprinted Marino's progress report: "For many years, officials of the various Italian organizations would use the word

Italian youth group was part of the Folk Festival Society's Royal Visit programme at Stanley Park, May, 1939. Front row, left, Flora Filipponi, Rita Iaci, Flora Culos, Rina Brandalise, Nita Trevisan. Second row, Maria Clementi, Ada Trevisan, Anita Panichelli, Gloria Ruocco, Lina Gatto. Third row, Elisa Martini, Alice Marino, Ada Corra', Ines Visentin.

Anita and Osvaldo (Ozzi) Panichelli.
Brother and sister team featured at Italian concerts, circa 1930s.

The Sons of Italy's 35th anniversary celebration was the last major banquet until war with Italy ended.

'cooperation' in discussions. Now I believe that this desired result is actually on the road to accomplishment. Last Sunday, the Sons of Italy, the Italian Ladies' League and the Italian Young Girls' Club had a successful picnic. It was attended by large numbers of representatives from the other Italian organizations. And I personally wish to thank all who attended. These include the family of our Vice Consul, *Cav.* Dr. Brancucci and members of the following associations: Italian War Veterans' Association, Vancouver Italian-Canadian Society, and affiliate associations, the Veneta Society, Circolo Giulio Giordani and the Circolo Roma ladies' club."[168]

One example of these groups cooperating related to the Sacred Heart Parish's school construction project. In November 1939, Marino Culos sent out personal letters to his membership asking that they "provide a favor". He asked that they proliferate a chain-letter campaign by sending letters to three of their friends—asking each to do the same—requesting donations to the new school. The Veneta Society, and Vancouver Italian-Canadian Society and their Italian Ladies' Leagues also solicited donations from their memberships. The women's groups sponsored 11 special booths at a fundraising bazaar and helped sell raffle tickets, which, with a number of individual donations, netted the fund $2,168.25.[169]

Privately, Marino conveyed a less liberal view about the pro-Italy organizations. In a letter dated Aug. 17, 1939 to Father Antoniolli of Canon City, Colorado, he confided, "The attitude of the people of the community is somewhat changing to a desire for better understanding. Since you left Vancouver there have been orga-

nized several more groups. One that has the obsessed desire to be 'the example' of good Italian tradition is the Associazione Ex-Combattenti. The name itself suggests its purpose but it goes further—it will eventually be used to take the leadership in future community mass organization. This body was organized by Gregorio Fuoco, who is the secretary of the Figli d'Italia and secretary for the Circolo Giulio Giordani."[170]

VICS Circolo Giovanile meet at McLean Park for inaugural members' photo session, 1937.
Marino Ghislieri facilitated Dr. Brancucci's plan to establish an Italian youth club.

First row, Fred Padula, Nicola Di Tomaso, Dante Faoro, Tony Ricci, Jimmy Ricci, (unidentified), Italo Quercetti, Bruno Barichello, Ernie Maddalzzo, Americo Cavasin, Second Cavasin, Ernest Giardin, John Miotto, Ernie Pastro, Enrichetta Benetti, Mario Ghislieri, Elio Maddalozzo, Tom Pavan, Fred Pavan, (unidentified), Mario Crema, Lily Geremia, Norma Geremia, Enes Petrin, Mary Basso, Laura Vincent, Mary Padula, Pietro Cecarini.
Second row, (unidentified), Bruno Qercetti, Ivo Barichello, Joe Barazzuol, Joe Agostino, Rita Santaga, Dennise Carniello, Leta Faoro, Mary Stefani, Evelyn Piovesan, Angie Bianchin, Delfina Basso, Annie Miotto.
Third row, Midge Santaga, Tony Padula, Rinda Durante, Gina Zanon, Eva Zanatta, Vickie Giardin, Antonina Pitton, Lina Maddalozzo, Rina Maddalozzo, Irma Zamai, Rose Agostino.
Fourth row, Peter Culos, Bruno Facchin, Gina Grigoletto, Nori Canal, Angelina Stancato, Dave Giuriato, Almalfa Bifano, Ines Giuriato, Bruna Facchin, Theresa Stancato, Armida Pitton, Dora Giardin, Carmela Stancato, Annie Barro, Josephine Lastoria, Elda Grigoletto, Charlotte Barro, Gilda Piovesan, Josephine Dal Secco, (unidentified), Gloria Papini, Delfina Rossi, Joe Callegari.
Fifth row, Davino Basso, (unidentified), Norma Martini, Elda Dotto, Nellie Santamaria, Dea Meorin, Vera Martini, Nora Piovesan, Dora Filippone, Gabriella Ghislieri, Emelie Barazzuol, Emma D'Andre, Clorinda Piccolo, Rosina Signori, Gino Callegari, Rino Faoro, Cirillo Braga.
Sixth row, Luigi Giuriato, Vittorio Basso, Oronato Facchin, Lino Giuriato, Vico Dal Secco, Gerard Del Secco, Lino Dotto, Mary Peppe, Alfred Pais, Remo Vincent, Emilio Girone, Rosi Zanatta, Herman Ghislieri, Fred Ghislieri, Bruno Girardi, Nino Sala, (unidentified).

Nicola Masi, Italian consul (front row, fifth from left), with Giulio Giordani members and friends, circa 1930.

The Internees
Gli Internati

By March 1940, Canada had been at war with Germany for six months. However, the 'Phony War' which persisted in Europe shrouded the movement of the 'bootjacks' soon to march under the Arc de Triumphe in Paris. In this relatively tranquil atmosphere, members of the Sons of Italy celebrated the society's 35th anniversary. A banquet held at the Hastings Auditorium featured a magnificent menu of regional specialties. These included *antipasto alla fiorentina, spaghetti "Catelli" all'uovo, alla bolognese, pollo arrosto, alla torinese, frutta alla siciliana, torta alla romana, caffe' d'Etiopia, panini alla friulana* and *vini delle provincie Meridionali.* The active founding members were introduced and acknowledged while Dr. Brancucci spoke of the glorious *Patria.*[171]

National security and contingency plans were developed by the Royal Canadian Mounted Police prior to Italy entering the war on the side of Germany. This is evidenced by a RCMP 'Secret' document dated May 29, 1940 in which Norman Robertson, chairman, wrote a memorandum to The Rt. Hon. Ernest Lapointe, P.C., K.C., Minister of Justice and Attorney-General of Canada. Commenting on a report that his committee comprising J.F. MacNeill, K.C., Superintendent E.W. Bavin and himself, he stated, in part, that [the Committee] "has examined the records of persons of Italian nationality and origin who might be considered capable of committing sabotage and other acts which would be detrimental to the welfare of the State *in the event of war with Italy.* The Committee recommends the arrest of the particular persons whose names and addresses are listed in Appendices I and II to this report."

Item 3. in the same document stated, "The persons whose names and addresses are listed in Appendices I and II are members of the *Fascio.*"

Item 4.: "The Fascist Party in Canada is an integral part of the Italian Fascist Party (Partito Nazionale Fascista), its members subscribe to the same undertakings as members of that Party, and its officers are appointed by and work under the direction of the Italian Fascist Party which is itself an official agency of the Italian Government. Every member of this Party pledges himself to obey implicitly and without question the orders of *Il Duce* and of his representatives.

The oath of membership taken by its members of the *Fascio* reads as follows (translation): 'I swear to execute without discussion the orders of *Il Duce* and to serve with all my strength and if necessary with my blood the cause of the Fascist Revolution.'"

Item 10.: "It is recognized that many Canadians of Italian origin may have joined the *Fascio* without enthusiasm and under various forms of social pressure and that such persons may in the event prove themselves to be well disposed toward Canada in wartime. The Committee feels, nevertheless, that it should be strongly impressed on such persons that their own unguarded conduct has put them in this position of probation and given their fellow citizens reasonable grounds for doubting their loyalty to this country."

Twenty-nine of the 33 Vancouver men listed in the RCMP report would soon be arrested and interned under the provisions of the War Measures Act.[172]

As the Italian war machine was about to be unleashed in Europe, Angelo Branca convened a meeting in his office June 4, 1940. Invited were representatives of the various Vancouver Italian-Canadian organizations and a number of businessmen with no affiliation to any of the organized groups. Branca chaired the meeting attended by W.G. Ruocco, Marino Culos, Nick Di Tomaso, Louis Rossi, Charlie Peneway, Joe Nadalin, Louie Graziano, Carlo Casorzo, Sam Minichiello, W. (Bill) Berardino, Paul Girone, Luciano Zanon, Pete Angelotti, Jack Tonelli, Luigi Giuriato and Alberto Boccini. After submitting a five-point proposal, Branca told them the time had come for Italian-Canadians to declare publicly their loyalty to Canada. The attendees influential within the organized groups were requested to ensure that the mutual aid societies and their leaders supported the proposal.[173]

Marino quickly arranged a meeting of the Sons of Italy executive at which time he gained its approval to officially support the objectives of the Canadian Italian War Vigilance Association.

Marino's anti-fascist stand was widely shared by members of

Vancouver Canadian-Italians proclaim loyalty to Canada.
Advertisement placed in the News Herald by Angelo Branca's war vigilance organization following Italy's declaration of war, June 10, 1940.

Registration card carried by Italians
Hundreds of Vancouver's Italians were required to report to the RCMP, Little Mountain Headquarters, during the war.

Alice and Santo Pasqualini, circa 1935.

the Italian mutual aid societies. However, the men who had joined the Circolo Giulio Giordani were now viewed with suspicion by the authorities. Bruno Girardi was shocked by this development. He believed the Giordani club's *raison d'être* had been "cleared" by government officials. It simply did not occur to him that his loyalty to Canada would be questioned.

Santo Pasqualini, who found himself in a similar situation, explained how he came to join the Giordani. Apparently, it was a simple case of *quid pro quo*. Struggling to make a go of his bakery operation during those lean Depression days, Pasqualini had looked for opportunities to solidify business arrangements which in 1940 started to show great promise. Already a member of the Figli d'Italia, he was quick to agree to join the Giulio Giordani as a way to show appreciation for the bakery product business the club gave him. He also believed his membership qualified him for discounted fares or a free trip to Italy during the Holy Year celebrations scheduled for 1940. As a result, he and his wife planned to take their children to meet his parents in Italy.[174]

In the early morning hours Monday, June 10, 1940, scores of RCMP officers swooped down on a number of unsuspecting Italians and with lightning precision rendered them in custody as enemy aliens. The RCMP also visited Marino but merely to demand he turn over the society's official minute books and other documents. In addition, the police instructed him to inform the Sons of Italy membership that no large society gatherings, meetings or festivities, were to take place while a state of war existed between Canada and Italy. Marino complied fully with these dictates.[175]

The Royal vice-consul Dr. Giuseppe Brancucci was late for work that day; indeed a rare occurrence. He had heard of Mussolini's declaration of war from a private source. Bursting into the office, he exclaimed to a startled staff, "*Siamo in guerra!*"

"We are at war," sounded a bit odd to Nellie Pitton. "Of course, we are at war—with Germany," she recalled thinking at the time. As Brancucci shouted orders, the 20-year-old secretary instantly understood the gravity of the situation in which she found herself. She was a Canadian-Italian loyal to her country. However, there appeared no escape from her dilemma.

Shouting instructions to his employees, Brancucci began systematically to cull personal papers from folders in his filing cabinet. Grace Fabri, an office clerk, went about collecting the documents that he wanted destroyed. She was assisted in this endeavour by Cleofe Forti who gathered diplomatic papers, *Fascio* membership lists and other consular files. The staff worked feverishly transporting cartons of papers via the elevator to the sub-floor furnace room of the Marine Building. The burning of files continued until the RCMP arrived and confiscated the remainder of the documents.[176]

When the smoke cleared, Brancucci made a hasty exit from the country, subsequently taking refuge in the New York Italian consular offices. Forti turned up in Argentina via the U.S. Although she eventually got back to Italy, Brancucci was not as fortunate. In October 1942, he was arrested and detained by agents of the FBI at Yonkers, N.Y.[177]

On June 10, more than 300 of Vancouver's Canadian-Italians attended the inaugural meeting of the Canadian Italian War Vigilance Association of Vancouver held at the Hastings Auditorium. The association's founder, Angelo Branca, delivered a stirring keynote speech following which the assembly declared unanimously that:

"Irrespective of any possible action to be taken by the Italian nation in the present conflict, the Canadian-Italians are unequivocally behind the war efforts of the British and Canadian governments and have sworn allegiance to His Majesty King George VI.

That they will endeavor to give all possible assistance to the authorities with reference to any so-called Fifth Column or other subversive elements.

That they will make to local authorities full disclosure of any so-called Fifth Column or other subversive elements.

That they will arrange a system of registration of Canadian-Italians who are British Citizens by birth or naturalization and also of non-naturalized Italians, voluntarily.

That they will approach the authorities to ascertain all

> "We kept going down in the elevator. I was mortified. Trip after trip with all these boxes of papers, putting them into the furnace. "I recall very well being in the Marine Building and we burnt as much as we could until the RCMP came. They impounded everything and I had had my eye on the Olivetti electric typewriter which was the first of its kind. And during the time of all the fuss, all I could think of was the typewriter. I don't know where it went, but it was the first Olivetti electric typewriter here in Vancouver."
> —Nellie Pitton Cavell

Vancouver's Canadian-Italian War Vigilance executive members collect money for Canada's war effort.
Second from left, John Branca, Angelo Branca, Charlie Penway and from right Tosca Trasolini and Marino Culos.

possible ways wherein they may assist federal, provincial and municipal governments."

Copies of the resolutions were forwarded to Canadian Prime Minister Mackenzie King, B.C. Premier Duff Pattullo, and Vancouver mayor Lyle Telford.[178]

The next day's banner headlines in *The Vancouver Sun* declared, "Canadian Italians Here Attest Loyalty to Allied Cause." The newspaper's lead news item on a section front page, stated in part, that "Angelo E. Branca, barrister, pro tem president of the newly formed organization, voiced the attack on Mussolini.

Winter scene at Kananaskis Internment Camp.
Guards often played cards with Italian prisoners. (National Film Board of Canada photo.)

"'Today an event, that shocked the world by the depths of its perfidious cowardice, happened—the declaration of war on the part of an arch coward and his blind and senseless followers against our country,' declared Mr. Branca.

"'He has, against the advice of the Holy Father, the Pope, cast the lot of a homogeneously Catholic people with the lot of one who has forbidden them their freedom of worship, denied them their God and repudiated Christian teaching.

"'He has desecrated the memory of those hundreds of thousands of Italians who, during the last war, fought side by side with the British and French.

"'We beg of Divine Providence, and we hope and trust and believe that Great Britain and France will triumph,' concluded Mr. Branca.

"Resounding applause followed his address, and it was several minutes before Mr. Branca could read communications from the Veneta Benevolent Society and the Italian War Veterans' Association, in which loyalty to the Crown and accord with the aims and objectives of the Vancouver Canadian-Italian Vigilance Association was expressed."

Branca's Vigilance group literally rallied around the Canadian flag. Affirmation of Canadian-Italians' loyalty was gained, plus a substantial amount of hard cash, donated by the attendees for the purpose of showing support of Canada's war effort. The officers of the pro tem committee slate of Branca, president, Louis Rossi, vice-president, Marino Culos, secretary, and First World War veteran Charles Peneway, treasurer, were confirmed by the 265 voting delegates.[179]

The Vancouver Italians arrested under the provisions of the Defence of Canada Regulations were primarily members of the Giulio Giordani. However, those under surveillance included Italian nationals, men associated with the Italian Veterans' Association and those who came to Canada following Mussolini's takeover of the Italian government in 1922.[180]

Of those detained in the first wave on June 10, a couple were released within a few days. The others were housed at the Immigration Building, north foot of Burrard Street, for about six weeks until Kananaskis Internment Camp at Seebe, Alberta, was upgraded and expanded to accommodate the Italians.

Olivio Marino was arrested at his place of work and quickly whisked away. This happened to his brother George as well. And because they were the sons of *Cavaliere* Carmine Marino, the police suspected them as being prominent Fascist members. This fact appears to have led to a police team decision to conduct a search at the family's East Vancouver home.

In the early light of day when Mrs. Marino stood before the laundry room window separating the clothes for a Monday wash, she glanced up and noticed three strange men briskly making their way to her house. Olivio Marino's wife opened the door and drew back as one of the men, pressing forward, demanded to know where her desk was located.

"Just like this. 'What desk?' I say. 'I don't have no desk,'" recalled Antonietta Marino.

Over her protests, they rummaged through her purse, then searched the house: upstairs, main floor, the basement. Finding no incriminating evidence, they prepared to leave. "Your husband is a Fascist. He's been taken away and you won't be seeing him for a long time," one of the detectives tersely stated. Actually, it would be 22 months before Antonietta would see her husband again.

Jimmy Ricci, a 12-year-old youngster at the time, recalls finding his mother in tears. "My mother came down the stairs and she was crying. 'They've taken uncle Vincenzo away,' she sobbed. The RCMP, when they went to pick him up at his home at 531 Victoria Drive, allowed him to take the key to his shop over to Benny Thomas because Benny was working for him," recalled Ricci.

"They took him [Vincenzo Ricci] away because he was an alien. That's what they said. He could become a problem because he belonged to the Italian society. They didn't come and say, 'Fascist' but they said the Italian society," he continued.

"My uncle was a shoemaker and was happy to be Italian. The only thing he seemed to be guilty of was that he was a veteran of the First World War and that he came to Canada around 1926. Patsy

"My father would get up early to go to the bakery and then would return home to sleep. My mother used to walk down with Lino and I and take over the bakery because all the baking had been done and the drivers had all the deliveries to do. So, she kept waiting, waiting, and waiting for him to come and pick her up. But he never showed. So, she walked home. The house was in shambles."
—Lina Pasqualini Iacobucci

Mrs. Pasqualini received an unsealed Prisoner of War Mail postcard from her husband a week after his arrest. Although the form printed card, post stamped June 15 at Victoria, did not disclose his whereabouts, it was clear that Santo had been interned under the Defence of Canada Regulations.

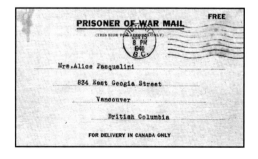

"I think the [Immigration] building was only two storeys. I could see his face. I could see the bars. And he was waving, and so, as a little girl of six, I walked across the tracks to talk to him. The guard who was standing there told me to get back. I mean seriously, what was I going to do?"

—Lina Pasqualini Iacobucci

Sketch of Santo Pasqualini, Petawawa Internment Camp, 1942.

Valente, who was my uncle's close friend and also a veteran, was sent away. Santo Pasqualini lost his bakery. Leonardo D'Alfonzo was all broken up—no family here except his brother—just an innocent little guy," Ricci concluded.

Pasqualini had been picked up from his East Georgia Street home within a few hours of Italy's declaration of war. The police roused him from bed where he had been sleeping after returning home from his night-shift work at the Paris Bakery.[181]

Mrs. Pasqualini, assisted by Elisa Martini, also worked at the bakery shop. On her return from the bakery, Mrs. Pasqualini sensed that something was seriously amiss. Informed by her boarder Louise that her husband had been arrested, she contacted Marino Culos and asked for his help.

It took Marino over two weeks to locate Pasqualini incarcerated at the Immigration Building. With this knowledge, he systematically began the process of petitioning Canadian authorities for Santo's release. The experience for the Pasqualini family, however, proved devastating, protracted, and alarmingly stressful.

The next day, Alice Pasqualini, with her two children, Lina, 6, and Lino, 3, on a tricycle, walked the four kilometres from their home to the Immigration Building located northwest of the Marine Building in downtown Vancouver.

Standing on the platform across from the Immigration Building, Alice caught a glimpse of her husband. Pasqualini waved to his wife and children from behind a second-floor window. Emotion overwhelmed young Lina. Waving and calling to her father, she darted across the railroad tracks to the building's entrance in an attempt to reach her father. But she was prevented from entering the building by a rifle-toting security guard. The tears that streamed down this innocent child's face were symptomatic of a tragedy which would forever haunt her dreams.

That brief glimpse of her father waving from behind the window bars was the last she would see of him for 25 months.[182]

Mrs. Pasqualini's inability to articulate well in the English language and her inexperience in running the family business led to the bankruptcy of the Paris Bakery. It also signalled the end of the family's only source of income. She was forced to ask for help.

Shortly thereafter, Alice Pasqualini became ill and was hospitalized.

The Zanon family rushed to her aid, as did the Luigi Moretto and John Scodeller families of Woodfibre, B.C. Other friends stepped forward but little more could be done. Lina and Lino, now deprived of both parents, were taken in by friends who cared for them until their mother's health started to improve following their father's release from the camp in July 1942.

Marino worked assiduously in an attempt to convince the

authorities that Pasqualini's place was with his family. He found the process painful and extremely slow. He also negotiated with a number of the creditors who vied for the remaining assets of the once thriving Paris Bakery business. One of the 23 letters Marino wrote relative to Pasqualini's internment and business problems was dated June 8, 1942 and addressed to the Deputy Minister of Justice, Ottawa. It read as follows:

"Re Santo Pasqualini (40-257). Once again, I wish to ask of you a favor. This time my reason is to avert probable serious consequences in the home of Mr. Pasqualini.

"On Tuesday, April 28 the Advisory Committee heard testimonials in favor of Mr. Pasqualini. To this date, Mrs. Pasqualini has not heard anything from the Committee.

"Mr. Pasqualini is a baker by trade and made his living by operating a bakery in Vancouver. When the authorities placed him under custody and later when interned, Mrs. Pasqualini did her best to carry on the business. It soon got the best of her and her health broke down. The business was closed. She has been under the doctor's care almost continually since then. A few days ago she suffered a serious relapse. The worry and nervous strain caused by the detention of her husband and the fact that she knows that the majority of internees have been released has created a most difficult mental disposition upon her, causing a very serious state of mental depression as well as physical suffering. The enclosed Doctor's certificate will bear witness to her condition.

"She is taking care of two small children. What has to be done with them if she should be taken to the hospital is a very serious problem. How long she will take to snap out and get well is something difficult to determine. No relatives live here."

Marino expressed the view that if Santo could be at home to assist with the care of the children, Mrs. Pasqualini's health would surely improve. He concluded with:

Cartoonist Otto Ellmaurer, a German prisoner, created a pictorial record of life at Kananaskis Internment Camp.

My Dear Wife:

I have received your letter of the 5th and I can't tell you how sorry I am to hear that it is necessary to sell the bakeshop. Naturally I will be guided by your advice and if there is no way of carrying it on then there is no alternative but to sell. I must leave that decision to you because you are on the spot and know best the conditions.

However, if your decision is to sell, it seems to me that the price of $1,250 is awfully low. You know that the oven alone cost me almost $1,700. Then there is all the rest of the equipment and the two trucks. It certainly seems that someone is taking advantage of our bad luck. Therefore, I want you to try to save one of the trucks for me. If I have a truck when I get out I'll be able to start something right away so as to support you and the children. Without this truck it would be very difficult indeed. So, see what you can do along this line. Try to get the best one if you can, but any one will do in a pinch.

Then there is the question of the rent owing by Pappas. Don't let him get away with it. He is responsible for all the rent due under the lease, even if the lease has not yet run out. So make some deal with Pappass [sic] that if you release him from the lease, he will give you a note covering a part of the future rent and all of the overdue rent. Thus, even, if he can't pay now, he may do so later on.

About the debt owing for the flour, etc., try to arrange to pay only part of it so that there will be some money left for you and the children. Do the best you can on this. Write at once and let me know what you are able to do re the suggestions contained in this letter. The papers you mentioned haven't arrived yet, but when they do come I'll hold the matter until I hear from you again.

Love to you and the children. Have courage and some day all this trouble will be over."

Your husband,
S. Pasqualini

"Sir, I do not know exactly what Mr. Pasqualini has done, however, this much I can assure you of—he is an honest, hard worker who loves his wife and children. What more can I honestly say!

"I beg of you to recommend the speedy consideration of his case to the Advisory Committee which heard the testimonies from seven persons in Vancouver and to forward a letter so that it may help to further show that his release will be a Godsend and that it may save Mrs. Pasqualini from a most complicated and grievous situation."[183]

Pasqualini had been shipped out with a number of his friends including Mario Ghislieri and Bruno Girardi as part of the first contingent of Italian internees sent to the Kananaskis internment camp. They were soon joined by other detainees from Vancouver.

The second wave of internees included Erminio (Herman) Ghislieri, age 27. He and his brother Fred were among 18 men ushered aboard a special CPR train on a warm summer's night in 1940. The group, transferred from the Immigration Building cells in Vancouver, was destined for the internment camp located near Banff, Alberta.

Like the "enemy aliens" who had made the trip less than two months earlier, Ghislieri and his friends were fettered for part of the trip and confined to specific pullman cars. In spite of their anger and frustration, an air of guarded optimism prevailed. As the whistle signalled departure and the train chugged slowly through the sleeping city, Ghislieri made a concerted effort to clear his mind of the events surrounding this most bizarre experience. His thoughts now turned to the exciting prospect of being reunited with his father at the internment camp.

The stop at Seebe was a brief one. In chain-gang formation, the men stepped off the train and climbed into waiting military trucks. Although the 11-kilometre ride to the camp was uneventful, Herman felt a sense of exhilaration at seeing the nearby hills on which he had often skied when he worked at the Banff Hotel.[184]

It was 10 a.m. when they approached the gates to their forced exile in a camp nestled picturesquely in the foothills of Alberta's majestic Rockies. The camp presented quite an imposing site: high barbed wire fences, search lights, armed guards. The level of anxiety felt by the new inmates was somewhat reduced as they neared the gates to hear a chorus of rousing shouts from the German internees. The Nazis had orchestrated a demonstration in honour of their 'Axis' partners, singing patriotic songs and giving the Nazi salute in defiance of the armed guards whose attention had been diverted by the arrival of the new internees. The Italians were incredulous.

Once in the triangular compound and past the commandant's quarters, the Italians were marched to the quartermaster's building under the surveillance of armed guards, including those manning the towers. After turning over their personal effects, each of the internees was searched and then given a uniform. The government issue comprised a pair of blue denim jeans, shirt, underwear and socks plus a jacket. On the back of the jacket was sewn a 13-inch red circular target.

"Fred and I had our reunion with dad and our friends, then we were issued identification disks. Mine was number 538," stated Ghislieri nostalgically.

"Next morning the new recruits marshalled on the parade ground, answered roll call, and had a look around the complex," he continued.

"The camp was built as a triangle," Herman recalled. "The prisoners' barracks started from the north and came south in rows. In the western part of the compound there was a kitchen, ablution huts and latrines. In the southern tip of the triangle was located an office for the camp prisoners' spokesman and a guard room. In the southeastern corner there was the isolation hut called the 'cooler,' which was a jail inside the wire fence for those who broke camp regulations.

"The camp's population of 795 prisoners comprised 25 Ukrainians and other Communists, 47 Italians, with the balance being made of Germans. Integrated among the German-Canadians was a crew of 50 or more nationals from a captured German merchant ship. A similar comparative percentage mix was reflected in the nationals assigned to each hut.

"In my hut we were 12 men. There was Ennio Fabri, the lawyer, and his father, and Piero Orsatti, the singer, and Santo Pasqualini, the baker, Angelo Ruocco, the tailor, and then there was Fred Lenzi from Summerland, and Carlo Casorzo, Fred and me. Most of the rest were Germans," recalled Ghislieri.

Max Bode, a congenial German from Saskatchewan, was the prisoners' senior camp leader with Ennio Fabri representing the Italians. These leaders communicated the commandant's orders, directives, and general information to the individual hut leaders who in turn briefed the others.

The hut leader, a position which alternated regularly, assigned men to fetch wood for the hut's two drum stoves, to remove and clean the latrine pails kept inside for emergency use, and to the clean-up detail. The prisoners were in complete charge of the maintenance, kitchen, work schedules, and social activity planning.

The day began with a gong at 0630 hours precisely. After making their beds to military standards and visiting the ablution huts, the men would assemble in the dining room at 0700. After the first

Photo of Lina and Lino sent to Kananaskis Internment Camp.
The children did not see their father, Santo Pasqualini, for 25 months.

of four or five daily parades and inspections, duties were assigned and the prisoners went to work until 1130 hours. The duties included clearing the wooded areas adjacent to the compound, trimming trees and working in the forestry camp. These assignments represented no physical hardship to the prisoners who were paid 20 cents a day in the form of yellow paper chits with which they could purchase items at the camp commissary. Lunch was at noon, dinner at 1730 hours. The evenings and Sundays were free for recreational activities, handicraft workshops or for writing correspondence. Each person was permitted to write four letters and four postcards every month but the length and content of each was subject to rigid rules and censorship. Pasqualini made beautiful small furniture items including jewellery boxes. He and others including Nino Sala and Fred Ghislieri, once back home, proudly displayed their artistic creations.[185]

Kananaskis internees' art projects
Fred Ghislieri excelled at wood carving.

Tony Cianci, 60 when detained, likened life at Kananaskis with being on a grand vacation. Food was in abundance and Italian groceries, ordered by family members, often arrived via Tosi's on Main Street. Cianci loved to eat the delicious Italian meals prepared by Nino Sala and Emilio Muzzatti and devoured more than his share of Santo Pasqualini's pastry creations. After light duties, he would play cards or a game of *bocce* with some of his older friends.[186]

"Cianci used to cut my hair in the concentration camps [sic]," recalled Bruno Girardi. "He was a number-one guy, eh, number-one funny guy. I told him, you and I are going to decorate the camp around. I put you in charge and said, I am your assistant. We approached the guard and I said, my partner and I have to go out and get a tree. Good idea. The Bow River was here, so we sat down, drank, smoked cigarettes, and slept," reminisced a smiling Girardi.

No Italians attempted to escape. However, a lone German gained his freedom briefly by exiting through a tunnel dug under the kitchen to the outside fence. "He was a baron, very arrogant and a real Nazi. I think he acted out of a sense of bravado because he was highly regarded by his fellow Germans," stated Ghislieri. In three days the baron was back.

The guards serving at Kananaskis were of the Canadian Home Guard. Many of them had

Kananaskis Internment Camp nestled in the Alberta Rockies.
B.C.'s Enemy Aliens were first interned in Alberta. (National Film Board of Canada photo.)

served in the First World War. The guards as a group were relatively easygoing and enjoyed playing cards and drinking wine with the gregarious Italians. There was a medical officer, however, who was "a mean and prejudiced son-of-a-bitch". Allegedly Dr. Gillespie so infuriated the Germans that one night when walking to the hospital he was accosted, grabbed and beaten. In fact, a number of the Germans from Calgary threatened him, "If not this year, next year. We'll get you!" The commandant's reaction to the alleged attack on one of his officers was swift but only mildly punitive. He ordered that the normal 11 o'clock curfew be withdrawn in favour of confining all inmates to their huts every evening for two weeks.[187]

"Soon after I arrived in Kananaskis," recalled Girardi, "it was in the mountains and I got a hell of a sore throat. So, I went for medical attention and the nurse actually helped me but the doctor was a major in the army. He was an asshole. He was always mouthing everybody. 'I'll look after your goddamn tooth'—he started to push me. I put him to the wall and I gave him a shot; bang! So, I walked out. Five minutes later the MPs come. They said they knew he was an asshole too." The incident was soon forgotten.

Girardi regarded his stay in the camps as a holiday when compared to the hardship experienced by the wives and children left grieving at home. While he was in Kananaskis, his wife Emma had been refused health-care attention because she was the wife of an enemy alien.

Dora Ruocco, an executive member of the Italian Ladies' League for 12 years, was shocked and mortified that the society for which her husband Willie Ruocco had laboured for so many years should suspend his membership. In an apparent retaliatory move, she resigned as secretary of finance of the Lega. Her husband, miffed, puzzled, and terribly hurt by the Sons of Italy's precipitous actions, arranged for his son Andy to return items to the society which had been held in safekeeping at his Europe Hotel offices.

These included furniture and the old piano which originally was purchased for the society's Italian Language School. A month later, the piano was sold to Sacred Heart Parish for the nominal amount of $35.[188]

A few weeks before the RCMP arrested Ruocco, Angelo Calori died.[189] As executor of his former father-in-law's estate, Ruocco attempted to administer the provisions of Calori's will from Kananaskis. This proved to be a difficult assignment. He managed, however, with the help of Victor (Ennio) Fabri who provided legal advice and handled much of the correspondence. Fabri had a vested interest in this exercise, however, as his mother-in-law, Rosa, was Calori's step-daughter. Calori's other daughter, Lina, now deceased, had been married to W.G. Ruocco.[190]

Santo Pasqualini also benefited from Fabri's generous coopera-tion. In his case, the former baker was confronted simultaneously with a bankrupt business, agitating creditors, and a critical situation at home. His wife was in the hospital and his children were living in separate homes of friends. During this critical period, Fabri's profes-sional assistance proved extremely beneficial.[191]

Speaking in sympathetic tones, Ghislieri recalled part of the Pasqualini family's crisis: "I was very close to Santo because I used to write some of his letters when we were in the camps. Yes, and he was quite a good friend being a *combattente*, he would do anything for dad, you see. Santo used to come to our house, sometimes being accompanied by Alice. So, before I was released [from Petawawa], I promised Santo—he was worried about his wife because she was sick—I would go and see her. At that time she was at the old Vancouver General Hospital. When I saw her, I was amazed to see her in that condition. So, I spoke to Father Bortignon and said, what can be done because that's no place to keep that woman. She needs better care than that."

Fortunately, Mrs. Pasqualini's health improved significantly fol-lowing Santo's release from Petawawa. But the experience took a devastating toll on the family's health and resources. To this day, they have received no financial compensation whatsoever for having endured this travesty of justice.

Internment camp life had its exciting moments. Rivalry existed between the Italians and Germans but basically it was friendly in nature in those early months of the war. When the Germans chal-lenged the Italians to a game of soccer, a team was quickly formed.

"Bruno and Attilio Girardi, Fred and I and a couple of others could really play soccer," stated Ghislieri. "The team was made up of eight because the field wasn't big enough for 11 players on each side. Anyway, we beat them. They couldn't swallow that, Germans beaten by the Italians, you know. They never asked us to play again," remi-nisced Ghislieri. "In fact, the relationship between our two groups deteriorated in the following months. The Nazis at Kananaskis no longer could abide Italians because Italy's armed forces would not fight for Hitler, particularly in Greece where they were beaten, and in Albania and Africa," he concluded.

In 1941, Kananaskis became an exclusive German prisoner-of-war camp. As a result, all non-German POWs were shipped by rail to Petawawa near the Canadian military training base. The camp was located about 160 kilometres north of Ottawa on the Ottawa River between Pembroke and Chalk River.

The Italians from Western Canada immediately sensed a difference in attitude between themselves and their *paesani* from Quebec and Ontario. Among their new compatriots were high-profile professional people accustomed to getting their own way. Although basically a good element, it appeared to Herman Ghislieri to be tinged with "a little bit of the Mafia". A few of the rich Italians had become camp work-foremen and actually hired people to do their bidding. These underlings would shave them, cook and serve their meals, and do their camp chores. The authorities seemed oblivious to this arrangement.

This situation was quite a change for the group from Kananaskis. They had come to appreciate the solitude of the Rocky Mountain forests and missed the manageable arrangement which existed between themselves and the guards. Petawawa represented more bustle. And the prevailing structure, influenced by Italians who enjoyed special privilege, wasn't of their choosing.

In *Dangerous Patriots*, authors William Repka and Kathleen M. Repka quote Bruce Magnuson, a former prisoner at Petawawa, as saying, "There were also Italian Fascists from Montreal and Toronto [at Petawawa]. It was interesting when we were on work parties, people like the millionaire Franceschini, the Montreal industrialist, and Maciola, the big construction millionaire from Timmins, were the foremen. The wealthy Italians were also able to get certain privileges. They could pay people to do their chores in the camp."

However, there were certain conditions at Petawawa which represented an improvement for those being relocated from Alberta. For example, the camp boasted a hospital staffed by eight doctors drawn from among the 600 Italian internees. Moreover, the new

Italians transferred to Petawawa, Ontario.
Work-gang escorted by military guards. (National Film Board of Canada photo.)

accommodation afforded more privacy; large bathrooms were actually attached to each hut. And they accommodated 50 men instead of only 12 which was the case at Kananaskis.

Friction between the Italians and Germans continued as the war progressed. This included arguments and fights over which group would be the dominant influence in the kitchen. Their frustration often was taken out in the boxing ring. A couple of Italians took on all comers, winning their share of the matches. But there were a couple of memorable losses to the German side, in particular a fellow by the name of Clark who finally vanquished the Italian champ.

"Among the Italians in another hut, there was a young swarthy type who used to be a boxer. Broad shoulders and so on, he was the Graziano type, a brawler. He could fight, let me tell you. But maybe he was out of shape when he challenged this Clark who was about 20 pounds lighter. They put a ring outside. It was afternoon. For the first couple of rounds this Clark, all he could do was just to stand up, see, because this [Italian] guy was a tough fighter. He was strong. But later on in the rounds, he started to weaken. And this Clark, he was a smart boxer, started to pummel him. They went 10 rounds and this guy was nothing but pulp. He really gave him a beating," recalled Ghislieri.

Petawawa Internment Camp offered benefits.
Guards entering camp grounds. (National Film Board of Canada photo.)

The Department of Justice set up a commission chaired by commissioners Hyndman (1940), Cameron (1941-42) and Miller (1943) to hear the complaints of the internees regarding their detention as enemy aliens. Although no charges were ever laid against the Italians, the authorities regarded those who had signed the *tessera*[party membership card] as members of the Circolo Giulio Giordani as being suspect.

"The reason why some were detained for about a year or a year and half, and so on is because the authorities had no case against them. They had to prepare everything. And when I went—when they called me—to appear in front of the commission, I was there for three minutes. They asked me my name—said, 'Have you ever been a member of the Fascist Party?' No, not in the sense of being a member of the Fascists. I said, I was a member of Giordani Club because I used to teach gymnastics, and so on. And as it was—I said—it was supposed to be a cultural club. We never had any direct political connection with Italy. And that was it. That was my case! Two weeks later, I was released," stated Ghislieri.

Of the three Ghislieris, Fred was the first to be sent home. The next was Herman. Within two weeks of Herman being released, he received his call to report for military service. On being inducted into the army, he was told that his incarceration in internment camps had been classified as a 'mistake'. Subsequently, he was discharged from the Canadian Army due to a back injury sustained during training. His father wasn't as fortunate. Mario Ghislieri spent a total of three years in detention. He was transferred to Fredericton from Petawawa with seven or eight other B.C. Italians, all of whom had been identified as former leaders of important Italian organizations. On his return to Vancouver, the senior Ghislieri declined to resume an active role in the affairs of the Vancouver Italian-Canadian Society.

Fortunately, Herman landed on his feet. He was reinstated at the Hotel Vancouver in mid-1943 and began a brilliant career culminating with the top position, catering manager. He attributed his success to his family background and an indomitable spirit. Because he was bright and conversant in English, French, Italian, and had a smattering of Spanish, and German, he surfaced as a true professional in his field. His health dictated early retirement, however, but not before his entrepreneurial nature led him to acquire the Ferguson Point Tea House with

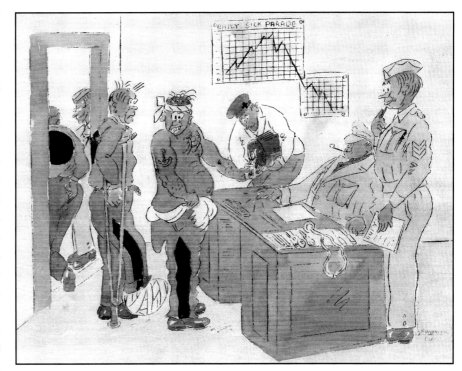

Prisoner-cartoonist finds humour in camp life.

Emilio Barazzuol. Later he completed stints as general manager of North Vancouver's Coach House Motor Inn and manager of the Quilchena Golf and Country Club in Richmond before becoming a food service instructor at Vancouver Vocational Institute.[192]

Bruno Girardi, born in Vancouver in 1913, believed he was interned because he had been publisher of the Italian-language newspaper. Appearing before the commission, he stated that some of the offending articles that he translated and ran in *L'Eco Italo-Canadese* had been picked up from *The Vancouver Sun* and *The Province*.

"Cameron, Taschereau and White were the three commissioners inquiring about our activities," Girardi began. "So, I said to them, nice and plain, look, I am surprised to be standing here by myself—between two RCMPs—I should have on this side the editor of *The Vancouver Sun* and that side the editor of *The Vancouver Province* because whatever I wrote in my newspaper was nothing but a translation from the daily newspapers. And I said, furthermore, may I say one thing, as far as I am concerned you are not here to see if I am guilty or not—you want to justify my guilt. As far as I am concerned you are nothing but a kangaroo court. Hey, I tell you, White turned whiter, Cameron, impassive, Taschereau he reacted, 'Wait a minute now that is not true.'

"I am sorry sir, but you are not here to see if I am guilty or not—you are here to be sure I am proven guilty. Because I was interned without any cause, without any reason. I was not even given an opportunity to debate my guilt or innocence. He said to me, 'You know, Mr. Girardi would you mind getting your wife to send me some letters of reference and I will see what we can do.' I said, I am sorry sir, I will not write to my wife and ask her to go out and get letters of reference—because if I did that—I would be admitting that I was guilty. And I am not. I am here on a holiday. A week later, I was released. I was released a week after Pearl Harbour," recalled Girardi.

Mrs. Tate's son-in-law Giancinto (George) Marino regained his freedom in late 1941 after having been incarcerated in the camps for 16 months. Arrested at the National Harbour Board where he worked, George's experience was similar to that of his brother Oliver who had been picked up by the police four weeks before. George's story, however, has an ironic twist to it. Shortly after being arrested, his son—the sole family wage earner—received notice to report for duty in the Canadian Army.

"After being held at the Immigration Building for six weeks, my father and others were taken in leg irons to the train station and shipped to Kananaskis," recalled Elain Butz.

"There was no money, so we had to leave school. My sister Gloria [Bowe] started working at 14 and I at 15. Until we went to work, the only means of support we had was from my brother, age 23. But that all but stopped when he was conscripted," continued Mrs. Butz.

Rino Baesso also was released in December 1941. In a memorandum to the Acting Minister of Justice, Commissioner S.T. Wood of the R.C.M. Police stated:

"1. The undersigned has the honour to report that Rino BAESSO of Vancouver, B.C. is an Italian National, who arrived in Canada about 17 years ago. He is a Shoemaker by trade, is married, and has two children who are at the present time in Italy and unable to return to Canada.

Sketch of Herman Ghislieri
Ghislieri posed for drawing while interned, circa 1941.

"2. In July last year this man was interned by order of the Registrar General of Enemy Aliens on the recommendation of the Inter-Departmental Committee, after they had studied BAESSO'S file in connection with his alleged pro-Fascist and pro-German beliefs.

"3. At the time, the Government was being pressured by the Public to take very stringent action against all Enemy Aliens, who were not known to be absolutely loyal to the British Empire.

"4. A review of this case has now been completed, and in the view of the fact that organized Fascism is non-existent in Vancouver, and as we have no definite proof that this man ever engaged in any subversive activities, the undersigned is satisfied that the release on parole of BAESSO would not be detrimental to the best interests of the State, and it is therefore, recommended that this Subject be conditionally released from Internment."[193]

The 632 Italian internees—from all parts of Canada—spent an average of fifteen and a half months in camps located at Kananaskis, Alberta; Petawawa, Ontario; and Fredericton, New Brunswick.[194] Yet, not a single one of the B.C. internees was charged with acting in any way prejudicial to the welfare of the State. By not being charged as enemy aliens, the internees became victims of the system and prevailing war hysteria.

A majority of the active members of Vancouver's society of Italians were known to and often investigated by the RCMP. Hundreds of Italians, including Italian nationals and those who emigrated to Canada after 1929, were required to report regularly to the RCMP headquarters located near Little Mountain in Vancouver. Later the Italians would report to an office at Vancouver's main post office building. Firearms had to be surrendered to the police and many individuals were required to leave Vancouver to relocate in the Interior of the province.[195]

"Government regulations required that my husband not remain on the coast while Canada was at war with Italy. It had something to do with his citizenship status. Therefore, Bert and I, with our infant son Nino, moved to Michele-Natal in the Kootenays. Gina Benetti's father, Emilio Sanvido, left his family in Vancouver for the same reason. He was looking for work in Calgary when he heard I was going to Michele-Natal. As a result, he came to Michele as well and lived about a half-block away from us. When we were settled, he and others would come regularly to our place to visit or to have meals with us," recalled Elisa Negrin.

Angelo Branca, who had stated categorically where his loyalties lay, provided legal advice to many of the families of the interned. He

"When Mussolini started the war, I was working at the airport. I had a nice job. I didn't do much. The foreman, who I knew since I come from Italy, came over and said, 'Iacobucci, that's it.' I said, what's the matter? 'Mussolini has declared war on the Allies,' he said. What the hell do I have to do with that? I lost my job."

—Gabriele Iacobucci

Ottawa, Ont. July 9, 1942 to M. Culos
"Re Pasqualini Minister of Justice signed conditional release today."
—F.P. Varcoe, Deputy Minister of Justice.

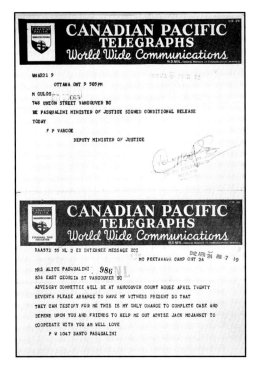

Santo Pasqualini finally released!
Telegrams announce end of injustice to
Santo Pasqualini and family.

also represented a number of the Canadian-Italians who were required to report monthly to the RCMP. Notwithstanding, the RCMP also maintained a dossier on Branca, the young accomplished barrister.

Among the records filed in the office of the Custodian, to the Inter-Departmental Committee, Ottawa, there is a memo marked 'secret' regarding the disposition of internee Aristodemo 'Big Marino' Marino (Marin). In part, it contains a direct reference to the RCMP's interest in Angelo Branca:

"Re Aristodemo Marino, Vancouver, B.C., [hereafter referred to as the Subject]

"The above named is the sole remaining person listed under Appendix III at Vancouver, whose disposition has not been decided. It will be recalled that the matter has already received the attention of the Inter-Departmental Committee, at which time it was decided to hold the matter in abeyance pending the completion of an investigation into the activities of Angelo E. Branca, Barrister, who had become interested in the case and who was also the originator of the Italo Canadian Vigilants [sic] Association. The activities, of which, appeared questionable.

"2. The file on Branca is attached hereto and contains two recent reports dated the 9th and the 16th instants respectively. A perusal of these reports disclose that little in the way of tangible evidence indicative of disreputable methods has been obtained. A review of report dated the 7th instant and appearing on file [with the] Italian Fascist Party, British Columbia, disclose that Branca is presently undergoing two weeks military training on Vancouver Island with the 2nd Battalion Irish Fusiliers in the Non-Permanent Militia.

"3.With respect to the subject, the files of this Force disclose that he was a strong Fascist and pro-German. He was a member of the Circolo Giulio Giordano Lodge of the Fascio, Vancouver. Following the roundup of Italians at the inception of the war with Italy, Gregorio Fuoco, Secretary of the Vancouver Fascio, supplied a list of the membership of that branch in his record of interrogation completed in the form of a solemn declaration. In this list, the subject is shown as having 'left the organization last year'.

"Your attention is directed to second paragraph of memorandum dated the 19th ultimo submitted by the Officer Commanding "E" Division. It will be noted that our Secret Agents state that the subject retained his strong Fascist leanings after he left the Fascio. Also he may not have attended the meetings. Attention is also directed to paragraph three of memorandum dated the 16th instant in which the Officer Commanding "B" Division stated that the release of the subject at this time would not reflect clearly to Branca."[196]

During this period, Branca continued his leadership role in the Canadian Italian War Vigilance Association. In a notice of meeting dated Feb. 20, 1941, signed by Angelo Branca and Marino Culos, the subject of establishing a "Free Italy Movement" in the City of Vancouver was introduced. The memo read in part, "The meeting is simply to marshall opinion of citizens of Italian Origin in this Country, as has been done in England and the United States and all who are in favour, and who are against the Facist [sic] Regime, and will do whatever can be done by them through force of unanimity of opinion to bring about a free Italy with a Free Parliament so that the government of the country might be based directly upon the will of the people rather than upon force and totalitarian power as has been the case and is, as it is at the present time."

The meeting took place at the Hastings Auditorium, Feb. 23. Marino Culos, a keynote speaker, read the following statement:

"Somehow, tonight, I feel as though I want to say so much on this subject. I am so enthused and so wrapped up with it all that it would take a couple of men to hold back my energy. The whole matter is so important and so deserving of our most profound thought that to miss this opportunity of exchanging views would be to commit an injustice to our sense of responsibility.

"This movement is so powerful in my opinion, that perhaps I may forget that you, under this great system, have your own ideas and that further, my opinion on the problem may not be in harmony with yours. So, let's get together and examine some of the facts. Democracy gives us the freedom of expressing our opinions. Democracy is broadly accepted as the right and practice of free people to share their government and to conduct it in such a way as to give the fairest treatment to all classes.

"And what makes it virile? What makes it strong? Simply this: The will to make it function. Once the will weakens, or collapses, democracy vanishes and something more sinister, more ugly, takes its place. Freedom dies. When freedom dies that something becomes an uncontrollable monster that knows no bounds. It preys on the helpless and destroys their joy of life. Shuts out the light of free thinking people.

"There is a war on. Nations have been plundered. A great number of innocent people have been murdered. This greedy monster has run amok in Europe.

Asked by The News-Herald *what action they thought people should take in response to the demand that they overthrow their leaders and sue for peace, their replies indicated their conviction that Italy should withdraw from the war. A number of Vancouver Italians interviewed in 1943 were agreed Italy was continuing [in the war] under threat from Germany.*

Peter Iaci: "I think they'll surrender all right—because they have nothing to fight for. I left Italy when I was a child, so I don't know about the younger generation, but the older people don't like the Germans. They fought against them in the last war."

Captain A. Vincenzi: "It is a very fair proposition and I think it would be a very good thing for Italy to take advantage of it before it is too late."

Peter Giovando: "I wish they had given an ultimatum before—but I don't want to make any predictions as to what Italy will do. I said she wouldn't enter the war."

Alberto Principe: "I don't want to think about it. I hope the Italians do give up, but I don't see how they can. You see, I figure there are so many German soldiers in Italy that they couldn't rebel if they wanted to."

E. Passerini: "I think it's a good idea, but whether it'll do any good now I don't know. I know that most of the Italians don't like to fight for the Germans."

Frank Iaci: "Italy certainly ought to give in. She'll have to sooner or later, because the people are just fighting on air—under German domination—and they hate it."

"Fascism, too, has tried to show our democracy just how useless it was to carry on. Fascism has met a serious setback. Italy's soldiers in Africa have no faith in Fascism and in a war that is merely based on greed and conquest.

"We, here, now realize what this ugly thing means and naturally we despise it.

"Even though many of us have been subjected to minor restrictions because of the war, we still enjoy the ownership of our homes, our freedom to operate our own business and have all the other privileges that a democratic government gives to all its citizens.

"It is therefore necessary to develop the idea that whatever may be the nationality of the citizen, he has a personal responsibility to the Commonwealth of which he is a part, because in a democracy the welfare of his family, the success of his business, his profession or his trade and his personal well-being depend upon a consolidated and harmonious community.

"This is the purpose of this movement and it is Mr. Branca's desire to impress upon you this personal responsibility. To tell you that this is no time for fear! Rather it is a time of high courage!

"We must work together for democracy. Those of us who have been naturalized have repeated the oath—the oath to the British Empire—that we shall always be loyal.

"How else can we work together but to organize? Could any other movement or name to such a movement be better than 'The Free Italy Movement'?

"In New York a few days ago, 1,500 Italians rallied to the call of the Mazzini Society. Many professors of Italian origin were present and as speakers, denounced Mussolini and fascism.

"Whatever other may be the purpose of the Mazzini Society in New York, the name Mazzini, Giuseppe Mazzini, brings to my mind the Italian patriot's ideals towards a unified Italy, his organization of a 'Giovine Italia', and its motto: 'God and the people.'"

"Nazism is entirely lacking in the higher principles. A short paragraph in *Mein Kampf* reads: 'An important factor in getting a lie across is the size of the lie. The great mass of the people in the simplicity of their hearts, are much more easily taken in by a big lie than by a little lie.'

"This simply means fooling the people.

"As reported, Gaetano Salvemini of Harvard University, said that if Hitler wins this war, Italy becomes a German Colony and if the Italians want to free themselves from Hitler and Mussolini, they must want a British victory.

Jimmy Scatigno and nephews Silvio and Victor Ruocco.

"We don't want to be tied and blindfolded, we want freedom and the truth.

"Therefore, we, Italians and Italian-Canadians should do our utmost to help preserve such a parliamentary state.

"We should organize our efforts so as to get the maximum results.

"We should do all in our power to safeguard our freedom.

"No intelligent person can dislike us just because we are Italian. We, ourselves, are not traitors to our land of origin just because we fight Fascism in Italy and elsewhere and boost with our might the Democracy of this Empire.

"We, all of us, are Canadian citizens and it is our solemn duty to stand by our Democracy.

"So, my friends, if you should feel in this matter, as I do—show your desire by becoming a member of the 'Free Italy Movement,'" concluded Marino.

Branca stood at the podium, flanked by supporters Louis Graziano, Jack Tonelli, Paul Girone, Santo Brandolini and Marino Culos, and delivered an inspiring oratory. He was quoted in the next day's newspaper under the heading, "City's Italians Hit Mussolini". The following is an excerpt: "Mussolini has earned for himself and, unfortunately, for a peace-loving nation, the despised condemnation of the world. His African empire is gone. His 40,000,000 people are on the verge of starvation, broken morally and physically; he is the virtual vassal of his co-conspirator, Hitler, who will soon give him the German heel. Next to Hitler, he is the most despised character in the world."

The news item continued, "At the conclusion of the meeting, which was attended by Canadians of Italian extraction, a committee was appointed to write the Dominion Government, to seek federal support for the movement. The committee will also attempt to ascertain from Ottawa in what manner it may best assist the British Empire's war effort."[197]

A number of innocent people became casualties of the government's programme to neutralize potential saboteurs. Not only were they uprooted from their homes and jobs, often they were ostracized by neighbours and friends for being enemy aliens. No one seemed to be listening to their protests of innocence.

In the case of 62-year-old Frank Federici, however, the Canadian government did act judiciously and with compassion. Within a month of his arrest, and in a secret memo to the Minister of Justice dated July 12, 1940, the RCMP recommended that Francesco Federici be released from internment. This decision was taken primarily because Federici had not been a member of the Fascio since 1932.[198]

Peter Ruocco also had been arrested June 10, and he too was released the following month. In his case, an internal memo from the RCMP—marked "secret"—was sent to the Minister of Justice on July 25, 1940. It read in part as follows: "This man, who attained citizenship in Canada prior to 1929, was recommended for internment and was interned as a result of information and evidence mistakenly attributed to him...it is recommended that this man be released unconditionally from internment forthwith."[199]

The Peter Ruocco family suffered many indignities associated with the internment question and the contradictions of war. Prior to being detained at the Immigration Building, Ruocco's son Silvio attempted to join the Canadian Forces.

A recruitment officer allegedly refused Silvio's application to join the military on the basis of his racial origin. This happened in spite of the fact that two of Silvio's uncles had served in the army during the First World War. These were his dad's brother Jimmy Scatigno, who served in the Canadian Medical Corps, and his mother's brother Fio Teti who made the ultimate sacrifice at Vimy Ridge as a member of the Canadian Army.

James Sinclair, MP, was aghast at the way Silvio had been treated. He introduced the details of this unacceptable and discriminatory recruitment practice to Parliament. As a result of his intervention, Silvio was given his opportunity to fight for his country which he did with distinction overseas. While in England, he sustained serious injury including a broken neck following an explosion at an airdrome which caused several fighter bombers to blow up.

"I presented Mr. Sinclair's letter to the recruiting officer. He looks at it and says, 'Well, I guess we've got to take you'. This is an Englishman. 'I guess we'll have to take you,' he said. So, I kissed the Bible and everything and he said, 'Well, look, would you like to change your name?' And I said what for? 'You wouldn't want to live with an Italian name in this country after the war.' I looked at him steely-eyed and said *'bacia il mio culo!'*. He didn't understand that I said, 'Kiss my ass.' Good thing. He might have put me in irons," stated Silvio Ruocco wryly.

His brother Victor who joined up six months later, however, paid the supreme sacrifice in the service of his country. After taking part in bombing raids over Germany, he was stationed in B.C. He remained on active duty with the Pacific Squadron at Pat Bay, Vancouver Island. But in 1944, he volunteered to fly personnel to the U.S. During one flight, the wings of his plane iced up at 10,000 feet and his aircraft crash-landed on Whidbey Island, WA. Everyone on board was killed.

As if the family hadn't endured enough because of this bloody war, two weeks later on a street in Vancouver, Victor's son Eddie, 4, suddenly darted away from his mother's clutches. The youngster ran

My Brother and I by Silvio Ruocco
Tearful remembrance of brother Victor
who died in the service of his country.

Oh, well do I recall the day
When, as two small boys, we used to
play . . .
The fights we had over each other's
toys,
For we were just a couple of boys

How fast the years did pass us by!
Until we two joined up to fly.
He was so proud of his uniform blue,
And his eyes always so steadfast and
true.

Each night to God above I'd pray,
"Please let me be the one to pay."
But it was he God took by the hand
To lead into that promised land.

And now, alone, as I wing through the
sky
I know I wasn't . . . of who was to die,
For always up there, he's at my side,
Waiting for me on that long last ride.

This life, I know is just a phase
To find those worthy of God's praise,
So, as I fly there in the sky,
I know we're together . . . My Brother
and I.

into the path of an oncoming streetcar and was struck down and killed. The family, including the child's great-grandmother, Sabina Tate, was devastated.

With controlled emotion, Silvio spoke of the tragedies and concluded, "My parents were heartbroken and I did not help by informing them that I intended to complete my air crew training. Laura May and I then returned to Lethbridge where I was to complete my bombing and gunnery training. It was at this time and with a very heavy heart that I wrote the poem *My Brother and I*."

Silvio's son David, a school teacher and former soccer great, speaks admiringly about the poem, "It makes me feel proud to know that he could write such a poem. It is a confirmation of his artistic and creative talents. And his poem also keeps the history of his brother's name alive for us—a reminder that he did exist. I have stated often how I wish I could have met him. My uncle was an athlete, a cyclist. We might have had some things in common. My friends are always impressed with my dad's art—paintings, sculpture, drawings—which is all around the house. The kids in the family would bring people around just to show off my dad's art pieces."

Elmo Trasolini with captured German airplane.
Trasolini (standing) fought near parents' hometown in Italy during WWII.

Chapter 19

Remember the Soldiers
Ricordati dei Soldati

In a significantly controversial interpretation of its constitution, the Sons of Italy Society suspended members interned under the War Measures Act. In a letter to the families of the member-internees, wives were informed of their husbands' suspension. The families learned that although suspended members would neither pay dues nor receive benefits, they would be welcome to reapply for membership when released. A condition of re-entry, however, was a doctor's medical certificate, the normal requirement of a new applicant.

As the society became aware of an individual's release from the internment camp, its correspondence secretary would send the person a registered letter. In the communique, the society encouraged the suspended member to 'rejoin' the organization as he would be welcomed back subject to the presentation of a medical certificate from his physician.

This procedure presented quite a challenge for Marino Culos, the society's president, as many of the ex-internees harboured resentment towards those who had joined Branca's anti-fascist organization. Marino, secretary of the Canadian Italian War Vigilance Association kept a diary during this period. Specific entries in the journal provide an interesting perspective to events associated with memberships held in suspension.[200]

The war years were the most turbulent experienced by the Sons of Italy and its members as the executive attempted to deal rationally with emotionally charged issues. The challenges faced during the war, and post-war periods were considerable. One of the most memorable was the issue involving the re-entry of its suspended members which included the high-profile former president, W.G. Ruocco. For months Ruocco spurned all overtures to rejoin the society. He particularly objected to having been asked to submit a medical certificate to validate his re-entry application. His request that this condition be withdrawn was refused. Although he eventually returned to the society he helped create, Ruocco never resumed an active role in society affairs. Nor did he forgive those whom he considered responsible for invoking the membership-suspension clause.

On Feb. 3, 1946, Bruno and Attilio Girardi were re-admitted to the society. This action brought to a happy conclusion the society's active quest to reinstate members who had been suspended in 1940.

Due to the pressure endured during this period, Marino began to question his own resolve in wanting to continue as president for a seventh consecutive term. The deliberations at the election of officers meeting of Jan. 7, 1945 reflected his dilemma.

Marino opened the meeting held at the Hastings Auditorium by reviewing the challenges his administration had faced during the war years. He was pleased to report on the success of the Comitato Ricordo Soldato as administered by the Lega. The single most difficult issue, he stated, was the one associated with the membership suspensions. Marino reminded the assembly that members who served in the Canadian Forces also had had their memberships suspended during the war. He then announced, for the good of the society, his intention to not continue as president.[201]

After much discussion, Charlie Braga, a member suspended when interned, stated a willingness to accept a nomination to stand for the office of president. However, the ensuing discussion regarding the presidency and its aspirants turned into a polemic shouting match. In the process, the meeting became prolonged and members became decidedly more agitated as questions on moral and ethical issues persisted. Finally Marino, anxious to put an end to the squabble, declared himself a candidate for re-election. Braga then withdrew. Within a half hour of Marino resuming the chair, the old administration either had been re-elected by acclamation or by ballot, and the business of guiding the society again became the priority.

At the close of the meeting, Frank Comparelli, another former suspended member, congratulated those responsible for the good work accomplished in carrying out the responsibilities of the society. He wished the new administration well in its future deliberations but the internal harmony to which he referred was never fully realized by the society especially in the short term.

December 29, 1941

At about 3 p.m. I came face to face with—first Dora and then W.G. Ruocco. A tense moment. Dora changed her facial expression and became serious while W.G. seemed unprepared. I spoke and remarked that I had heard of his mustache—He asked what I thought of it whereupon I said that it was my opinion that I preferred him without them [sic] to which he said, "Cianci thinks I look better with it." They left.

—from Marino Culos's journal

In a written statement, Marino Culos informed the general membership regarding the rationale leading to the suspension of interned members. He stated that, (translation) "The question under examination is not whether the members interned are guilty of being a threat to the state or whether their arrest under the Canada Defence Regulations was justified. We did not know the reason then nor do we understand today the reason they suffered this humiliation. However, we have known from the beginning that we would be unable to communicate with these [interned] members [in order to obtain the answers to these questions].

"When a person is interned in a concentration camp [sic] he is considered a prisoner of war. These camps are under the jurisdiction of the military. One who is so interned does not have the freedom that a [Canadian] soldier is able to enjoy. Therefore, if we can rule that a member [of this society] who is a soldier [in the forces] cannot continue to be a member, how can we permit one who is interned to continue to receive benefits from the society? This rationale is the reason we have enforced the article [of the constitution under which suspensions are allowed].

"And because these members, estimated to be 15, are unable to defend themselves, we will in good faith permit them to be reinstated once they have been set free from the camp. I believe, therefore, that this point of clarification constitutes our legal and constitutional position and that the members in question are not being expelled from the society."

The programme of the Comitato Ricordo Soldato (Remember the Soldiers Committee) to which Marino referred had been proposed by the Lega in January 1944. The idea to send care packages to men and women serving in the Canadian Forces—whose parents were members of the society—was immediately endorsed by the Sons of Italy executive. A committee comprising Marino Culos, Zefferino Bordignon and Raffaele Caravetta, the society's vice-president, was appointed to work with the Lega and its representatives. Bordignon, an accordion manufacturer, had a son in the army. Two of Caravetta's sons were in the Forces: Orlando in the army and Mario in the navy.

Raffaella Trasolini, president of the Italian Ladies' League, is largely credited for the Lega's initiative. She, along with colleagues Dora Trono, Phyllis Culos and Nellie Pitton, represented the Italian Ladies' League on the Comitato Ricordo Soldato. In addition, Trasolini's daughter Tosca, along with Mary Castricano and Nellie Pitton purchased, packaged and posted the care packages. Care packages were completed and sent in March 1944 and March 1945.[202]

Raffaella's involvement seemed pre-eminent as she had four of her five children serving in the Canadian Forces. Her sons were on active duty: Norman, a captain serving in northern Europe, Salvador, a staff sergeant, Medical Corps, and Elmo, a member of the famed Canadian Princess Patricias. And her daughter, Fulvia, was a sergeant in the Canadian Women's Army Corps assigned to the U.S. Army Liaison Office, a branch of G-2 (intelligence), Western Defence Command.

Elmo was Raffaella's youngest child. At age 21, he couldn't wait to follow his brother Norman into the fray. But it wasn't easy—to be accepted for active duty, that is. "Well, I tell you. When I got shipped to Calgary, they were making up a draft; those to be sent overseas. Well, we were all out on the parade square with all our equipment and everything else. My name was not called. I had to step out. The rest of the guys moved on. I missed two or three drafts to go overseas and I started to get suspicious. And I had heard that due to the fact I was an Italian, I was not to be placed where there were fortifications or anything like that. So, I deliberately got into trouble, had to, kind of got called on the mat and got punished. I swept and washed the floors while making my way into the major's office. And I saw on the wall—and my name was on the wall—that this man was not to be placed any place where fortifications were located. Boy, I was just raving. But I think Sal had something to do with it—I'm not positive—but he raised so much damn hell. So, when the next draft came, I went," stated Trasolini.

Trasolini participated in Operation Husky as a member of the invading forces which landed in Italy in the summer of 1943. He saw action in several bloody battles including the victorious campaign over the formidable German troops of the Hitler Line.

Following the liberation of Torrice and Frosinoni, south of Rome, Elmo received a letter from his mother. "She wrote asking that if I was close to her home town of Torrice to visit the relatives and to let her know how well they were doing," he recalled.

"I obtained permission from my unit commander to go back and attempt to find my relatives. Once in Frosinoni, I entered an *osteria* [a bar] and looked around and saw a bunch of guys just sitting around drinking. There was one guy—wearing a white suit—who looked prominent. So, I asked him, 'Can anybody here speak English?' He answered, 'I do. And what can I do for you?'

"Well, I said, I am looking for the Raino and Trasolini families of Torrice. He took me to the town and said, 'This is the Trasolini from Canada.' Holy mackerel, things just exploded. People came, came from all over. I became the centre of attraction—I was still armed and in full battle dress—when invited to sit at the head of the table," Trasolini exclaimed.

"I couldn't speak Italian, which I really regretted. But I was treated as a god, the centrepiece. And everybody, including my cousins Eddy and Johnny, who were only around nine and 13 at the time, just stood there smiling, talking and looking at me," remembered Trasolini.

Robert Bevilacqua sought front-line action in Europe and the South Pacific. Front left, twenty-year-old Bevilacqua and his twin Abbey were eager to get into the fray but armistice kept them in Canada.

"And the custom too, the men sat down and the women stood behind. I had the best bed; full of corn husks. Unfortunately, I was only able to stay overnight. And I only had meagre rations; cigarettes and chocolates. I gave them all I had," Trasolini concluded.

Not all of the Canadian servicemen were prepared to follow the likes of Elmo Trasolini into active service in Europe. Rather than wait to be conscripted for possible active duty, a number of men enlisted voluntarily to serve in the Home Guard. These recruits agreed only to fight within the borders of Canada should the country be attacked by an enemy force. This condition might have developed had Japan's invasion of the Aleutian Islands in 1942 progressed to include B.C. or the Yukon. These enlistees sometimes were referred to as Zombies.[203]

Thank-you notes were received by the Lega from forces personnel stationed in Canada and abroad. Orlando Caravetta, in training at Medicine Hat at the time, promptly sent a card of thanks. Prior to the war, Caravetta had been one of the Italian Language School students. His textbook, *Letture classe prima*, included a description of Mussolini which in retrospect reads rather ironically: "*Il Duce*. All Italian children love Mussolini, the leader of the new Italy who never ceases his efforts on behalf of the *Patria*."

Lance-Cpl. Eugene Paone's stationery had "On Active Service" as a heading. His letter was date-lined C.E. Branch Adm., Headquarters First Canadian Army, April 25, 1945 and read as follows: "I received your present of 600 cigarettes today. And at present am loath [sic] how you received my name. Thanks to the ladies of your organization for their act of kindness to a stranger so far away."

Vic Mauro's letter dated May 6, 1945, was sent on Armed Forces stationery: HMCS *Matane* c/o CFMO Great Britain, London England. He wrote, "Just a short note to let you know that I received the cigarettes which you so kindly sent and to thank you very much for them. The English cigarettes, when we can get them, are expensive and not nearly as good as Canadian cigarettes. So, the two cartons you sent are more than appreciated. I wish I knew how to thank you enough for them. I'm afraid I'm not much at letter writing so I guess I'll have to let it go at that. Thanks again and all the best of luck."[204]

Special invitations were extended to servicemen attending society banquets at the end of the war. "When I got back from service in the air force, the Veneta Society had two or three tables of ex-servicemen at its banquet. They threw a big banquet at the Silver Slipper for us: Tony Negrin, some other fellows and my brother Ugo who had just returned from overseas with the New Westminster Regiment. I was in uniform and feeling pretty proud to be honoured like this," recalled Bill Canal.

Chapter 20

The Banquets

I Banchetti

Top: **VICS banquet: 1945.**
Vancouver Italian-Canadian Society banquets were a major social affair.

Bottom: **Sons of Italy 40th anniversary banquet: 1945.**
Large gatherings of Italians were again permitted to assemble near the war's end.

*A*t the regular monthly meeting of the Sons of Italy held March 2, 1946, Marino Culos submitted his resignation as president. He cited personal reasons for his decision: to take a course of study in higher accountancy. Guiding the society through the war years, he said, to a position where it once again had a bright and promising future—a mandate of his administration—was now complete. He felt it was time to leave.

Honorary life president, Frank Pio Rita was unanimously elected to replace Marino for the remainder of his term. Following a number of speakers who praised Marino Culos for his contributions to the society, the members endorsed a recommendation by Armando Comparelli and president Rita that an honorary director-for-life status be conferred upon the resigning president. Marino, who would remain an active member, accepted the honour with humility and dignity. This award was followed by the presentation of a pen and pencil set at the next meeting, April 7, 1946.

Among the new breed of dynamic leaders of the society, Bruno Girardi was most popular. He had joined the society in 1936 but had not taken an active part in its affairs primarily because he was preoccupied with publishing *L'Eco Italo-Canadese*. Following his tenure as vice-president in the Rita administration, Girardi was elect-

VICS junior members were part of the festivities.
Francesca Quercetti, Joey "Chick" Venturato, Irma "Bebe" Miotto and Eleanor Halladay pose for photos after presentations to the Lega executive and to the mayor of Vancouver, circa 1938.

ed to the chair in 1948, becoming the first and only Vancouver-born president of the Sons of Italy. A prominent local businessman, Girardi held partnerships with his brother Attilio in a number of enterprises including a grocery store and a ship chandler operation. His entrepreneurial spirit led him to sponsor *Musica Italiana*, a popular Sunday radio programme. Its success helped to increase CKWX's listening audience by as much as 70% within the programme's time-slot. And in the early 1950s, Girardi was the first to obtain papal approval to broadcast from inside a Vancouver Catholic Church on Easter Sunday and Christmas Day. These and other Girardi initiatives did much to enhance the awareness of the Italian presence in the community during the post-war period.[205]

Every newly elected president chose a password to be used by members during the year. These passwords were a holdover from the days when fraternal organizations met in relative secrecy. It would be whispered to the sergeant-at-arms by members entering the meeting hall. Primo Mazzocca, a tall and sturdy individual, supervised the password verification procedure for the Sons of Italy for over 20 years. Although the practice was largely ceremonial, the use remained an integral and popular custom throughout the life of the society. Girardi chose the password *Unita'* (unity) for his first administration and *Carrelli* (Giovanni Carrelli, the society's first president) for his second term. Rita's had been *Avanti* (forward).

The agenda also followed tradition: roll call of the table officers and directors, reading of the minutes of the previous meeting, treasurer's and other financial reports, plus the report of the sick committee which included submission of medical certificates signed by attending physicians.

To verify one's claim for sick benefit, a member first visited a physician. Following treatment, an application form was completed by the attending medical doctor. It included information regarding the kind of sickness treated, fitness of patient to work, and the date the member returned to work. On receipt of a doctor's certificate, the membership would vote approval of payment. In addition to the doctor's fee, a member was entitled to receive $1 a day for the number of sick days, less a three-day grace period. Maximum cash benefit in any one year was $53 with a member's lifetime total amount received not to exceed $404. After being visited by a delegation from the sick committee—for years headed by Luigi Pressacco—the member in question would receive a letter which provided details of the sick benefit and a cheque from the corresponding secretary. Marino, who wrote scores of these letters, typed by his wife Phyllis, always added a cordial and personal note of best wishes.

In the event of a death, survivor benefits would include the option of having the deceased buried in the society's plot. The family would receive $135 less $94.55 (circa 1960) for the cost of the grave, perpetual flowers and headstone as prepared by Rizieri Stefanini of the Kingsway Monumental Works. In addition, flowers would be sent by the society to the church funeral service.

Committee chairmen presented progress reports and following the reading of the correspondence a vote would be taken dictating the action to be taken. The liaison committee chairmen interacting with the Italian consulate, pastor of the Sacred Heart Church, and the organization's physicians (circa 1925–1936: Dr. E. Zito, Dr. M. Fox and Dr. D.A. Tomsett; circa 1937–1966: Dr. P. Ragona) also would be asked for their comments. The president, who served as director on the Italian Ladies' League executive, would detail the society's current and projected activities with the society's affiliate. Towards the end of the agenda, any items relating to good and welfare and new business would be discussed.

Following discussion on good and welfare, the regular order of business would be suspended and applicants for membership introduced. Once presented, the aspirants would be asked to step out of the room while members in good standing decided whether or not to ratify their membership applications. After a review of each applicant's qualifications, a small three-compartment ballot box carried by an official was brought forward. The first two sections of the box exposed white and black round agates commonly referred to as peas. The third compartment which had a removable lid contained a circular hole. The official would present the ballot box individually to each member in good standing. A white or black pea would be selected and deposited through the opening. If at the end there were three or more black agates in the box, the person in question would be notified that his application for membership had been rejected. Usually, however, applause would emanate from the meeting room signalling acceptance.

The final procedure was an attendance lottery for a cash prize of $1 or more. Often the consumption of *panini* [sandwiches] and wine at the end of the meeting precipitated a rehashing of the more sensitive issues previously discussed.

The society's designated physician for 30 years was Dr. Paul Ragona. The only son of a prominent physician in Palermo, Dr. Ragona travelled to London upon graduating from medical school. Following completion of his studies, he immigrated to

Dr. Paul Ragona and fellow Italian medical school graduates in Italy.
Dr. Ragona, second from left, provided medical services to Sons of Italy members for 30 years.

Sons of Italy banquet: January 1946

Canada living and working in Calgary before settling in Vancouver in the late 1930s. Dr. Ragona's courtship, marriage and life with his wife Emmy reads like a story-book romance. She left the comfort of a pre-ordained and privileged lifestyle that centred around Naples, Capri and Palermo to follow her betrothed—a struggling doctor—to the wilds of the New World. Emmy Ragona had been born to an aristocratic family. Her titled mother was Princess Rosa Lagana' Alliata, a member of the Sicilian *nobilita*.

On arriving in Vancouver in 1936, Emmy instantly fell in love with Vancouver. Her marriage to Paul, which took place in Victoria a few months later, was witnessed by Mr. and Mrs. Pietro Colbertaldo and Mr. and Mrs. Italo Rader. After a brief honeymoon, Dr. Ragona returned to Calgary. His bride, however, did not follow

him. Rather she explained, "I said to Paul, in Calgary there is no sea. And I am not going. Without the sea, I cannot live. And that's why he came to Vancouver." The Ragonas eventually set up housekeeping at the 'Villa Capri' in Point Grey where they remained until his death in 1976.

Later Emmy Ragona was to confide that although she vacationed in Italy regularly, she never pined for her former life because life with her husband had been so complete. "Paul was my father, my mother, my brother, you know. I don't think there was another man like that," she mused.

In Girardi's administration, new members were encouraged to speak about their impressions of the Sons of Italy and how they thought they might contribute to the well-being of the society. The

Sons of Italy, Lega and Giovani Italiane combine to sponsor the 1947 banquet.

successful applicants were sworn in and then greeted individually by the members—hand shakes all round.

On March 5, 1950, following acceptance as a new member, Joe Parisi addressed the meeting stating, (translation) "My impressions of the Sons of Italy Society are really very good. Through its numerous and diverse activities, the society is able to keep alive the memory of life of the mother country for Italians who find it necessary to adopt a new country and to live abroad."

Thirty-one new membership applications were approved in 1948. Bruno Girardi won the competition for signing up the highest number with 13. The next year, the coveted title with prize was awarded to Marino Culos who brought in eight of the 30 new members. Their names were added to a plaque on which a permanent list of top achievers was recorded. The name Joe Politano occupied a special category as recipient of a gold medal for outstanding work as a successful membership recruiter.[206]

Rev. Father Victor Gallo's ordination to the priesthood is celebrated by Sacred Heart parishioners, 1947.

Concurrent with these membership drives was a resurgence of juvenile or junior memberships. Children, sons of active society members, soon swelled the membership rolls. In the 1940s, these

young people included Louie Barillaro, Fred Borsato, Bruno Carretti, Dominic Ciarniello, Attilio L. Girardi, Lino Pasqualini, Larry Politano and Victor and Raymond Culos.[207]

The author, looking forward to his ninth birthday the following month, happily joined his brother Victor in front of the executive. As they faced their father who was flanked by other table officers including a smiling Felice Cianci, Marino asked his sons to repeat the Oath of Membership—in Italian. As neither one of the boys spoke Italian at the time, the experience was an unforgettable embarrassment for all concerned.[208]

Sacred Heart Church, Official Opening
The new church is Father Bortignon's crowning achievement, Oct. 23, 1949.

"When I became president there were between 110 and 120 active members. Within two years, I brought it up to close to 200. The old people are good for directing. The young people are there to work. You need a director but the festivities committee workers know what to do," stated Girardi.

"The only difference of opinion I had with Marino Culos was that he wanted to look at the past, and to look after the past. I didn't. I wanted to forget it. Look after the members while they are alive, not when they are dead. They always wanted to stay within the confines of the constitution and *bumba a bumba*," he continued.

Girardi's brother Attilio headed up the new Sports Committee. Its members soon organized the Sons of Italy Sports Club which sponsored a soccer and softball team. Committee member Attilio Costanzo obtained Al Principe's cooperation in securing the use of the 64 Club on Hastings Street and also contracted for a gymnasium. The soccer team, the forerunner to Peter Mainardi's Columbus Soccer Club, had an excellent following as it provided much entertainment for young Italians whose first sports love had been playing football in Italy.

Midge Santaga was a member of The Sons of Italy Sports Club and the Girardi Brothers' soccer teams.

"We had a number of skilled soccer players who started for the

When Cece Nicholls, the much honoured lacrosse player-coach, visited the Union-Prior Street area and witnessed the exceptional calibre of play by the Italo-Canadians, he exclaimed, "I've discovered a virtual gold mine [of talent]." Indeed, some of the most exciting lacrosse, soccer and softball ever played in the Vancouver area during the 1940s, 1950s and 1960s came from this phenomenal talent pool of Faoro, Genovese, Venturato and the brothers Crema, Cervi, Durante, Maddalozzo and Santaga.

Kindergarten students were among the inaugural enrollment at the new Sacred Heart School, 1940–41.
Back row, left to right, Roy Bianco, Louie Bianchi, Stanley Tully, Robert Boussier, Lawrence Boussier, Edward Esakin, Walter Limiski, Raymond Culos, Edward Soltis. Front row, Dora Gatti, Mary Giuriati, Gloria Giuriati, Violet Guerino, Josephine Limiski, Lena Torresan, Betty Tully.

Sacred Heart Communion class
The parish's Catholic families were required to send their children to Sacred Heart School and to encourage them to receive the Sacraments. Circa 1943.

Society's team including all-star player Ernie Durante and his brother Joe, George Bogdanovich, Lino Cervi, Larry Crema, Don Faoro, Elso Genovese, Mike Rossi and Chick Venturato. And the final game—for the under-21 league championship—was decided in a hotly contested game with the Norburn," recalled Santaga.

The score was one-nil for the Italians as the team suffered a major setback when one of the team's half-backs was handed a red card for retaliating after being fouled.

"Jones came into Lino Cervi with both knees: right in his back. A normally placid Cervi jumped to his feet, swung around and with a single blow broke the guy's nose. We were then playing one man short and just barely hanging on. With two minutes to go, referee Blundell blundered and made a controversial call. Norburn was awarded a penalty kick and made good its shot. We lost the cup in overtime. Regarding the Cheece's foul, he appeared at the compulsory hearing and was completely exonerated for having retaliated because of the severity of Jones's vicious attack," stated Santaga.

"A few years earlier, I had played for the Girardi soccer and softball teams. I had so much respect for Bruno and Attilio Girardi because they really got involved. Not only did they sponsor us but they wouldn't miss a game. Attilio was a very good soccer player. God was he good. We formed the Girardi Bros. team and at the end of the first season of play we were champions," concluded the former centre-half.

A new and refreshing atmosphere prevailed as dozens of new arrivals to Vancouver joined the Sons of Italy. These included Anthony and Frank Iuele, Fiorenzo Benincasa, Lu Moro, Gerry DiSilvo and Leo Tesan. They wanted youth activities, greater emphasis on sport, music and drama. They also wanted an English-for-Italians language school, and above all a casa d'Italia facility. Joining the resurgence movement were a number of men of experience who had either allowed their memberships to lapse or who had become inactive. These included Onofrio Fiorito, Fred Ghislieri, Cirillo Braga, Nino Sala, Santo Pasqualini, Gregorio Fuoco and Antonio Paolo Borsato.

Father Joachim Bortignon, the society's *prede*, was awarded an honorary membership by the Girardi administration. As pastor of Sacred Heart and energetic builder of the new church, Father Bortignon had been a friend and the spiritual leader to the members of the Sons of Italy since 1936, the year his parish officially became known as Italian.[209]

However, all administrations suffered the same malaise: lack of participation and interest on the part of a majority of its members. After attending the meeting at which they were inducted, many neophyte members would drop out to resurface only at the annual election-of-officers meeting. A sense of frustration was felt by a majority of new members upon becoming witness to the long and often protracted discussions on the constitution. Some became incredulous by the constant in-fighting and the self-indulgent posturing on the part of a few individuals. Whenever this atmosphere of animosity and confrontation prevailed, absenteeism resulted. Generally speaking, however, those who did not attend the meetings regularly supported their society's banquets and picnics.

Marilyn Pettovello: First Communion
Religious instruction was offered to all Catholic children.

Sacred Heart's St. Cecelia Choir, 1948.
Second row, from left, Gina Sanvido, Marie Morrison, Angelina Mazzocca, Charlotte Barro. Front row, Irma Borsato, Ida Visentin, Marcella Stefani, Gloria Genovese, Armida Pitton, Mary Maddalozzo, Lina Maddalozzo.

1950 Sons of Italy 45th anniversary

1951 Sons of Italy, Circolo Sportivo
banquet

1951 Sons of Italy October banquet

Lu Moro was vice-president in Girardi's third and fourth terms as president. Moro had come from Italy at age 11 with his mother to join his father in Trail, B.C. He enlisted in the Canadian Navy in 1942, and in the same year was married to Virginia Cima. Following the end of the war, they settled in Vancouver. The Canadian Lacrosse Hall of Fame [team-builder] member and former star lacrosse player with Trail's 1938 Champion Golden Bears, Moro helped form a major sports element within the structure of the Sons of Italy activ-

1952 Lega's 25th anniversary, held at the Cave Supper Club.

ities.[209A] In addition, he spearheaded an amateur dramatic club with major cooperation from Fiorenzo Benincasa.

Relating to his induction into the Canadian Navy, Moro offered some interesting comments. "I had been classified as an enemy alien. I was living in Trail at the time and with others I was transporting a juvenile hockey team to Vernon. It was winter and in order to by-pass the Cascades [mountain range], we decided to go through the States. At the U.S. border, they wouldn't let me pass because I was an enemy alien and as such had been reporting regularly to the authorities. When I joined the navy, I said to Sergeant Williams where I reported that I was leaving to report for duty the next day and I wouldn't be coming in to sign [report] anymore. He says, 'You

Father Giuseppe Della-Torre, pastor of Sacred Heart Parish for over 25 years.

The Italian Choir preserves its cultural heritage through musical performances.

take this transfer paper to the Victoria Provincial Police [sic] and report to them.' I said, you know what you can do. You can wipe your bum with this. I threw it at him and said, no I am not! Look, I'm joining the navy and you are not making me sign anymore."

In April 1951, Moro's committee presented a concert and variety show at the Hastings Auditorium. Leading the list of entertainers were Rino Cechetto lip-singing Al Jolson favourites with accompaniment by Ugo Sartorello, and Anita Panichelli and Carmelina Barillaro, talented soloists who performed under the direction of *Maestro* Piero Orsatti. Also featured were F. Salfi and Emilio Gallo, mandolin and guitar aficionados. In addition, Margherita and Marianna Basile and Antonio Iuele, singing and dancing specialists, plus Giuseppe Donati, tenor, and Gloria Ghini, soprano, highlighted the list of performers.

Marino Culos volunteered to establish an English language school in 1949 for the many new arrivals who now held membership in the society. Rose Cianci (formerly Mrs. Puccetti), a student and colleague of Cleofe Forti, agreed to serve as instructor along with Marino. The twice weekly sessions were very popular and had an enrollment of 50 students in the second year of operation. The large turnout necessitated moving the Sunday classes conducted at the Culos residence at 748 Union Street to the larger classroom at Sacred Heart School. Attractive diplomas were presented to the graduates at the Christopher Columbus banquet in October.

One of the graduates was Vincenzo Calla who registered for English classes in 1949. "I never forget Mr. Culos and Mrs. Cianci. They helped me when I needed help most. They were wonderful. They teach me English, you know, and Mrs. Cianci would give me sheets with the verbs to take home and study. I needed to learn English and they were the first to help."[210]

When Rose Cianci and Marino Culos completed their terms as instructors of the English language classes, they asked to be replaced. Girardi appointed vice-president Benincasa along with Lu Moro and Joe Politano to the School Committee. Commencing in November, classes were expanded to include Italian language courses. Girardi and Moro provided instruction for members wanting to learn English. The president, with Fiorenzo Benincasa, taught those interested in the Italian language. For 50 cents a month, students received four weekly lessons.

At the June 1951 general meeting, Father Camillo Santini of Sacred Heart Parish and Italo Rader were appointed honorary members. Rader, first post-war Italian vice-consul to address the membership of the Sons of Italy, is remembered for his general interest and support of Vancouver's Italian mutual aid societies.

During his first term as president, Girardi awarded Fourth Degree Honorary memberships to W.G. Ruocco, Angelo E. Branca, Marino Culos, Gettulio Falcioni, Antonio Cianci, Achille Pini, Cesare Anderlini and Father Joachim Bortignon in recognition of their special service to the Society.

Girardi liked Father Bortignon very much, primarily because the priest was so "down to earth". The two men shared a strong belief in Italy, a view duly noted by government and ecclesiastical authorities in 1940. While Girardi protested his incarceration at Kananaskis, Father Bortignon was transferred to a parish near Hamilton, Ontario. "Although not a *confinato*, Father Bortignon was very proud to be Italian. But I guess because he was a priest, they couldn't fool around with him," Girardi opined.[210A]

Sacred Heart Bazaar: Lega's booth
Craft products were donated to the church by scores of women representing the various Italian women's organizations. From left, Rose Cianci, Phyllis Culos, J. Sartore and Dora Trono

Vancouver Italian-Canadian queen contest, Seymour Park, 1950.
Reginetta Italiana contestants introduced by Lino Giuriato and John Benetti. Rose Sorrenti, (VICS Lega president), looks on as Mary Durante Maddalozzo (seated) is proclaimed queen.

New era immigrants like Agostino Martin (at mike) brought dynamic leadership and challenging expectations to Vancouver's established society of Italians.

Chapter 21

The New Order

La Nuova Era

*A*lthough he attempted to gain support for the purchase of land on which the elusive Casa d'Italia could be built, Girardi was forced to pass the challenge to subsequent administrations. In spite of keeping the dream alive, the society never did succeed in its quest to acquire a banquet and/or sport facility. There had been an opportunity to purchase the Hastings Auditorium, in which the Sons of Italy previously held shares, for $70,000 in 1951; a proposition highly supported by Marino. However, with a bank balance of only $7,000 to $8,000 the majority of the active members vetoed the idea. Aside from the question of financing, some opponents of the proposal no longer considered the location of the old Silver Slipper Hall to be within Little Italy which now was centred in the Nanaimo and Hastings streets area of Vancouver's east end.

In addition to his leadership role with the Sons of Italy, Girardi established a service to assist immigrants that included a games room near the corner of Main and Hastings streets. In 1948 Girardi gave impetus to the movement to found the Italian Immigrants Assistance Centre and the Italo Canadian Activities Committee. Through these organizations Girardi successfully garnered the support of post-war arrivals, many of whom were determined to promote a new definition of purpose for the mutual aid societies.

"The Centro Assistenza had money in the bank and everything was paid for and the facility crammed full every night," recalled Girardi. "Then a few guys tried to make some money and they came up with an excuse to sideline me. I couldn't very well be president of that association because I wasn't born in Italy. I told them, let me tell you what I think will happen. In six months from now, you won't be in existence any more because everybody will try to dip into the money," he prophesied.[211]

"We had a group of people who were always there to see if they could make money. Marino Culos and I put money into it. We didn't take it out. One thing I can say about Marino Culos, he was straight down the line. He was a good man for the society," Girardi stated.

Fiorenzo Benincasa, the bright and youthful leader of those pressuring for change, became president of the Sons of Italy in 1952. At age 27, he held the position which so far had eluded Gregorio Fuoco, the *paesano* who sponsored his membership application. Fuoco, born in Spetano Piccolo, a town approximately 500 metres from Benincasa's birthplace in Calabria,[212] chided the newly elected president for leaping ahead of him in quest of the prestigious office. Destiny, however, would not deny Fuoco for he would become president in 1964.

"It felt good to join the society. I felt that we were among some very good people. These very good people, at the time, helped to make you understand that Canada was a good country. We had a saying, 'provided you did your best, sooner or later the sun will shine on you'," Benincasa stated.

Six years out from Italy, Benincasa was adept at identifying with the needs of the post-war immigrant. As a result, he became an effective proponent of the 'new order' agenda. However, to some of the old-guard members, including Frank Rita and Marino Culos—who had been there, done that—Benincasa's desire to give new definition to the society's established programmes and activities met with an entrenched conservative attitude. There appeared little room to manoeuvre.

"When I was president, I came up with the idea to amalgamate the Italian societies. I thought, we are all Italians here, now why—what the hell we had to have so many separate societies? Because maybe two families didn't get along? And that was the Vancouver Italian-Canadian Society. I can't say whether that was against Branca and the Veneta, or against Marino Culos, against Bruno Girardi, or against me from the Sons of Italy. I don't know. I used to go around almost every Sunday to each house to talk about amalgamation. Marino didn't like it," recalled Benincasa.

Frustrated by the lack of support from the older members for the idea to purchase land on which to build a Casa d'Italia,

Fiorenzo Benincasa, post-war president, championed the societal aspirations of contemporary immigrants.

Girardi's Travel Bureau became the official travel agent for the I.I.A.C. and the first Air France charter group left for Milan Dec. 6, 1956. The fare was $325 return.

Frank Rita, a bastoncino from Castelgrande
Rita, with trademark walking stick (bastone), was one of the Sons of Italy's most able and respected presidents. Circa 1950s.

Benincasa turned to other young men for support. This new generation of member partially succeeded in its desire to offset what Benincasa termed "the repressive forces" from within. Many of the conservatives, notably Angelo Branca, were cautious about buying a hall or constructing a Casa d'Italia because of the Veneta's experience with the Hastings Auditorium during the Depression.

"Before I was married, I brought in Joseph Tosi, my future father-in-law. And everybody including Marino liked to see him come in because he was a successful businessman and one who had not previously been involved in the societies," remembered Benincasa.[213]

Because of his age, Tosi was accorded an honorary membership. This he was pleased to accept commenting, "If you want to do something, you just let me know, and I will do the best I can." Benincasa took these words to heart. He was convinced that if Joseph Tosi and his brother Peter had decided to do something grand for the Italian community, anything would have been possible.

Peter Tosi was a gifted and respected businessman with a penchant for languages. He captured the retail and wholesale Italian importing food business and became wealthy in the process. Although his frugality is legendary, most of Vancouver's Italians are not aware of his compassionate character which he often displayed in aiding those temporarily in financial difficulty.

"Tosi was an outstanding man," commented Gina Sanvido Benetti. "During the Depression, he said to my mother and father, 'Don't worry about paying me. When your children grow up they will pay me.' He was such a generous man. Of course, my father did go out of town to work and he paid him back. But that is the type of man he was. He was not afraid to help," she said.

After a brief work experience in Montreal and Calgary, Tosi established himself in Vancouver by opening a butcher shop on the 500 block Union Street in 1908. After breakfast, he would leave his home at 4:30 a.m. for his daily walk to the meat wholesalers located near Columbia and Water streets. There he would hand-pick sides of beef for delivery to his premises. "He was the first one down—and that's why he had good meat. He sold a lot of meat in those days," stated his son Angelo. "A little later and with a team of four horses hitched to a rickety wagon he and Cecil Cima would go down to the waterfront to pick up his rice shipments. Italian *risotto* rice. It was packed in 100 kilo bags which they would take back to his place on Union Street," he continued.

At age 47, Peter married Lina Casorzo at Sacred Heart Church in 1931. They moved to the present location of Tosi's Italian Imported Foods establishment in early 1932 and settled into an above-the-store suite of apartments which served as the family home. Tosi was the prime supplier of pasta, pure virgin olive oil, salami and select cheeses: Parmesan, Romano, Provalone and Gorgonzola. The formula for his famous Genoa salami came from his parents and the quality cheeses were imported from his brother's cheese factory located in Novara, Province of Arona in the region of Piemonte.

In addition to his burgeoning retail trade, he enjoyed a brisk business with hotels and restaurants while serving and supplying Italian grocery stores with many of their consumer products. Staff was kept to a minimum but Carlo Franceschini was Tosi's dependable associate for the greater part of his business career.

As a teenager, Emma Lussin Maffei worked for Peter Tosi. "When Tosi's wife got sick, he hired me to look after baby Angelo. Mr. Tosi treated me nice as he did with my whole family. And he could enjoy a good laugh too. I worked in the cannery with Irma and Mary Zanatta, Lina Negrin, Mary Dalfo, Mary Padovan and Maria Carretti. We worked piecework. My first cheque was for 25 cents. So, my mother went to Tosi and asked to cash the cheque. She ordered dried raisins which came from California from which you made wine. Tosi said fine and added up the bill: around $25. 'I'll have Cecil Cima deliver it,' he said. My mother asked, 'How long have you been in business? Shouldn't you be looking at the cheque before cashing it? Well, he almost had a stroke 'cause he had given her $25 for a cheque made out for 25 cents," Emma recalled.

"In celebration of the Lega's 25th anniversary, we had a big Christopher Columbus banquet at the Cave Supper Club," recalled Benincasa. "It was very well organized by Marino, the chairman of the banquet. But I had a little bit of an argument with him because me, as president, he put my seat, you know, my chair, at one end of the table that did not belong to the head table. I would say it was deliberate because in a sense, Marino was a little bit jealous of me," he surmised.

Benincasa's administration was quick to act when asked to support victims of a landslide in Italy caused by flood waters emanating from a ruptured dam. "With the other Italian societies, we organized a benefit banquet at the Hastings Auditorium. I think we made $1,600 or $1,700. It was a great success. And there was me and Lino Giuriato, president of the Vancouver Italian-Canadian Society. When it came time to address the people before the concert started, he wanted to do all the talking. I said, my society is 10 times as big as yours. So, he went on the stage and I went on the stage too," he chuckled.

The memory of war is a tragic nightmare for Benincasa. In 1943 he had entered the Police Academy in Rome from his home in Spetano Grande, Province of Cosenza. A graduate of a three-month accelerated training course, he soon became a member of the

Fiorenzo Benincasa's grandfather, Francesco Benincasa first came to America from Calabria in 1876. As a child, he lived and played in the area near the site where the fratelli Bandieri had been killed in 1848, a story he often repeated throughout his life. Antonio Benincasa, Fiorenzo's father, spent a total of 55 years in the U.S. and Canada, going home only periodically to be with his wife and family—the numbers of which increased with each visit. An illness prevented Marietta Benincasa from immigrating to Canada with her husband.

Agenzia Pubblica Sicurezza stationed at Bari. Within two weeks of his posting, American bombers pounded the city's industrial sites. Because of Bari's strategic position on the Adriatic, the Germans mined the seaport lanes in anticipation of the Allied Forces arriving by sea. The Americans soon moved in.

"Around November 1943, 13 of the American fuel supply tankers were blown up, knocking out all of the windows in Bari Vecchio. Over 12,000 people were killed that night," recalled Benincasa.

Another post-war immigrant who knew first-hand about the travesty of war was Iolanda Pitton. She arrived in Vancouver in 1949 and soon joined the Italian Ladies' League. Iolanda was an excellent seamstress and made numerous traditional Italian costumes for special events. On one memorable occasion she, Teresa Pettovello and Mario Colonello combined to make costumes for a complete group of performers at a musical sponsored by the Famee Furlane. And in 1952 she assisted with the arrangements for the Lega's silver anniversary banquet and dance programme.

Iolanda's memories of the war include a meeting of historical note. Attached to the Italian legation in Albania, Iolanda Pitton (nee Comin) spent several years in Tirane, the capital city, as a member of the viceroy's residential staff. In April 1941, she was a witness to the ravages of war, as many Italian troops wounded in the battles raging on the Greek frontier were removed to crowded hospital facilities in Tirane.

"So many troops coming from the front. Wounded. 'Oh *signorina*, help me.' So many. Make me cry, really. I bring chocolates. I would sell my dress because they need help. They had nobody there. You could not send information from Tirane to Italy. Every letter was censored. My mother would receive my letters; whole pages blacked in," Iolanda recalled.

At one point, Iolanda was an aide to the Countess Edda Ciano, Mussolini's daughter, who was attached to the Italian Red Cross. En route to Albania, the ship on which she sailed was torpedoed and sunk. Although many lives were lost, the countess survived the ordeal to continue her work in Italian-occupied Albania.

"I was working for the new Tenente Generale d'Italia in Tirane and Edda was working for the Red Cross. That time Albania and Greece was fighting. She came into the same palace where I was working. She wanted me to follow her to *Grecia* beyond the border region with Albania. We were sleeping in the royal residence, Palazzo Reale; she in one room and me in the next.

"On this particular morning, somebody knock the door. I did not expect. '*Signorina, Il Duce vuole parlarle con te,*' he said. He wants to talk to you. I said, yes, but I am no ready because he just wake me up. About 7 o'clock in the morning. Very early because we travelled

Iolanda Comin Pitton.
Pitton, an effective Italian women's league exective member, met Benito Mussolini in Albania during World War II.

all day, the day before. I remember Edda: *Contessa Edda, si chiamava.* Contessa because she married to Count Ciano. And she said, 'Iolanda, we sleep tomorrow morning late, and we take rest. I said, fine. I don't worry about waking up early. But this guy who open my door—I said, who is that?—he said, the secretary to Mussolini.

"I say maybe he is drinking or something. So, he opened the door. He said, '*Il Duce*, he wants to talk to you before he goes back to Tirane in Albania. I said, okay. I'll be ready in 10 minutes, maybe 15.

"So, he is sitting at the table. So *autoritario*. But nice person, friendly. Very friendly. For me just the same a father. I got no concern, beautiful impression, the first time I saw him. He gave me the confidence to talk to him, you know. This is a very nice for a big leader. So, he asked me so many questions, 'Where do you come from?' I say, I came from north Italy. 'What are you doing in Tirane.' I said, working for the government. He said, 'Oh.' He had so many compliments for me because I had a lovely job. And in the meantime, the time of the war is no easy because it is scary, so many things happen.

"He say, 'You tell my daughter, Edda, she no got to leave early tomorrow morning. No, this morning because she got to take rest because last night she looked so tired. She needs to rest.' I said, okay, fine. And he went out.

"At the door, already the press was at the door. The reporters asked, '*Signorina*, what did the *Duce* say?' I said, 'nothing, he just asked me something about the Contessa'. That's it.

"But there was a little emotion because I never expect so early in the morning. I thought about it all day," Iolanda concluded.

Cross marks Italian military cemetery
Iolanda Pitton assisted the wounded and dying in Albania.

Chapter 22

Sons of Italy celebrates its 50th anniversary, 1955.
From left, Marino and Phyllis Culos, Emma and Bruno Girardi (Raffaele Caravetta looks on)

Precious Memories
Memorie Preziose

Carlo (Carl) Pepe, a former member of the Young Canadian-Italian Athletic Association's boxing division, is the owner/operator of the Olympia Tailors which he established in 1947 on Hastings Street near Nanaimo. Interestingly, he became a tailor solely by chance. In 1941, Carl was in the habit of frequenting a small shop near Vernon and Hastings streets which was owned by a "little Jewish fellow and gentleman". The proprietor regularly cleaned and pressed Carl's suits and trousers.

"He was about 80 years old. And one time the place was closed. So, I got in touch with him and asked if he would teach me to sew a little bit. Then one day I said, 'How much do you want for rent'. We settled on $7.50 per month. I stayed for three years before going into the [Canadian] Army. After the army, I opened this store," recalled Pepe.

The Fabulous Fifties started as a decade of celebration for the Sons of Italy and its affiliate the Italian Ladies' League. There was an air of optimism in the community as hundreds of new arrivals gave a youthful presence and much needed stimulus to the old societies. British Columbia was in a state of continuous growth and jobs were plentiful for skilled labourers who recognized opportunity. Italians were among the successful post-war immigrants who prospered and grew with Vancouver and the province.

The Lega celebrated its 25th anniversary amid this era of growth and prosperity, with a highly successful Christopher Columbus banquet and dance at the Cave Supper Club, Oct. 9, 1952. It was a night filled with nostalgic utterances and Marino Culos was in his element. As chairman of the festivities, he introduced W.G. Ruocco, the founding director and organizer of the Lega, Enedina Fabri, its organizing chairperson, Frank Rita, the Sons of Italy's honorary president for life, A.E. Branca, Q.C., leading spokesperson for the Veneta Society, and Italo Rader, Italian consul. Among the senior politicians in attendance were Vancouver mayor Fred Hume and Dr. Lawrence Giovando, MLA for Nanaimo. Other politicians regularly supported the Italian community's celebrations but none with as much enthusiasm and interest as Senator Ray Perrault.

Following a greeting from president Fiorenzo Benincasa, Ruocco delivered a sterling speech. He congratulated president Phyllis Culos for her leadership and praised the Lega's members for their outstanding contributions to the men's society and to the Italian community at large over a period of a quarter of a century. He then introduced Maria Balma, a founding member of the Lega. Balma, 79, the Italian Ladies' League's senior active member, was flanked by Louisa and Rosemarie Ricci both of whom assisted her in cutting a special commemorative cake. Also witnessing the event was Filomena Pulice, who would live to be 100, and would in time become the Lega's oldest member.

Three years later, the men marked the 50th anniversary of the founding of the Sons of Italy. Billed as "The Greatest Italian Event of All," the sell-out dinner and dance was held at the Commodore Cabaret, at 872 Granville Street. Guests paid $3.50 for a scrumptious four-course dinner that included wine. The attendees were treated to the swinging dance music of a 12-piece orchestra.

The society's four surviving founding active members were accorded celebrity status. Achille Pini, Antonio Cianci, Cesare Anderlini and Gettulio Falcioni had been fraternal brothers and members in good standing of the Sons of Italy for 50 years.

W.G. Ruocco, during his leadership tenure, had been accorded the highest honours for his outstanding service to the society. He is listed as one of the society's founding members in *Souvenirs 'Ricordi'*, circa 1935. However, on this occasion he was not recognized as a founding member because he had not become a dues-paying member until January 1906. Conversely neither was Frank Federici recognized. Apparently his membership also had been allowed to lapse

Phyllis Culos, president for 18 years.

Society's 50th anniversary celebration held at the Commodore Cabaret.
From left, Millie and Joe Agostino, Tommy Paonessa, John Alvaro, Emma Paonessa, Rose Alvaro, 1955.

Lega executive members, circa 1955
M. Brilaro, J. Sartore, E. Gazzola, M. Balma, T. Trono and A. Angelucci.

Teresa Pettovello, Mary Pettovello, Rose Cianci and Iolanda Pitton.

Emila Montico, Nellie Cavell, Maria Carretti and Maria Longo.

at some point along the way. Although Federici became a centenarian and survived to outlive his contemporaries, it is Cesare Anderlini who is regarded as the last surviving active member of the Sons of Italy. Anderlini died in March 1976.[214]

Commemorating the society's 50-year history was a natural for Marino Culos who was serving his ninth term as president in 1955. He again produced a souvenir booklet, *Memorie Preziose*, and complimentary copies were distributed to the banquet guests. The front cover page featured an illustration of the Greek-style pillars that Marino had drawn for the society's 1935 calendar. Included in the booklet was a congratulatory message from Angelo Branca, Q.C., followed by several profiles of the society's leading contributors including Frank Rita. It also contained a compendium of events, with photographs, from the society's golden years. It proved to be another excellent keepsake.

A year after this memorable festive occasion Frank Pio Rita died. The man described editorially by the *Highland Echo* as having been "an outstanding pioneer of the community" died at his home, Oct. 16, 1956 in his 72nd year. Rita was an outstanding Catholic and a member of the Knights of Columbus (Fourth Degree). The Simon Fraser Assembly of the Knights of Columbus provided an Honour Guard at his funeral service at the society's section of the Mountain View Cemetery.

Following his father's death, a grieving Joseph Rita wrote to Marino,

"On behalf of my mother and brother Arthur may I express to you the gratitude we feel for your kind and loving attention to the details of my father's funeral. It is so comforting to know that the final temporal rites are in the hands of one who, through a lifetime of affection and true friendship merits the duty.

"Certainly there was never any doubt in my father's mind as to who should be in charge. He was most specific in reminding us of your position in this matter.

"As you know, my father was a man of firm convictions and was also a fine judge of people. I have never known him to err in his assessment of another's character.

"Thus the esteem and affection he felt for you, serve to secure forever the affection I now have for you. For him to have placed you so highly in his affections is the purest guide I know to your true worth. He esteemed and respected you with a fervor he granted to but few.

"For this reason above all others our family was comforted to know we could lean on you.

"With regard to his years of devotion to the Sons of Italy

Iolanda Pitton and Teresa Pettovello
Lega members dressed in Friuli regional costumes.

Society, I need not remind you of the zeal he displayed during his active days in the society. To him, the society was one of the prime factors in his life, ranking with his family, his church, and his work. His expressed desire to be laid at rest with his old friends in the society plot, bears testimony to this.

"I will appreciate it if the rules of the society permit this letter to be read at the next general meeting. I regret my inability to express myself in the Italian language but perhaps you might be inclined to translate this letter for the meeting. Affectionately."

A week earlier, the Lega had lost the gallant Sabina Tate. A pioneer resident of B.C. since 1896, Sabina had lived in Vancouver for 53 years.

Maria Balma: Lega's oldest active member
Dr. Black introducing Mrs. Balma to the applause of Father Armand Oliveri and Angelo Branca, 1958. Atlas Studios pix.

Sabina Tate's obit was carried in the *L'Eco d'Italia*, which had been founded by Piero Mainardi and his colleague Pierino Mori in March 1956. The Italian newspaper was the first post-war publication of its kind in B.C. Trail's Fred Tenisci, Nanaimo's Andy Ercolini, and Kamloops's Cuzzetto, regular contributors to the publication's forerunner, *L'Eco Italo-Canadese*, again reported from their respective communities. Merchants supporting the popular and editorially liberal newspaper included grocers Bruno Girardi, Peter Tosi and Ray Benny. Also running display advertisements in the weekly newspaper were the Empress Taxi and Olympia Tailors.[215]

Mainardi's and Mori's hard-hitting editorials—often right of centre—advocated improved services for new arrivals from Italy. They challenged the mutual aid societies and lobbied the Centro Assistenza Immigranti Italiani to meet the recreational and information needs of the new flood of Italian immigrants to Vancouver. Within the first year of publication, the newspaper spearheaded a drive for the establishment of an Italian Immigrants' Assistance Centre at 570 Granville. This support led to 152 Italian immigrants being registered for job opportunities with the centre, of whom 47 were placed by May of the following year. The agency became a significant entity despite difficulties in being accepted by various unions.

Among the executive of the Italian Immigrants' Centre were a number of outstanding members including Rina Bidin and Iolanda Pitton. In 1958 Rina Bidin provided a leadership role in sponsoring the group's amateur dramatic production of the comedy *Scampolo*, starring Franca Paoli. It was held at Britannia High School.

Building on these successes, Mainardi, with Dr. Gianni Azzi, Ennio Andreutti and Father Armand Oliveri of Sacred Heart Church Parish, provided leadership in founding the Columbus Soccer Club. Some of the Columbus team members previously played for Sacred Heart. "We had acquired several good players with Graziano Franzon, and some needed a bit of financial help, which of course, we could not give, because we didn't have any money. We had always made it with handouts," recalled Father Armand. "Father Joseph Scanagatta, who was there before me, had done a lot to develop the Sacred Heart team. He even played in some of the games," concluded the Salesian priest. Successive Columbus championship teams captured the hearts and support of hundreds of local Italian fans.[216]

At this time Marino Culos was busy getting the executive members of the various Italian organizations together under the auspices of the Comitato Attivita' Italiane: Committee for Italian Activities. In effect what had been created was an umbrella organization which coordinated the social calendars of the societies while each entity remained independent. In addition, the Committee's mandate was to secure a Casa d'Italia.

In his book, *The Italians in Canada*, A.V. Spada writes, "All the societies meant well, but the community suffered from the divisions. In 1935 W.G. Ruocco, president of the Figli d'Italia, tried, unsuccessfully, to bring them all together in an executive committee. This was accomplished in

Columbus Soccer Team
Back row from left, Graziano Franzon, Tony Canta, Dino Dal Pos, Paul Lisowski, Bill Newhaus, Roy Nosella, Frank Sealey, John Comuzzi, Don Pighin, John Azzi, circa 1961.

Nino Sala and kitchen staff
Sala coordinated scores of Italian banquets and wedding receptions. Front centre, Edie Harris's smile captured by photographer.

Italian Activities Committee Banquet.
Banquet profit went towards the Casa
d'Italia building fund, 1959.

1956 when Marino Culos, also a leading member, became the first president of the Comitato Attivita' Italiane."[216A]

The Comitato's executive group grew to include Bruno Girardi (Italian Immigrants Assistance Centre), Piero Mainardi, Pierino Mori, and Cesare Tofini (*L'Eco d'Italia*), Giovanni D'Appolonia (Famee Furlane), Angelo Gatto (Italia Bicycle Club), Marino Culos (Sons of Italy), Phyllis Culos, Elisa Negrin, and Teresa Bosa (Italian Ladies' Leagues), Angelo Branca (The Veneta Society), Mario Ghislieri (Vancouver Italian-Canadian Society), *Professoressa* Stefania Ciccone (Societa' Dante Alighieri), Dr. Salvatore Saraceno, Italian Vice-Consul and Father G. Della-Torre (Sacred Heart Church Parish).[217]

Father Della-Torre, a Salesian priest, came to Sacred Heart in 1952. He would remain to serve his flock there for the rest of his life. His 27-year tenure as pastor, by the grace of God, became the longest in the history of the parish.

The Hon. Angelo E. Branca would write, "What a modest man! What a beloved Pastor! Beloved alike by his parishioners, by his peers, by his superiors and by everyone else.

"Onward ever! Never complaining, never finding fault with anyone. A few words of wisdom and his encouragement to so many of his parishioners who need some moral uplift.

Sell-out crowd at the Hastings Auditorium.
President Luigi Barone (front right) and friends, including Lina and Gianni Savio.

"The Sacred Heart Parish has always been a very important parish in this city and it has ministered to many Italians who have come to Canada to settle and adopt Canada as their home. All the problems to which immigrants fall heir, fell into the lap of Father Della-Torre during this time, and whether those problems were of a spiritual, a temporal or other nature, he always, always listened intently to his friend and parishioner and endeavoured to solve the problem, or get someone to help him do it.

"I think that record of achievement is one which should give great happiness to Father Della-Torre when he thinks of those things."[218]

Head table guests, Mayor and Mrs. Bill Rathie, Vi and Angelo Branca, Phyllis Culos.

John D'Appolonia (standing) at Cave Club
Italian societies sponsored multi-group concerts during the 1960s. Cathay Studio photo.

Italian Activities Committee concert
Vancouver's Italian societies sponsor successful concert at the Cave Supper Club, circa 1960s. Cathy Studios photo.

In October 1958, the Italian Activities Committee dedicated its Columbus Day banquet to the celebration of the B.C. Centennial. As president, Marino Culos coordinated the event calling upon old friends Nino Sala and Santo Pasqualini to prepare a special dinner at the Lion's Gate Memorial Hall.[219]

Events that marked the Italian community's participation in B.C.'s 1958 centennial year included a folkloric music festival held at the Cave Supper Club. Featured speakers at this event were Dr. V. Bifulco, Consul for Italy, Father Giuseppe Della-Torre and Angelo Branca, Q.C. And the entertainment segment was conducted by Giuseppe Ricciotto. The performers, dressed in traditional costumes depicting many of the regions in Italy, provided excellent entertainment to a sell-out crowd. Also taking part in this grand social event were the Famee Furlane entertainers, the 35-member Sacred Heart choir and the Italian Orchestra.

"We delighted in presenting our culture through our music, dance and language, so that everybody coming to the Comitato's *feste* could see and enjoy it," stated Agostino Martin, a member of the Famee's troupe and an alternate delegate to the Italian Activities Committee.

"Regarding the Comitato, the members seemed prepared to do anything that would be good for the Italian community. I can't say for everybody. Some people are honest and sincere. Others are there for personal reasons—for glory—I don't know what. The intention of the Comitato, in part, was to create activities in which the Famee Furlane club, and others, could take part. We all took great pride in bringing forth our individual and regional cultures," continued Martin.

The Famee Furlane was the brainchild of a few immigrants from northern Italy including

Famee Furlane Entertainers
Ralph Ricci provides accordion accompaniment. Cathay Studio photo.

Marion Culos dancing the Tarantella
Famee Furlane entertainers perfoming at Italian Activities Committee sponsored festival, circa 1960s. Photo by Zonta.

Agostino Martin. In the early 1950s, they met informally at the Waldorf or the Astoria hotels to discuss the possibility of organizing a distinct organization. Once they developed their idea, they approached the patriarch of their clan, John D'Appolonia, the successful architect. With his initial guidance, the proposition flourished. By 1956, the group was well established. And within two years the Famee had its constitution and had been registered as a society.

"We were talking about putting this thing together until we came to know D'Appolonia. And when we presented this idea, he favoured us very much. He was enthusiastic about it. He saw a group of people very enthusiastic. So, we worked out all of these things and came up with a group. Mind you, at the beginning everybody was very enthusiastic to be a part of this association. But many of them did not last very long. Having a job was their priority. It was a

Special invitees, Dr. and Mrs. Paul Ragona.

Progetto Casa d'Italia, Comitato Attivita' Italiane.

case of taking what work was available and to relocate if need be. And never say 'no' to taking a job out of town. In my particular case, I went to the Arctic Ocean to work on the DEW Line. I stayed 22 months there; 600 miles into the Arctic Circle. And the attitude of the non-Italian people—I wouldn't say everybody, but certain individuals—was very tough with us. We were often called D.P. [displaced person], you know. Very common name in those days. We never got mad. We accepted everything. And we have been and have done [the kind of work] what others did not want to do," stated Martin unapologetically.

"When our group joined the Comitato, Marino Culos was president. And every time we proposed something, he would support us. He understood what our group could do. When he asked the groups to organize a *festa*, the Famee said, 'Let's do it'. But then other oppositions came about. Yes, so, even Marino had difficulties sometimes, you know. So, to avoid a little bit of bickering, we would rather withdraw or reduce our level of involvement. And so, some of the things we would have liked to do didn't happen," concluded Martin.[220]

Another spectacular event presented that year was the bicycle racing events at the Empire Cycle Bowl (China Creek Park) which headlined expert Italian, Canadian and American cyclists. Thrilling the crowds with brilliant finishes were 1958 North American Open champion-class riders, Luigi Zanatta and Mario Brunoro. Other cyclists for the Italian Bicycle Club were Bianco Fiori, a junior rider and Secondo Andreola, a young Italian rider who displayed great promise.

Chapter 23

The Italian Activities Committee
Il Comitato Attività Italiane

Italian Activities Committee, 1963
From left, back row, Gilberto Gatto, Tony Fabris, Angelo Gatto, Agostino Martin. Front row, Cesare Tofini, Phyllis Culos, Dr. Guido Pagano, Father Joe Della Torre, Teresa Bosa, Ottavio Bevilacqua. Roma Studios photo.

In 1959, the Italian Activities Committee put forward a plan to build a Casa Italiana on a parcel of five available lots and hired an architect to prepare preliminary drawings. The dream of acquiring an Italian centre continued to arouse interest. A new and committed supporter was Giovanni Bertuzzi, a spirited individual who would become president of the Sons of Italy within four years.

Although the Sons of Italy Society was determined to do its share, like the other mutual aid societies, its position of influence was in decline. Membership stood at 130 amid growing disinterest. The loss of Frank Iuele, its effective president, who had accepted a job out of town was a decisive blow. Liquid assets totalled slightly more than $7,000 in 1959. And its election-of-officers meeting in December only drew 15 members.

Marino Culos wrote to the retiring president regarding the results of the election and added, "Mr. Iuele, your absence has made a hole in the good ship 'Figli d'Italia' causing it nearly to sink."[221]

In an attempt to address concerns regarding membership numbers and member apathy, Luigi Barone, Iuele's successor, appealed directly to his colleagues. In a communique entitled "Personal Letter from the President" dated March 30, 1961, Barone made reference to a recently held meeting at which society orator, Antonio Cianci proposed that each member bring in at least one new member each year. Barone asked for their cooperation in attracting men of commitment to the ranks of active participants.

The president reminded his members of the oath they had taken upon joining the society: "I will on my honour and as a person and citizen, do all I can in the best interest of the society for as long as I am a member." He then asked rhetorically, "Why have you not remembered these sacred words more often?"

Barone concluded his missive by stating, "Dear brothers, the life of the society and the continuation of its mission to foster solidarity and unification between the Italians is conditional on your active interest. It is not sufficient to be a member, but necessary to be a part of the process."

Marino Culos remained active in the Sons of Italy and continued to influence the society's affairs primarily as secretary of finance and as confidant to president Barone. The greatest share of his energies, however, were devoted to the Comitato Attivita' Italiane, the organization to which he was re-elected president in November 1961.

In his acceptance speech, Marino applauded the tireless efforts of colleague Angelo Gatto. He further proposed and received unanimous support from the membership "to elect him [Gatto] an honorary member meritorious, in recognition for his unselfish and constant dedication to the initiatives of the Comitato Attivita' Italiane".

A few months later and in a surprise move, Marino Culos turned his attention to federal politics. As Liberal candidate for Vancouver East, he waged a forthright but phlegmatic campaign during the 1962 federal election. In the process, however, he received a leg-up from the influential Angelo Branca who provided considerable support. Branca, preeminent within the Liberal Party, was instrumental in arranging for Senator David A. Croll to speak in the riding on Marino's behalf and in inviting cabinet ministers Jack Pickersgill and Paul Martin to do the same.[222]

Although the Sons of Italy was not permitted constitutionally to become involved in partisan politics, its directors were pleased to promote one if its ablest representatives. In a letter dated June 7, 1962, secretary Raffaele De Luca

Marino Culos congratulated by Paul Martin
Culos wins Liberal nomination to represent Vancouver-East in the 1962 federal election campaign. Although Liberal vote doubled, Culos lost to Harold Winch.

Branca campaigning for Marino Culos
flanking Angelo Branca left, B.C. Liberal Party leader Ray Perrault, right, Senator David Croll.

wrote to the membership outlining Marino's qualifications as a spokesperson for Italian constituents and referred to his contributions in glowing and optimistic terms. Scores of members attended a special rally in support of Marino's quest to become a member of parliament. Although he doubled the vote his party recorded during the previous federal election, Marino lost his bid for elected office.

It was suggested by those close to the campaign that Marino did not always display the temperament required to be successful in federal politics. His honesty, intelligence and personal integrity were never in question. However, under stressful conditions, he often displayed a petulant characteristic unpopular to those with whom he closely campaigned. Although he never again sought federal elective office, Marino continued to be involved in federal elections as the appointed Returning Officer for Vancouver East.

Following the election, Angelo Gatto, a future Italian consul (pro tem), wrote a letter to *L'Eco d'Italia*. The newspaper gave page-two treatment to Gatto's treatise in its Oct. 31, 1962 edition. His message was clear: it's time for the Italian community to support the Comitato's plan to acquire a *casa nostra*. His was an emotional and emphatic call to action which drew immediate support from the community's leaders.

In April 1963, the Comitato Attivita' Italiane sent out a questionnaire under the signature of Antonio Fabris who succeeded Marino as president. Italians and Italo-Canadians were reminded of the committee's objective—to purchase or construct a *casa d'Italia* within two years, and appealed to those interested to support its fund-raising campaign.

As a result, *L'Eco d'Italia* launched a determined, emotional and feisty six-month campaign to support the Comitato's objective. In its first editorial, the Italian newspaper exclaimed, "The campaign therefore has started. Any doubts and every 'if' and 'but' must be set aside. We have to give it all we can because the end result will result in a happy ending. With 18,000 Italians to support it, a *'Casa'* can become a reality. Failure to make this campaign a success, however,

A lighter side of the L'Eco d'Italia *was presented in* The Vancouver Sun, *April 2, 1962, with this story line: "More than 300 members of Vancouver's Italian community turned out Sunday to greet actress Sophia Loren and actor Vittorio de Sica.*

"An article in last week's edition of the Italian-language newspaper L'Eco d'Italia *said the screen stars were arriving aboard a special train at 4:40 p.m.*

"But instead the expectant fans were met at the Great Northern station by members of the paper's staff bearing a large sign. It read [in Italian]: 'April Fool'."

Angelo Branca's daughter Dolores Holmes described her father as a people person. "My father was the first Vancouver Canadian-Italian to be called to the Bar. He was followed by Vic Fabri, David Comparelli and Vic Paletti. And of course, there have been many others since then. "Because my grandparents had the store, dad knew everybody in the Italian community. And most of these people couldn't read or write in English. So, for years his practice was largely from this Italian block.

"Ines Falcioni was his first secretary. She married Vito Treselli, a captain in the Italian merchant marine. They settled in Trieste just before the war.

"He liked people and he liked being with them. He was really exceptional in that he could maintain that contact with—I don't mean the 'common man' in the sense of that, but I mean—a person who was not a lawyer or in the legal profession. And he could stay friends with politicians of all parties. Whereas most of us wouldn't have had the self-confidence to be able to handle it. He, on the other hand, never had a problem with self-confidence," mused Judge Holmes.

"Dad stopped in to see my grandmother [Teresa Branca] every morning, and every night. When I started to work at the office, we would leave the house about 8 o'clock and would get down to 2nd Avenue and Main Street and go into the house. My grandmother would have coffee going. We would sit down at the kitchen table, have a cup of coffee, maybe 15 minutes, then leave. We would leave the office at 5:30 or so and stop at my grandmother's. She would be getting dinner ready for herself and we would go in. Dad would have a little 'cicchet' [drink of liquor] and I would have pop or whatever. We'd do this just to see how she was. He was like most Italians, possessing a strong feeling about family," she concluded.

will be an admission that we Italians of Vancouver are not yet socially mature."[223]

The bi-weekly newspaper continuously devoted its editorial opinion space exclusively to publicize the campaign which, in one issue, included a reproduction of Antonio Fabris's questionnaire.

The caption to a photo which appeared in *L'Eco d'Italia*, April 19, 1963, read, "At the last meeting of the Comitato Attivita' Italiane its members approved a donation [from its resources] of $4,500—the first contribution towards the construction of the 'Italian Home'". In the photo were pictured some of the community's strongest proponents of the plan: Ottorino Della Schiava, vice-president of the VICS; Gilberto Gatto, president of the Veneta Society; Felicetta [Phyllis] Culos, president of the Lega Femminile of the Sons of Italy; Antonio Fabris, president of the Comitato; Dr. Guido Pagano, consul; Angelo Gatto, president of the Italian Assistance Centre; Father Giuseppe Della-Torre, Sacred Heart Parish; Agostino Martin, president Famee Furlane; Teresa Bosa, president of the Veneta's Lega; and Ottavio Bevilacqua representing the Sons of Italy.

As the campaign progressed, donor profiles and photos were incorporated within the newspaper's editorial content. Enrichetta Benetti was the first to be profiled. "As a respected member of the Italian community and former president of the Veneta and Vancouver Italian-Canadian Society's Ladies' Leagues, Enrichetta Benetti was first to return a completed questionnaire. She has invested $500 in the project."

One the community's most popular sons, Angelo Branca, donated $1,000.[224] Next to pledge $1,000 was stalwart Giovanni S. D'Appolonia, a founding member and first president of the Famee Furlane in Vancouver. These and other prominent leaders including Father Giuseppe Della-Torre, Angelo Gatto, Dr. Tommaso Merler, Dr. Mario Seraglia, Antonio Paolo Borsato and Triestino Marotto also were included in the newspaper's first published donors' list.

The critics also made their debut. Pasquale Asporito, in a letter to the editor, dated May 31, 1963, wrote, "Some time ago, I saw the picture of the members of the Comitato [in your newspaper] but I have yet to see the names of the president and the consul included among those listed as donors. When these important people give $100 each, I will give a thousand!"

Another reader stated dissatisfaction with answers given at a meeting of the Comitato regarding the loss of the Veneta Society's Silver Slipper Hall in the 1930s. He asked for assurance that this kind of debacle would not be repeated if the present proposal to build a community hall received the go-ahead. The newspaper went on the attack, castigating the 'pessimists' and defending the proponents of the proposal. This action prompted greater interest in the campaign—pro and con.[225]

A number of people—members and non-members of the Societa' Veneta—have suggested that their families lost money investing in the Veneta's Silver Slipper Hall.[226] Although undocumented, a few of these people allege that the Branca leadership was lacking as the rush to sell shares manifested itself. Guido Bianchin, however, disagrees vehemently with this view.

"Don't believe any of it. My dad was involved pretty good with that. When they built it, they sold shares to the members. That's the way it was. Pietro Cecarini had shares. My father had shares. Antonio Pastro had shares. Even Antonio Piovesan, Gildo's father, had money in it. They used to hold banquets and dances there too. Then one thing led to another and I guess some of them [shareholders] panicked and wanted their money back. Not too much money in those days. A dollar was a dollar in the Depression; goddamn hard-earned dollars. They had to pay them off; it developed into a panic situation. They got a buyer like the Swedish people. So, they decided to sell it and pay off the shareholders. There's a lot of hanky panky talk about the Brancas taking money. Don't believe that. That's a lot of bullshit! Now, they sold it to the Swedes and nobody came out a loser," stated Bianchin.

L'Eco d'Italia's May 31 donors' list recorded additional contributions by Comitato members Antonio Fabris, Gilberto Gatto and Ottorino Della Schiava. The list soon grew to include Agostino Martin, and Marino and Phyllis Culos.

Critics then suggested that the Comitato was light on members representing southern Italy. Some Canadian-Italians, it was reported, were not completely in favour of the proposed name, "Casa d'Italia". The editorial writer ended his column dated June 21 with a quote described as being from "a well-known Italo-Canadian", "Let's build the house now and think about its name later!"

Paolo Seminara, an aspiring businessman and operator of the Continental Barber Shop at 1st Avenue and Commercial Drive, pledged $1,000. Seminara, who arrived in Vancouver from Sicily in 1952, admitted great personal enthusiasm for the campaign. In a statement to *L'Eco d'Italia*, he said (translation), "It is not likely that our people will fail to recognize the value of having a place in which we can come together as a community."

Alex Macdonald, MLA for Vancouver East, lent his support to the Comitato by stating his

One of the hundreds of Italians who went to Angelo Branca for legal counsel was Tony Bruzzisi. "I went to Angelo Branca in 1951 when he had his office at Hastings and Main. When I told him I was Francesco Bruzzesi's [sic] son, he agreed to help me with a customer who owed me a lot of money. He had bought gas, tires and everything from me at my gas station in North Van. The guy ended up in jail because he had taken a woman on another real estate deal. He ends up in jail and I end up with a judgment [but no money]. But Angelo Branca didn't charge me one cent for all the work he did. And that's something!"

Jack Pickersgill in Vancouver-East.
Marino's 1962 election campaign supporters: from left Nino Sala, Phyllis Culos, Jack Pickersgill, John Azzi, Marino Culos, Grant Lenfesty.

willingness to approach the provincial government for assistance to the Italian Home funding campaign. Macdonald made a nominal cash donation, thus adding his name to the growing list of 125 donors. However, it would be another decade or so before anything formal was heard from government sources regarding a project grant.

John Savio became the 50th person to donate $100. Although the total stood at $15,466, the promotion's momentum faltered.

In a page three news item dated Aug. 2, 1963 *L'Eco d'Italia* stated, "For the first time since the campaign began, no new donations have been received."

Sensing the urgency of the situation, the Vancouver Italian-Canadian Mutual Aid Society, soon to celebrate its 30th anniversary of incorporation, donated $2,000.

But alas, at the Comitato's information meeting held on Sept. 19, president Fabris stated clearly that the prognosis was not good for a successful conclusion to its fund-raising efforts. Unless a major source of new donors could be identified, he cautioned, the executive would have to reconsider its options. The end was definitely near.[227]

In mid-October 1963, *L'Eco d'Italia* substituted its *cause celebre* with a plea for support of the "Chain of Solidarity" fund-raising campaign. It appealed for cash donations in aid of the survivors of one of Italy's most catastrophic disasters in modern times. On Oct. 9, an estimated 2,500 people had died in the Vajont Valley in the province of Belluno, Italy, amid ravaging flood waters.

The progress of the four-week appeal, to which hundreds responded, ran as an editorial lead in a format identical to the Comitato's fund-raising coverage. The first individual to donate to the new cause was Italian Consul, Dr. Guido Pagano.

The community was very impressed with the Paganos as is evidenced by the reception given to Mrs. Pagano at the Lega's 35th anniversary banquet. *Presidentessa*, Phyllis Culos, on behalf of the Lega awarded *Signora* Flavia Pagano an honorary membership. The presentation, which included a beautifully inscribed certificate, received the warm endorsement of the assembly. The citation acknowledged (translation), "This certificate of honorary membership is given Mrs. Flavia Pagano in recognition of her support of the Italian community."[228]

At the Christopher Columbus Day banquet, held under the auspices of the Comitato Attivita' Italiane, an appeal for financial support for Casa d'Italia was organized. As a result of the fine efforts of Pia Tofini and Frank Iuele approximately $500 was added to the Chain of Solidarity coffers.

Nothing further was mentioned editorially regarding the status of the Comitato's project until the new year. In the Jan. 10, 1964

"My father was broken-hearted over the loss of the hall. It was caused by the Depression and was really very devastating. I guess they got into some financial difficulty and some people lost their investment. My dad got nothing back. We got nothing back."

—Bill Canal

Lega's reception for Flavia Pagano
Italian consul's wife awarded Honorary
Membership in Italian Women's League.

issue of *L'Eco d'Italia*, however, the Comitato's president Antonio
Fabris announced the suspension of the fund-raising campaign.
Provision then was made to reimburse the donors of the proposed
Casa d'Italia.

As if seizing on the momentum generated by the Comitato,
Angelo Branca immediately embarked on a mission to merge the
mutual aid societies into a single entity. The old societies, he
warned, had become ineffectual and were in danger of collapse. By
1963 and with more time to devote to the community, Judge Branca
was ready to embark on unifying the societies. He could devote
more time to the community, now that he had left his very demand-
ing law practice to accept an appointment to the B.C. Supreme
Court, Trial Division.[229] He began his journey by advocating the
establishment of a strong and determined organization as a prereq-
uisite to the acquisition of an Italian community centre. Most of the
Comitato's members, wanting to keep the dream alive, readily
acquiesced.[230]

Firstly, *Giudice* Branca sought and gained approval from the

Sig.ra Phyllis Culos
Leo Tesan

Oggi come prima
Una donna s'avicina;
Con la sua abilita'
Da' il cuore alla societa';
Il pensiero e' cosi' grande
Che nessuno lo sapra'—
Avanti sempre con ardore
Per il bene delle societa'.

**Dr. and Mrs. Guido Pagano and Irma
and Angela Gatto were special guests
of the Italian Activities Committee.**

Veneta, the society to which he was honorary life president and the Vancouver Italian-Canadian Society for his merger proposal. Secondly, he sent out feelers to the Sons of Italy and Famee Furlane groups while getting agreement from the fledgling Circolo Meridionale to join the Confratellanza Italo-Canadese.

The Circolo Meridionale had been established in 1962 by a group of men whose roots were of southern Italy: Abruzzi, Molise, Lazio, Campania, Basilicata, Apulia, Calabria and Sicilia.

The club's founding executive members included Antonio Spartano, president; Cesare Tofini, secretary; and Tony Moscone and Renzo Montagliani, vice-presidents.

Montagliani, an enterprising tailor, was an original proponent and prime organizer of the first Italian Market Days on Commercial Drive. He credited two of the club's executive with the Circolo Meridionale decision to join with the old societies to form the Confratellanza. They were Antonio Spartano, a close friend of Judge Branca, and Cesare Tofini, the Italian newspaper publisher who was a leading activist on the Comitato Attivita' Italiane.

Celebrating a successful banquet.
Banquets represented the Italian community's major social occasions.

The young club, which held regular meetings and festive banquets and dances, had other talented members including Andy Stefanucci and Loreto Zaurrini. These bright young men were to fit nicely into Judge Branca's organizational plans. Branca recognized the importance of having the Confratellanza embrace all Italians interested in joining the society. Its membership wouldn't favour one particular group as was the case when the Veneta became an entity in 1911. The move spoke well of Judge Branca's astuteness as an effective community leader.

"When it came time to vote on the amalgamation question, the feeling with all the members of our club was very optimistic. We had an open vote and the membership was unanimously in favour. The reasons were that we would have a good leader in Judge Branca, and we would gain in association with the older and bigger Italian societies. Plus it was the only way we could hope to have a Casa d'Italia. So, we felt secure," stated Montagliani. The Circolo Meridionale became a full participant of the Confratellanza, Jan. 1, 1967.

The situation regarding the Sons of Italy offered a greater challenge. It was the community's oldest society with a membership greater than the combined memberships of the other two mutual aid societies. In addition, its affiliate, the Italian Ladies' League, with an impeccable record of loyalty to the men's group, comprised a strong and formidable membership. Marino Culos, the arch-traditionalist, was expected to resist any attempt at a merger.

In January 1965, the Sons of Italy celebrated its 60th anniversary amid rumours of amalgamation. At its banquet, another fine touch was displayed: a printed programme featuring the creativity of Leo Tesan. His contribution was a compendium of witty poems describing eight of the society's leading individuals: Antonio Cianci and Cesare Anderlini—the two surviving charter members still active in the society; Marino and Phyllis Culos; W.G. Ruocco; and Felice Cianci; plus two deceased members—Giovanni Carrelli and Angelo Calori. Marino wrote to W.G. Ruocco who had not attended due to illness in the family regarding the success of the *festa* and concluded his letter by stating, "The snow and fog did not deter those interested from attending."

Later in the same month the society, anticipating a communique from Judge Branca, instead received a letter from the Supreme Lodge, Order Sons of Italy in America. Writing from his New York office, publicist Dominic Massara invited the Sons of Italy of Vancouver to affiliate with his organization. Claiming "numerous" affiliates in both Quebec and Ontario, he suggested the lodge desired to expand its Canadian presence to include B.C.

Responding to Massara, secretary Gianni Savio stated that the society was unable to seriously consider the proposal at this time. He confided that "There was a proposition in Vancouver for the unification of two other fraternal orders and we may be drawn into the plan."

In April, Branca publicly announced the decision of the Veneta and VICS to amalgamate under the name Confratellanza Italo-Canadese. The 25 members in attendance also voted unanimously to invite the Sons of Italy to join with them in this historic undertaking.

From the outset, Marino Culos was personally against the Branca proposal. The mere thought of witnessing the demise of his beloved Sons of Italy Society was sheer agony for him. He openly solicited support for an anti-merger campaign and in this endeavour was joined by several stalwarts. But with the exception of recognized leaders such as Felice Cianci, a 50-year member of the society, and Bruno Girardi, a Branca antagonist, most of Marino's supporters kept an open mind. Girardi, however, was vociferous in his condemnation of the proposal. He suggested if anything, the Veneta and Vancouver Italian-Canadian Society should merge with the Sons of Italy.[231]

The author interviewed Felice Cianci, 90, in 1979. The following is a quote from the "Commento di Culos" column which ran in L'Eco d'Italia July 7, 1979. "A self-educated man, Mr. Cianci has derived a lifetime of pleasure studying grammar and literature, a select number of passages from the Bible and the works of authors such as George Bernard Shaw. [He stated] 'Happiness is a state of euphoria which only can be experienced in death. Therefore, I am not yet quite ready to experience true happiness.'

"In 1935, the society presented Felice Cianci with a special Honorary Certificate in recognition of his devoted service and 10-year tenure as secretary of correspondence."

In the article, Cianci's view of the Sons of Italy's first president is also recorded: "Giovanni Carrelli was an effective leader with sound organizational abilities, but generally speaking, a community cannot progress further than the capabilities of its leaders. Therefore, what is needed is a Billy Graham type to bring together all Italians from Friuli to Sicily under one society."

Louvre Hotel, Gastown, circa 1912
Tony Cianci turned a bank loan into a fortune—then lost it all!

Branca, however, captured the imagination of the young Italians with his logic and charmed his old friends in support of establishing one strong mutual aid society. Tony Cianci, founding member and a leading spokesperson of the Sons of Italy, sided with Judge Branca. Cianci viewed the proposal as the only way to ensure the preservation of his society's values and traditions. Nino Sala adopted a similar posture. Tony Borsato, member of the Sons of Italy and past president of Branca's Veneta Society, also advocated unification.[232] So did Joe Ghini, the bright and active member of the society's executive. Thirty-eight-year-old Louie Barone, president of the Sons of Italy, believed that a single society offering a single voice in the affairs of the community would serve to rejuvenate the popularity of the mutual aid society as an entity. Moreover, by merging the societies, he felt the acquisition of a Casa d'Italia would eventually become a reality.

Judge Branca, now a member of the B.C. Court of Appeal, was also very popular with the women's groups. When polled, a majority of the executive, including Phyllis Culos serving her 18th term as president, favoured Branca's proposal. The affiliate ladies' leagues were also having to deal with diminishing interest and participation from dwindling ranks. Amalgamation promised a quick fix to their membership problems. The combined active membership of the three women's lodges totalled 70. A merger would allow for a reduction in the 'duplication of effort' factor which resulted from having three independent organizations competing in the same market.

It soon became quite evident that the mood was for change among Vancouver's society of Italians.

For the membership of the Sons of Italy, the moment of decision was faced on May 2, 1965, at the Hastings Auditorium. After a brief discussion, devoid of any acrimony, a quorum representation voted to accept the invitation. Upon reflection, Barone commented that, "There had been a great deal of bickering and arguing during the last few meetings. The vote to merge wasn't a close one. It was conducted by secret ballot and only two or three people voted against the idea. Marino was against it."

Il Giudice had scored a hat-trick!

The terms and details of the accord, however, were still subject to review. The societies had a year to work out the details of the amalgamation plan. During this hiatus the antagonists continued the debate. In the end, however, a vast majority of those who first questioned the merger, including John Savio, acquiesced. A couple of events preceded Savio's decision to look to Judge Branca as the person to lead the societies on a more liberal path. First he disagreed with a plan advanced by Marino Culos for the distribution and control of Sons of Italy banquet tickets. And secondly, he didn't share Marino's expressed view that Branca would never build an Italian community hall.

There is some evidence, however, that Marino was willing to comply with the will of the majority. In his letter to Lino Maddalozzo of Abbotsford dated May 6, 1965, he summarized the results of the vote to amalgamate adding, "I think that this step is a good one for all Italians."

A few items under unfinished business preoccupied Marino's interest. On Feb. 6, he dutifully submitted the names of the society's directors to the Registrar of Companies in Victoria, in compliance with the Societies Act. The directors of the last administration comprised Luigi Barone, meat cutter; Gregorio Fuoco, shoemaker; Giovanni Bertuzzi, contractor; Marino Culos, accountant; Nino G. Sala, caterer; and Nicola Ciarniello, shoeshine business [operator].

Complimentary tickets for the Sons of Italy and Lega's final banquet and dance were sent to all members in good standing. Non-member spouses paid $3.30 for a ticket. It was held March 12, 1966 at the Royal Canadian Legion Hall, 2205 Commercial Drive, with 182 in attendance. A commercial photographer snapped a group photograph of the combined memberships of active members.

Felice Cianci, 90, receiving his gold medal from Rudy Bonoro.

Sig. Antonio Cianci e
Sig. Cesare Anderlini
by Leo Tesan

Dieci anni son passati
Dei quattro fondattori onorati
Solo due son restati;
Sono loro che pure oggi
Progrediscano nei nostri destini;
Gridiamo con gioia "eviva Cianci e
Anderlini".

Communicating his regrets, Ruocco wrote to Marino Culos explaining his situation and sadness in noting that the good ship Sons of Italy was sinking. Moreover, the letter stated in part that (translation), "I have noted with pleasure the precise control and preparation which have gone into organizing this banquet and feel secure that it will be a grand success. We are grateful for the invitation but don't believe we will have the pleasure of being with you

Strand Hotel Beer Parlour.
Partners "The Greek" and Millie Rossi with Jack Green and hotel waiters, 1940.

for the [society's] last supper. It is especially difficult now that the union of the societies is a *fait accompli*."

The finance committee held its last meeting May 8 at the Hastings Auditorium to review outstanding business and accounts. A final dues collection statement, prepared by Marino and audited by G. Di Fonzo, A. Del Bianco and J. Bordignon, was also discussed and approved. The amount of $4,576.48 in liquid assets would be

STRAND
REFRESHMENT PARLOR STAFF
—1940—

VICS celebrates its 22nd anniversary.
From left, John Benetti, Vancouver Italian-Canadian's president, Ralph Goodman, banquet presenter and Stan Callegari, society secretary.

Sig. Felice Cianci
by Leo Tesan

Cianci Felice,
Il vostro nome ce lo dice,
Portaste con voi la gioia, l'amore.
Lavoraste con tanto ardore
Portando alto il nostro tricolore.

transferred in June to the Confratellanza Italo Canadese account. The end was near.

Under unfinished business, the committee dealt with the issuing of final sick benefit payments. These letters written by Marino on behalf of the society carried an uncharacteristically formal tone. One such letter, dated May 28, 1966, was addressed to his old friend Gregorio Fuoco, "Dear Member. It is with pleasure that I enclose a cheque from the Sons of Italy in the amount of $11, payment of sick benefit. We wish you a full recovery. *Saluti*".[233]

In the early 1960s, the death and retirement of some of the society's most active members created a critical shortage of dedicated participants. In March 1960, Frank Spatari passed away and in July, Frank Comparelli died at age 74 years. Comparelli went peacefully while having his hair cut by Girardo Di Fonzo, a Sons of Italy vice-president and popular men's barber shop proprietor.

In January 1961, the society lost two dedicated members, Santo Pasqualini and Luigi Palazzini. Following a review of their contributions at the general meeting, a minute's silence was observed. Pasqualini, buried on what would have been his 62nd birthday, had remained loyal to the society and to Marino, his fellow Friulano to the very end. Palazzini, for decades the society's North Vancouver representative, was a gifted and accomplished tenor. He entertained the membership at numerous society functions and had been a source of pride to the Italian community. During the war, his company supplied and installed terrazzo in Canadian frigates in dry dock on the North Shore.[234]

Some of the older directors such as Felice Cianci retired from the executive. The society officially recognized Cianci, a Castelgrandese, as an "exemplary member". Joining the Sons of Italy in 1917, he served as secretary of finance and secretary of correspondence for more than 30 years and for his significant contribution was awarded a certificate of merit and a handsome wrist watch. Cianci had been a barber since coming to Vancouver in 1905. For many years, he was the owner/operator of a barber shop at 307 Carrall Street.[235]

The ranks of the Lega were also being depleted by the death of some of its most dedicated members. June 1961 marked the death of Maria Balma, also with roots in North Vancouver. The following month, Olivia Bordignon died. On Dec. 23, 1962, after four years of suffering, Ida Giuriato died at age 60. She had been a longtime active member of the Vancouver Italian-Canadian Society to which both her husband Luigi (Louis) and son Lino formerly served with distinction as presidents.

In private life, Ida Giuriato had worked side-by-side with Louis in the family business from their premises on the 400 block Union Street. In 1944, they pioneered the manufacture of canned ravioli in

Canada. Within a few years, Bonus Ravioli Dinner —"The Bonus is in the Flavour"—was selling across the country.

Speaking about her father's success as an entrepreneur, Ines Giuriato Cappon recalled, "Our store seemed to be the headquarters for the immigrants coming in. He was one who would help the immigrants to find work, especially in the logging camps. My dad would phone his contacts and often his efforts would result in these job-seekers being sent out to work. And of course dad never had a day at school."

"Dad became an orphan at 10. First his father died when he was six. They had gone to Brazil from Italy in search of their fortune. Instead his father died. His mother was left with six children in a strange country and not knowing the Portuguese language. So, they went back to Italy where his mother died within four years. As a juvenile, he worked for room and board plus 60 lire [estimated value six dollars] and 'a straw hat for a year's work'. When he was 15, papa left for Germany where he worked with construction gangs, sleeping in barns in the winter and on hay stacks in the summer.

New Dodson Hotel owners.
From left, Peter Minichiello, Louie Blanc, Art Minichiello and Gigi Pettovello.

Five years later, he was in Vancouver; a new country offered renewed hope for a prosperous future," she concluded.

In a major expansion in July 1958, Louis Giuriato and his sons Lino and David, both university graduates, opened a new plant in Burnaby. The $170,000-facility made possible the national distribution of their 22 products with the company remaining a viable operation until the untimely death of Lino, its president. A gifted speaker and brilliant student, Lino succeeded his father as president of the Vancouver Italian-Canadian Society in the late 1940s. He served successive terms as leader of the society until stepping down in support of John Benetti's candidacy for president in 1951. Benetti, in turn, guided the VICS through a successful term with the aid of a brilliant executive which included the capable and devoted Stan Callegari.

Longtime member, Antonio Zanatta, a pioneer resident of Vancouver, died April 7, 1962. And on July 1, 1963, Ottavio Bevilacqua, the society's dedicated vice-president, died from injuries sustained in a fall from a cherry tree in his neighbour's backyard.

While the Bevilacqua family was in a state of shock, Marino Culos went about making the funeral arrangements in a quiet and unobtrusive manner. To further ease the family's stress, Marino wrote to Ottavio's son Leo providing a list of the pallbearers: Giovanni Bertuzzi, president; Antonio Cianci, *oratore*; executive members, Zefferino Bordignon, Nino Sala, Girardo Di Fonzo and Marino Culos.

Felice Cianci delivered the eulogy and Phyllis Culos offered the following words of sympathy at the graveside on behalf of the Lega, "This is a very sad day for all those who knew Ottavio. Recently, Ottavio and I, among others, had attended a meeting of the Comitato Attivita' Italiane and when the meeting was over he obligingly offered to drive me home. On the way he talked of his family—his wife had enjoyed a well-earned vacation—his sons and his daughter were getting along fine—his grandchild was a lovely baby. It was easy to see that he felt God had been good to him. I felt he was a model husband and father. It is difficult for me to realize that he will no longer be with us. To Mrs. Bevilacqua and to his and her family, I wish to offer the sincere sympathy of all the members of the Lega Femminile Italiane [Italian Ladies' League] and I shall say a prayer asking God to take care of him and to watch over his family. Rest in peace."

Italian pioneers continued to decrease in numbers into the 1960s. The community mourned the death of Paul Girone in November 1965. He had established Powell River's first bakery, circa 1918 before settling in Vancouver. And Sabatino (Sam) Faraone passed away two months later.

A member of the society for 46 years, Girone was one of 32 or more Italians to own shares in hotel beer parlour operations in

Vancouver. George Cillis and Leo Paletti were his partners in the Broadway Hotel, Hastings at Columbia.[236]

His daughter Florence Mazzucco recalled how proud Italians were to be in the hotel business. "Whenever Italians owned a hotel or other business, they always held themselves up very high. They had pride and seemed to stand out within the Italian community. It was understandable too, that they should feel this way considering how difficult it was to get past the 'Macaroni-Girone' [prejudice]. And the ones who made it, well we really looked up to them," she stated.

Hotel Owners: Alvaro brothers
Nick, Frank, Johnny and Meco

Louie Valente, the former owner of the Astoria Hotel, also has a high regard for the memory of the pioneer Italian hotel owners. "When you owned a hotel in the early days, everyone played the part. You went to work with shoes shined. Many of the Hastings Street hotel owners would meet next to the Balmoral Hotel. The Granville Street guys would go to a Robson Street shine. But they all would have had their shoes shined; always immaculate with a white shirt and tie," stated Valente.

"These guys worked at their hotels too. Up to 14 hours a day between the time they spent behind the bar and walking around mingling with customers. You would take your jacket off but you would still have a vest over your shirt with a tie and stick pin. People gave them their respect. It was class," continued Valente.

Johnny Alvaro also has vivid memories of the way waiters dressed at the London Hotel Beer Parlour, an enterprise his father owned for many years dating back to 1936. "They would have the little white starched vests, black shoes and pants. And a black tie. It was the uniform back then. And it was mandatory and sanctioned by the union," he recalled.

During the Second World War the beer parlours did a roaring business. The war-time economy brought in a steady family trade but it was the hundreds of men employed in war-related enterprises that accounted for the hotel owners becoming wealthier.

"That was the time when the shipyard workers came in. They allowed the women to come in unescorted and to purchase beer in the section next to where the men drank. And the hotels had to close between 6:30 and 7:30 p.m. It was the only way the women could

Sons of Italy and Italian Ladies' League active members, 1966.
Societies' last banquet and photo opportunity before becoming part of the Confratellanza Italo-Canadese.

get their husbands to go home for dinner. That by-law was in effect until the 1960s," Valente affirmed.

Giuseppe Marino, the last member to be buried in the Sons of Italy's section of the Mountain View Cemetery, was born in Bellamain, Provincia di Bari. He joined the society in March 1927, and died December 1965. Two generations of Vancouver's Canadian-Italians remember Joe Marino as the fruit peddler with the boisterous and rhythmic voice. From the back of his horse-drawn wagon (and later his truck) he would bellow, "Wadda-ma-loan. Ah-pre-kotch and wadda-ma-loan," as he plied the streets of Little Italy selling fresh supplies of watermelon and apricots.

The Sons of Italy had funds set aside to deal with members'
special needs. A donor who asked to remain anonymous had previously donated $100 to this fund. Marino Culos gained the society's
approval—and the donor's blessing—to make the money available
to Joe Marino's widow.

This thoughtful and caring approach in times of bereavement
endeared the society and its officers to the membership. Often letters would follow expressing a spouse's or other survivor's appreciation. For example, Mrs. Gallazin wrote the society following the
death of her husband Lino in February 1963, "The attendance of
your members at the funeral and the tribute read at graveside was

Cemetery monument at Mountain View Cemetery dedicated in 1938.

much appreciated, and we thank you most sincerely for this evidence of your loyalty and friendship."

In this regard, Marino Culos received his share of kudos. Florence Scoppa wrote to him following the funeral service of Filippo Pepponi, a member who had no family residing in Canada. Her letter dated December 1964, reads in part, "Dear Marino, I'm writing in behalf of mom and dad to express our sincere thanks in the interest you took during the recent death and burial of Mr. Pepponi. We appreciated the efforts to have him buried with the Figli d'Italia members

in their special plot. We feel that this was truly a humanitarian act especially at this time of year and in behalf of such a lonely older man. I know that God will bless you and yours for your charity. Dad feels that the lodge would be nothing without you and your kindness in these particular cases."

Chapter 24

The Requiem and Birth

Il Requiem e la Nascita

Marino, with Phyllis at his side, contemplates the future of Vancouver's society of Italians.

*A*s the merger of the societies became imminent, Marino Culos conducted a private inventory on the results of his lifetime involvement in Vancouver's society of Italians. He had known many of the founding members, worked with the community's best, and had advanced the cause and reputation of the Italian community. As the baton of societal participation passed into a new era, Marino knew the race—for him—was over.

He confided his impressions to W.G. Ruocco in letter dated February 8, 1966. Over a period spanning 40 years, he had been protégé, nemesis and now cordial colleague. Marino's letter to the brilliant former leader, contained a nostalgic and conciliatory tone, (translation) "The Figli d'Italia suffers a great deal from the lack of people interested and those with the capacity to understand the affairs of the society and those who have the courage to make decisions. Notwithstanding, we can say with pride that we have been members of the Sons of Italy because it will be remembered as a grand society of major importance in the story of the Italian community of Vancouver. After having sailed across the community's seas and at times through tempestuous waters, our ship has arrived at its final destination. And now we are left to await the requiem of the Sons of Italy and the birth and the baptism of the new Confratellanza Italo-Canadese. *Preghiamo.*"

The Sons of Italy Mutual Aid Society officially ceased to exist May 1, 1966.

Although Judge Angelo Branca and the Confratellanza Italo-Canadese never totally abandoned the idea of acquiring a Casa d'Italia, the race to build an Italian community centre was lost to the Italian Folk Society of B.C., a federation of Italian associations formed in 1974. In 1977, this group of Italians, made up primarily of post-war immigrants under the leadership of Giovanni Germano, the Italian consul, succeeded in building the Italian Cultural Centre at 3075 Slocan Street, Vancouver.

The Italian Folk Society, now known as the Italian Cultural Centre Society, serves as an umbrella organization to a federation of autonomous Italian associations. The society obtained financial grants and organizational assistance from the B.C. provincial government and the City of Vancouver. It applied these grants toward the acquisition of land, construction of the buildings and in compiling library materials. In addition, the Italian Folk Society had the support of the Canadian and Italian governments.

Soon the Italian Cultural Centre Society's *"casa d'Italia"* became the focal point of the Vancouver Italian-Canadian community. Although the centre appeared to be a successful operation, it carried a significant debt load. This situation infuriated Judge Branca and a number of the Confratellanza executive. Branca was so vociferous in his attacks against Giovanni Germano and Gerry Visentin, the centre's administrator, that a serious split resulted between the two groups. Following the death of Judge Branca in 1984, however, the Confratellanza Italo-Canadese and the Italian Cultural Centre Society began a dialogue to resolve their differences. This process led to the Confratellanza becoming the Centre's 35th member in 1990.

Sig. Marino Culos
by Leo Tesan

Per voi o Marino
Come bello fu il destino:
Direttore a vita vi hanno onorato
Per la fede e l'amore che avete portato;
Lo avete portato con voi nella battaglia
Ma nel vostro cuore—
Era solo la "Figli d'Italia."

Rocky Marciano and Cap Capozzi toast to the success of the Confratellanza with a supply of the famous Calona wine.

Notes

Chapter 1

1. Nephew Peter Culos and Marino's five grandsons John Starcevic and Robert, David, Victor, and Adrian Culos served as pallbearers. The Confratellanza's honour guard included president Rocco Salituro, past presidents Mario Caravetta, Angelo Holmes, Lino Natola, and Rudy Bonora and executive member Gino Ramogida (1997–1998 president). And from the Lega: Armida Beasley, America Bianco, Bruna Defend, Enza De Filippo, Emilia Pastro, Teresa Pettovello, Lori Stefani, and Mary Thacker.

2. R. Angelo Holmes, son of Judge Dolores and Pat Holmes, was president of the Confratellanza Italo-Canadese 1991, 1992 and 1993. He had been inspired to provide a leadership role in the Italian community by his grandfather, the late Judge Angelo Branca.

3. In his eulogy, Peter Culos spoke with affection and admiration of his uncle's dedication to the Sons of Italy Society and his skill in producing promotional material for the society's candidate during the 1937 Queen Contest campaign. Although only nine years of age at the time, Peter vividly recalled his impressions while watching his uncle Marino produce beautifully painted posters with catchy slogans at the Union Grocery Store and Meat Market. Following their completion, young Peter would deliver the posters to the neighbourhood store owners who had agreed to display them. He was moved to say that it was this experience that influenced his decision to enter the advertising and marketing field in later years.

Chapter 2

4. Marino vividly recalled his first ride in a North American automobile and the sense of trepidation he felt upon arriving at his new home.

5. The author viewed the family home in S. Giovanni di Casarsa, and in 1990 spoke with a local historian regarding the evolution of the Culos name. It was determined that members of the Culos family had spelled their name in various ways over the centuries. (Translation) "A very old Prodolone family is that of Culos which has been spelled Colos, Colossio, Colossys." Evidence of this is found in Giuseppe Iop's *Prodolone Parrocchia, 1300–1970*, which lists priests of the Prodolone Parish in the Friuli region of Italy. The list includes Father Gio: Antonio Colos (1513), Father Zuan Daniel Colossio (1579), Father Domenico Colossio (1596), Don (Father) Osualdo Colossi (1763) and Father Marco Colos (1590). On pages 118–128 of his publication Iop lists the families which were resident in Prodolone including "Colos (Culos)—Ghelf—1607." Ancestors of the author lived in San Vito al Tagliamento (Colos, Colossi, Culos) before

moving a few kilometres to San Giovanni di Casarsa in 1850.

6. The by-laws of the Sons of Italy state that the society was organized for the purpose of helping its members in case of accident, sickness, and with funeral expenses. Another objective stated it was not to assist members charitably, but rather obligatorily from the general funds of the society. It is important to note that the society was not concerned with individual members' beliefs, thoughts or religion.

7. In conversation with Marino Culos whose published articles in *L'Eco Italo-Canadese* March 1940, provide direct references to Galetti's and Calori's contributions.

Galetti was president of the Sons of Italy for six years and is credited with providing effective leadership during the society's formative years. He was an early proponent of the establishment of a ladies' auxiliary and was one of the signatories of the founding of the Societa' Femminile Italiane affiliated with the Sons of Italy. He died in 1927.

In conversation with Al Principe, Lorenzo Politano's godson, who lived next door to his godfather's store; 1908–1920. Larry Politano gave the author his grandfather's flag to keep as a souvenir.

8. In conversation with Marino Culos whose published articles state that the first meeting of the founding members (Sons of Italy) was held at Ferrera's Italian Agent's office.

Prior to being appointed Italian consul in 1902, Agostino Ferrera had established himself as a successful Vancouver businessman.

9. Excerpt from the Societa' Figli d'Italia's minute book, November 1904.

10. In conversation with Marino Culos and an excerpt from the society's minute book, December 1910.

11. As recorded in the society's minute book, Mr. Federici was president in 1906. He died at the age of 101 in 1979. Obit in the author's column "Commento di Culos" as published in *L'Eco d'Italia*, Aug. 30, 1979 read, "In 1891, sponsored by an uncle living in the States, Francesco Federici boards an Anchor Line ship in Naples. The fare is $9. Crossing the Atlantic lasts 24 endless days."

The Vancouver Province did a major take-out Feb. 10, 1934 at the beginning of B.C.'s Italy Week which originated with the National Council of Education of Canada. Three distinguished Italians were to visit Vancouver on a Canadian speaking tour. Their mission was to interpret the new Italy of Mussolini to Canada and to link closer the bonds between the two countries. The special feature included this blurb, "The man who does not know Francis Federici and Umberto Tragella is ill acquainted in Vancouver. Federici is head of the barber shop of the Hotel Vancouver, a citizen here since 1900 and a member of the Rotary Club for the past 17 years. He has mementoes from the Prince of Wales, the late President Warren G. Harding, Gene Tunney, Harold Lloyd and a score of other notables whose friendship he gained. He is a lively talker with a host of reminiscences and one of the most delightful representatives of Italy in the province.

"Tragella is likewise in the Hotel Vancouver. For years he has been the maitre d'hotel. Anyone who has dined in the hotel remembers him, handsome in evening clothes, overseeing his crew of skilled waiters. Like Federici he has won the friendship of distinguished visitors and he has made a reputation for himself as host extraordinary."

12. In conversation with Marino Culos and by crosschecking membership lists of the Figli d'Italia and Societa' Veneta, circa 1911. Also, the following excerpt from an interview with Bill Canal. "My father worked for Filippo Branca at the store. As a result of his friendship with Branca, he became very active in the Veneta as a member of the Sick Committee."

Judge Branca, in his column "Branca's Page," which appeared in *L'Eco d'Italia* dated Nov., 1978, talked about the founding members of the Veneta Society. A summary suggests that there were 81 initial founding members, almost all from the Treviso and Venice areas. Branca listed a number of the society members including Carlo Franceschini, who worked for Peter Tosi and Luciano Zanon, the successful baker. Zanon was educated and extremely well read. Many of the members worked for the B.C. Electric repairing the streetcar tracks in Vancouver; these included Angelo Carniatto, Giuseppe Toffoletto and his friend Isidoro Pavan. He also mentioned Tessaro Quinto who eventually became a farmer near Abbotsford. "Giovanni Secco and family lived on the 300 block Prior Street and I can remember as a little boy delivering groceries to them from my father's store in the 900 block Main Street. Then there was the Piccolo family, Giovanni and Giordano, wonderful people. And Luigi Guerra worked on my father's farm in Burnaby during the First World War. Another very well-known character was Leone Brandolini. Brandy, as we used to call him, lived on the 500 block Prior Street. He raised a very fine family. Attilio was one of the boys and one of my life-long friends until he died. He was Chief Engineer at St. Paul's Hospital for many years. Another brother [Gillie] was the owner of the Melbourne Hotel. He married [Ermie] Pulice," stated Branca.

13. In conversation with Mr. Crosetti's daughter Emma McMillan and Filippo Branca's granddaughter Judge Dolores Holmes.

Judge Branca, in his column, "Branca's Page," dated Oct. 27,1978 wrote, "My father was one of the early merchants, having started his store way back in 1903. At first he was in partnership with John [sic] Crosetti and within a year or two after that, alone. I think he started [his own store] in 1905. He had an importing store of Italian foodstuffs on Main Street from 1903 to 1939 when he died. I think he was one of the most respected men who ever came from Italy to establish his home in the far West..."

14. Excerpts from an interview with John D'Appolonia in *L'Eco d'Italia*. Conversation with Luigi Possagno's daughter and an excerpt from an interview with Ernie Maddalozzo. "My dad had been slated to go to Australia but the war with Turkey intervened. He used to tell us that it was during the Libyan campaign that the airplane was first used to observe the enemy's military disposition and movements," recalled Maddalozzo.

Another prominent member of the community, Frank Mangarella, also served in the Italo-Turca war. Mangarella, who served on the Royal Italian Navy gunboat *Sardegna*, participated in the conquest of Tripoli, Misurata, Zuara and Sidi Said. During the late 1930s, he became recognized as a successful local fish-boat builder. In May 1940, 67-foot *Anna M*, sister ship to the *Adele M*, was launched for Frank Mangarella at the Stanley Park Shipyard.

15. Excerpts from an interview with Violet Benedetti and an interview with Edie Harris who both recall Anne Gatto's funeral.

16. In conversation with Marino Culos who excitedly described his reaction when his father got him to put his finger in the bullet hole in the door frame. The author has the pocket watch.

17. Excerpt from an interview with Al Principe, "He had the first team to cross Connaught Bridge—I've got pictures of this. My dad saw an ad: 'Beer Runners Wanted; Must Have Fast Team of Horses.' So, my dad checked it out—remember in those days it was Prohibition—near beer. If you wanted beer, you phoned the brewery and told them you wanted a case of beer—24 bottles for $2.40. Each brewery had runners. A barrel would have ten cases."

18. Newspaper articles re the Royal Visit, reviewed by author at Pacific Press Library.

19. Excerpt from souvenir booklet, *Fogolars 1979*, page 136. The author arranged to have Fred Dalfo, Marega's longtime apprentice and employee, interviewed for the *Fogolars* article.

20. Excerpt from *Souvenirs 'Ricordi'*, page 9, published by Marino Culos in 1935.

21. Excerpt from an interview with Caesar Anderlini, the nephew of Cesare Anderlini, a founding member of the Sons of Italy.

22. Excerpts from an interview with Mario Masi. *Bastoncini*: literally those with canes. According to Violet Benedetti, Phyllis Culos, and Mario Masi there were several members of this group including Nicola Masi, Francesco Federici, Antonio Cianci, Frank Rita, Antonio Villa, and the Ruocco, Erico and Cristiano brothers. The *bastoncini* considered themselves members of Vancouver's Italian elite.

23. Excerpts from the society's minute book, May 1912. Among the 10 signatories to the request for a special meeting was Egisto Casadei. He was a devoted member who worked assiduously for the society. Although he moved to Hayward, California in 1928, Casadei remained a dues-paying member until his death by suicide in 1952. During the intervening years he accounted for a consistent stream of correspondence to the society to which Marino Culos replied to a majority of the letters. Prior to his death, he had been in poor health, a result of a protracted illness and the effects of an operation which took place a few weeks before his death.

24. Excerpts from original correspondence from the Ettor and Giovannitti Defence Fund organizer, circa May 1912.

Historian MariJo Bulla's research of the subject appeared in the *Encyclopedia of the American Left* (1959) as follows: "Son of a modest doctor/pharmacist, Giovannitti was born in Ripabottoni, a small hill town of southern Italy in the region of Abruzzo-Molise. Upon completing school he emigrated to Canada.

"The effectiveness of Giovannitti and fellow WW I organizer Joe Ettor during the bitter Lawrence strike of 1912 made them marked men. During a confrontation with the state militia, a young girl among the striking demonstrators was killed. Although Ettor and Giovannitti were not present at the shooting incident and evidence indicated that a police officer's bullet had actually killed the young girl, they were arrested and charged as accessories to murder. After almost a year of imprisonment, Ettor and Giovannitti were found innocent by a jury and set free." (The above item was researched by David Sheldon, Burnaby Public Library.)

Chapter 3

25. In an interview conducted by the author in April 1992, Gabriele Iacobucci said, "When I joined the Sons of Italy in

1925 my sponsor was Vincenzo Sabatini. I stayed as a member with Marino Culos until we merged into the Confratellanza Italo-Canadese in 1966."

Gabriele Iacobucci married Rosa Pirillo in 1929 and they had four children. To Teresa, Danny, Frank and John, their father offered a simple but fundamental code of values which Mr. Iacobucci had learned from his father in Italy: "Don't bring shame to the family, work hard and respect everyone."

26. In conversation with Artemisia Minichiello, circa 1970 and Marino Culos, circa 1992.

27. Excerpts from *The Province*, circa Sept. 24, 1914 as provided by Elain Butz.

28. Excerpts from interviews with Violet Benedetti, Gloria Bowe, and Elain Butz. "Well, they put him in jail for life. What happened—I used to have people come into my store—they would say, he [Montenario] fell into the Fraser—well, that's a lie because he broke out. But Montenario, the police always told us he had drowned in the Fraser; well that's a lie. He went north where he stayed in hiding until he died," asserted Mrs. Benedetti.

The police court transcript of Mario Montenario's case includes the testimony of Detective Joe Ricci of the Vancouver Police Department. Ricci was the first Italian to attain the rank of detective in the force and was a prominent member of the Italian community. The counsel for the prosecution J.K. Kennedy questioned Ricci as follows: "[Q.] Did you warn him then? [A.] I did in the presence of Inspector McLeod. [Q.] In what language? [A.] Italian. [Q.] What was it he said? [A.] He said that he had shot the man. [Q.] Shot what man? [A.] Angelo Teti. [Q.] How many times did he say he shot him? [A.] He said about three times. [Q.] Did he say any of the circumstances at all? [A.] He said he had considerable trouble with this Angelo Teti for some time regarding some mortgage, some money, $2,300 and that is why he went out in the morning and shot him. I asked him if he ever had any trouble with Angelo Teti previous to this. [Q.] Previous to what? [A.] Previous to this date and he said, 'No, I never had any trouble for a considerable time.'

He said, 'The only trouble we had was a dispute over $2,300.' So, he went out and shot him. He said, 'I went out about seven o'clock in the morning and I put my gun in my pocket and Angelo Teti was in McKinnon's office in the seven hundred block on Main Street and I shot him.'"

Ricci was then cross-examined by Frank Lyons, counsel of the defence: "'Didn't he tell you that Angelo Teti had refused to accept the money to redeem the mortgage? Did he tell that? That Angelo Teti had refused to accept the money to redeem the mortgage pretending that he had nothing to do with it, that it was transferred to somebody else, and that he was trying to defraud him and his family out of the money?' [A.]'I think he did say that.'"

29. Excerpts from interviews with the late Fio Tate's sister Violet Benedetti and his nieces Gloria Bowe and Elain Butz. Also from an interview with Silvio Ruocco who has Fio Teti's citation and military decorations.

Chapter 4

30. R. Castrucci interviewed Rose Cianci in the summer of 1966. His article, published in *L'Eco d'Italia* July 5, provides a different twist to the Giuseppe Guasparri—John Lewis—story. His version suggests Joe Louis's [sic] 640-acre ranch was located near Hudson's Bay. And it was in this area of Canada that he traded with the Indians. Apparently, he made a fortune selling the furs and pelts.

Chapter 5

31. From the society's minute book, circa May 1915.

Article 17 (h) of the society's by-laws stated that any member who voluntarily or by compulsion entered military service would have his membership suspended until his return to civilian life and his sick benefit also was to be suspended during such time. In Article 16 the member returning to civilian life was eligible for reinstatement subject to furnishing a medical certificate stating he was in good health.

32. Excerpts from an interview with Silvio Ruocco who possesses a documented file regarding his family members' military service.

33. Excerpts from the society's minute book, circa 1917, 1919 and 1920.

Chapter 6

34. Excerpts from the society's minute book, circa 1917.

35. Excerpts from the society's minute book, circa 1921. A photo of the Sons of Italy's monument located at Mountain View Cemetery on which Ottavio Vanelli's name appears is contained in the Marino Culos file.

36. According to the society by-laws, members attending a funeral were required to be decently dressed and were to

wear the badge of the society. A fine not exceeding $2 could be imposed on absentees away without just cause. Moreover, a black and white ribbon bow was to be the emblem worn by all members attending a funeral.

The death benefit application was approved only if the deceased member was deemed to have been a member in good standing at the time of his death. A major breach in the relationship between Frank Rita and the society's administration, as represented by Marino Culos, occurred in 1942. Rita's brother Angelo died at a time when his membership dues were in arrears. As a result, the usual death benefit payment was denied to his beneficiary. Frank Rita was incensed and carried on a heated stream of correspondence with the society's executive stating his brother had been of the opinion that his current dues were paid. At one point Rita, the society's honourary president for life, asked to speak directly to the assembly. Moreover, he requested that a secret ballot be conducted at a general meeting on the question of whether or not the death benefit be paid. It would be his proposal to the membership that the money be paid based on extenuating circumstances. A special committee was set up to hear Mr. Rita's side of the issue. It became a protracted confrontation and stalemate. Rita, who became ill, did not attend society meetings until Dec., 1945. The author's research uncovered no record of a death benefit having been paid. However, Frank Rita became interim president in 1946 when Marino Culos resigned the chair.

37. In conversation with Marino Culos, Phyllis Culos, and Angelina Daminato. Author has copies of a number of the speeches delivered at the cemetery and related photographs.

The scenes at funeral services were often times heartwrenching. Marino Culos's diary has the following entry for Jan. 5, 1943, the day Mrs. De Paola was buried at Mountain View Cemetery: "Phyl tells me that Eugenio asked Cliff Cleary, the undertaker, to open the casket so that he could get one last look at his beloved wife. This request, however, could not be complied with. He had done this when his son was buried a few years ago and the casket was opened. The boy's grave is a few graves from that of his mother. Dominic Perrillo [sic]—Union Street—gave a worthy eulogy."

38. Excerpts from interviews with Angelina Daminato, Irma Pastro and Bill Canal.

When the society inaugurated its new monument at Mountain View Cemetery in 1938, Frank Comparelli chaired the proceedings. In his remarks he suggested that Providence had given each nation particular gifts based on the country's unique characteristics. He reminded the assembly that Italians were gifted artists whose talents lay in many disciplines as evidenced throughout the world.

Comparelli's speech appeared in *L'Eco Italo-Canadese* and was reprinted in *Memorie Preziose*, page 27, in 1955. (Translation) "This tradition is reflected in the masterful monument which we see here today. It is a source of pride to the Italian colony of Vancouver and in particular to the members of the Sons of Italy Society and the Italian Ladies' League. The idea and design for this monument came from the indefatigable Marino Culos whose work artistically portrays the concept of our fraternity. The workmanship is from the hand of our fraternal brother Rizieri Stefanini, a master craftsman."

Chapter 7

39. Excerpts from interviews with Elda Battistoni Venturato and her brother Cyril Battistoni. The Culos family often entertained the Battistonis at their Coquitlam farm, circa 1920s.

40. Excerpt from the society's minute book and from *Souvenirs 'Ricordi'*, page 13.

41. In addition to his active membership in the Veneta, Angelo Branca opened his own law practice in 1926 at age 23.

42. In conversation with Angelina Graziano Osborn and excepts from interviews with Ermie Pulice Brandolini.

The local daily press ran photos of Flo Toso-Enfante [sic] and Irmie Pulice and a lead story under the heading, "Two Italian Beauty Queens Are Selected," read in part, "Miss Toso-Enfante will be crowned Queen of Italy on Friday for the purposes of the Jubilee Celebration and henceforth will be known as the prettiest and most popular young lady of the Italian colony of British Columbia. To pretty Irma Pulicce [sic] will go the honour of being Miss Canada. She is the popular choice of the British Columbia Italian colony as the type to represent Canada. Misses Inez Falcioni, Evelyn Stefani, Ida Zuliani, Carmel Corra-Miller and Angelina Graziano are to be maids of honour to the Queen and to Miss Canada."

43. Excerpt from an interview with Peter Culos whose parents Antonio and Rosina Culos were sole proprietors of the Fior D'Italia Italian Restaurant following the death of Gaetano Papini.

44. Excerpt from an interview with Marguerite Girone McPherson.

45. Teresa Marchese continued as an active member and director of the Lega for several years. Her daughter Louise also joined the organization and became a source of great

pride to the Italian Ladies' League and the entire Vancouver Italian community as a brilliant medal-winning typist. Willie Ruocco was married to the former Lina Calori, Rose Anderlini's half sister.

At the time of her husband's and son's arrest as enemy aliens in June 1940, Mrs. Enedina Fabri was serving as president of the Italian-Canadian Red Cross Unit, a committee she helped establish following the outbreak of war with Germany. In a notice appearing in *L'Eco Italo-Canadese*, February 1940, she is quoted as stating, (translation) "Canadian women of Italian origin who have always showed loving devotion to the mother country are now wanting to help [Canada] their adopted country in which they and their families live. This invitation to attend the inaugural meeting of the Comitato Italiano per the Croce Rossa is directed to those who share this feeling."

46. Excerpt from an interview with Emma Crosetti McMillan.

47. In conversation with Marino Culos, excerpts from an interview with Louie Minichiello and an excerpt from *Souvenirs 'Ricordi'*, page 25.

48. An excerpt from an interview with Ermie Pulice Brandolini.

49. From correspondence from Giovanni Brait to Marino Culos and from *Souvenirs 'Ricordi'*, page 25.

50. Tosca Trasolini was featured in *Souvenirs 'Ricordi'*. In an article describing her achievements as a pilot, editor Marino Culos comments, (translation) "On Jan. 19, 1935, after intense training her dream is realized; she completes her first solo flight."

51. Excerpt from an interview with Sammy De Filippo and from an article in *Souvenirs 'Ricordi'*, page 27.

52. Correspondence from J. Berrutti, president of the Young Canadian Italian Athletic Club to John Branca, financial secretary of the Societa' Veneta dated July 3, 1933.

53. Excerpts from a letter dated Dec. 8, 1933 to Charlie Penway and Joe Nadalin, proprietors of the Columbia Hotel.

54. *The Vancouver Sun*, Oct. 4, 1954.

Chapter 8

55. The leading importer of California grapes for three decades was Donato (Dan) Minichiello. He received the franchise from his brother Sam who initiated the practice of purchasing special varieties of grapes from specific vineyards. Sam made a trip to Fresno in 1927 to choose the actual product intended for export to Vancouver. Later, as owner/manager of the family business, Dan refined this procedure by staying in California for up to two months in order to select only quality Zinfandel product for his clientele and to supervise the picking of the grapes by migrant workers from Mexico. Minichiello had an advantage over his competitors as he personally knew Alfonse Donati who shipped some of the finest grapes from the Fresno Valley area. Before his marriage to Frieda, Donati lived in Vancouver where he boarded with Dan and Cristina Minichiello.

Chapter 9

56. In conversation with Marino Culos and an excerpt from the Societa' Veneta's minute book.

57. Excerpt from the society's Majestic Hall rental schedule, circa 1930, in which names of those contracting for meeting rooms are listed.

58. Excerpt from the society's minute book, 1929.

59. Excerpt from the society's minute book, 1930.

60. In conversation with Marino Culos, letters from Culos to creditors, and information gained from a review of the motor vehicle transfer papers.

61. In conversation with Marino Culos and by comparing the names listed in documents obtained from government archives in Ottawa with lists of Italian war veterans reproduced in various issues of *L'Eco Italo-Canadese*, circa 1937–38.

62. Excerpts from an interview with Emma Green McMillan.

63. From an interview the author conducted with John Crosetti in 1979 for *L'Eco d'Italia*.

64. Information as printed on the programme dated January 1930, and from an interview with John Crosetti in August 1979. The following is an excerpt from the column "Commento di Culos," as published in *L'Eco d'Italia* (John

Crosetti commenting): "Although the Great Depression already had made an effect on our lives, this special social or *festa* attracted over 250 guests to a sit-down dinner prepared by Antonio Culos, the pioneer Italian chef who had become very popular as the owner of the Fior d'Italia Restaurant. I remember well, working most of the night stringing those streamers from one side of the hall to the other. The banquet was a great success, as most of our activities were in those days, especially because of the rivalry between our group and the Veneta."

65. Excerpt from interview with Clara Pini Preston.

Chapter 10

66. Excerpt from interviews with Nellie Pitton Cavell, Marguerite McPherson and Bill Canal.

67. Excerpt from an interview with Lily Castricano Albo.
   L'Eco Italo-Canadese reported on a Young Italian Girls' Club's dance Dec. 19, 1936. Spanish guitarist Emilio Gallo had been the featured musician whose repertoire that evening included popular Fascist tunes, "Faccetta Nera" and "Selassie:non e' chiu Imperatore."

68. Excerpts from interviews with Ermie Brandolini and Lily Castricano Albo.

69. Excerpts from interviews with Rinda Satti Dredge and Lily Castricano Albo.

70. Excerpt from an interview with Marguerite McPherson and excerpts from a news item in *The Vancouver Sun*, May 1935. "Officers and crew of MS *Cellina*, Italian vessel, with Italian residents of Port of Vancouver, on the occasion Sunday of dedicating the flag of the ship's Dopolavoro Club. The club is the Afterwork Club, a unit in the organization founded by Benito Mussolini to bring all ranks of workers together during leisure hours for cultural recreation.
   "Carmine *Cavaliere* Marino, titled '*cavaliere*' by Mussolini because he represents, according to Italian residents, all that is finest in the worker's character."

71. A direct quote from a news item in *The Vancouver Sun*, May 1935. Also excerpts from an interview with Carmine Marino's daughter-in-law Antonietta Marino. "I threw it away myself. I was so mad. [laughter] He stays home maybe I have to look at him and my husband is in the camp. I think I throw it away because I never seen it anymore," stated Antonietta. "For me he [my father-in-law] was good when my husband was in the camp. If I didn't

have him, I don't know. I would have to go to work. He looked after the garden. He was good really; I can't say he was bad. Sometimes I feel sorry, sometimes..." she concluded.

72. Excerpt from an interview with Emma Lussin Maffei.

73. Excerpts from the constitution of the American Dopolavoro Club. A copy of the Confederazione Nazionale Dopolavoro Fra Gli Italiani d'America constitution was obtained by Marino Culos from *The Voice of Italy*. The advocates of this umbrella organization claimed to be non-political, and were dedicated to marshalling the support of the "thousands of Italo-Americans" wherever they were resident in the U.S. in promoting the culture of [Mussolini's] Italy.

74. Excerpt from an interview with Lily Castricano Albo. The Castricano home was located on Hawkes Avenue a few blocks from the pier where the visiting Italian ships would be moored. Mary Castricano made her home available for meetings and socials to the members of the Italian Young Girls' Club, church groups and other community organizations.

Chapter 11

75. Excerpt from *Souvenirs 'Ricordi'*, page 16.
   In his "Branca's Corner" column of Oct. 27, 1978, Judge Branca made reference to immigrants from middle Italy. "There were not many from middle Italy except a bunch from Campobasso, including the Minichiello family which came here very early in the century and had quite an illustrious history in the community. And Nicola Di Tomaso was one of those very fine gentlemen who never ever spoke much but did a lot. He ran a grocery store at the corner of Hawks Avenue and Georgia Street for many, many years. He was a particularly close and treasured friend of mine."
   The author also mentioned Nick Di Tomaso in his *L'Eco d'Italia* column dated June 14, 1979. "Born in the little town of Civitanova del Sannio in 1884, this gentle and soft-spoken patriarch was extremely generous with his affection and loyalty to family and friends. *Compare* [godfather] Nick was special to my family having been a boyhood friend of my maternal grandfather Savario Minichiello, a friendship fostered by their parents, dating back to more than a century ago."

76. Excerpts from "La Rivista", a column by Marino Culos in the *L'Eco Italo-Canadese* dated Aug. 7, 1937. (Translation) "Under the direction of Mr. Durante, they

[New Westminster Italian Mutual Aid Society] built the Roma Hall which was opened May 24, 1932. The members were so pleased with his contributions that they presented Mr. Durante with a gold medal in recognition of his 'honesty' when he was society president and during his term as secretary and for directing the construction of the hall facility.

"In Italy when he was 18 years of age, he served in the Great War. As a designated military driver, he chauffered Generale Eugenio Vaccari and later Generalissimo Diaz when the latter was on an inspection tour in the Venezia Giulia region of Italy."

77. Excerpt from *Souvenirs 'Ricordi'*, page 15.

78. Excerpt from an interview with Cyril Battistoni whose father operated the Venice Bakery.

Chapter 12

79. Excerpt from an interview with Herman Ghislieri.

Mario Ghislieri was a signatory to the Societies Act application filed May 7, 1936, with the Registrar of Companies, Victoria, B.C. The other society executive officers signing the document, as witnessed by Pietro Colbertaldo, were Nicola Di Tomaso, Cesare P. Durante, Massimo Costa, and Pietro Canal.

80. Excerpt from an interview with Herman Ghislieri.

81. Data on Mario Ghislieri gained from excerpts in *Souvenirs 'Ricordi'*, page 16 and *L'Eco Italo-Canadese* dated April 3, 1937. In a secret memo written by Norman A. Robertson of the RCMP to The Rt. Hon. Ernest Lapointe, Minister of Justice and Attorney-General for Canada dated July 24, 1940, Robertson stated in part that "the persons named in this document are members in good standing with the 'Circolo Giulio Giordani' Lodge of the Fascio, Vancouver, B.C." Mario Ghislieri was among those listed.

82. In March 1935, W.G. Ruocco established Il Grande Comitato, the member organizations of which were Sons of Italy, its affiliate, the Italian Ladies' League, the Vancouver Italian-Canadian Society and its Italian Ladies' League. The Veneta Society did not participate. Excerpt from *Souvenirs 'Ricordi'*, page 17.

83. Marino Culos produced a Columbus Day Celebration programme dated Thursday, Oct. 12, 1933 to illustrate the animosity which existed between W.G. Ruocco and Eugene De Paola.

The 1933 banquet and dance was to have been organized "under the auspices of the Italian colony". Although the Sons of Italy had agreed on the date and a society minute dated Aug. 10, stated that the proceeds of the banquet and dance would go to the Italian School Committee, the Sons of Italy later changed the date of its social function to Oct. 11, "due to unforeseen circumstances". De Paola, first to organize Columbus Day festivities in Vancouver, was infuriated by this decision.

The front cover of the programme publicized the evening's entertainment: Bob Peroni, accordion solo, Paolo Gatto, National Hawaiian Orchestra, Berrettoni Brothers—a musical selection, Teresa Principe, soloist and selections by the Bologna orchestra. Dance music was provided by the Ceccarini [sic] orchestra. Speakers included Nicola Masi, Italian vice-consul, Piero Orsatti, local Fascist secretary and Angelo E. Branca, official orator. Eugene De Paola, chairman of the Columbus Day Celebration Committee, also spoke. His oratory, which included an attack on the president of the Sons of Italy, was reproduced on the inside pages. An excerpt from the text is as follows: (translation) "The discovery of America by Christopher Columbus took place Oct. 12, 1492, not Oct. 11, as the president of the Sons of Italy and his Feste Committee suggest. By changing the date for celebrating the great Italian navigator's discovery, the feelings of millions of people around the world have been ignored." The written tirade commended the Catholic Church and the 800,000 people who attended Chicago's celebrations Oct. 12, 1893, for observing the correct anniversary date and specifically admonished Ruocco (without actually mentioning his name) and the Sons of Italy for having the audacity to select a day other than Oct. 12 to commemorate the great Italian's exploits. The 800-word statement concluded with an invitation to the reader to come to De Paola's office and read the letter from the Sons of Italy dated Aug. 30, 1933, in which De Paola was informed of the date change. The message concluded, "Members of Italian community please note well that Oct. 12, 1492, is the real date of the discovery of America by Christopher Columbus, not Oct. 11, as suggested by the Sons of Italy. Be sure to inform your friends of this fact."

84. Excerpt from *Souvenirs 'Ricordi'*, page 17. Date of incorporation also appeared on the Societa' Cristoforo Colombo Inc. stationery.

85. Marino Culos spent approximately six months preparing the historical booklet, interviewing prominent members of the community and selling advertising to offset production costs. Marino was motivated to include advertising in his booklet as a result of knowledge gained from an advertising course he completed by correspondence from the Page-Davis School of Advertising, Chicago.

86. Montalban and Marino contributed articles to *L'Eco Italo-Canadese*. Correspondence suggests that this association led Marino to submit copy to Montalban's publication Italian Life, and Montalban's cooperation in editing Marino's Italian language copy for *Souvenirs 'Ricordi'*. Phyllis Culos handled the typing assignments in both languages.

87. Correspondence between Marino and Italo Rader, 1935.

88. Excerpt from a news article in *The Vancouver Sun*, circa 1953.

89. Excerpts from an interview with Norma Gallia Porter and an article in *Souvenirs 'Ricordi'*, page 23 and page 35.

90. At the time of the interview, March 18, 1992, Norma Gallia Porter was actively engaged in teaching music and arranging for musical artists to perform in the Vancouver area.

Chapter 13

91. What otherwise might have been a paradox, Francis Federici, by declaring his loyalty to the British Empire as represented by Canada, was stating disapproval of Italy's aggressiveness toward Ethiopia. And yet, he was arrested and briefly interned four years later following Italy's entry into the war as Germany's ally.

92. Correspondence between Marino and the editor of *The Voice of Italy* suggests his main interest was to gain publicity for and/or a review of *Souvenirs 'Ricordi'*.

93. The words "Defend and spread the spirit of Mussolini's Fascist Italy" appeared in issues of *The Voice of Italy*, circa 1936.

94. Excerpts from a letter written by Marino Culos to Dr. I.A. Manecchia, editor of *The Voice of Italy*, dated May 16, 1936.

95. Excerpt from an interview with Emma Lussin Maffei.

In a section-front-featured news item dated Sept. 20, 1935, *The Vancouver Sun* reported, "Canada Cuts Off Italy's Credit." Because of the war scare over the invasion of Ethiopia, Canadian businesses were warned to get cash for any products being exported to Italy.

"Canada Moves Against Italy," was the headline in *The Vancouver Sun*, Oct. 30, 1935. It was stated that Canada would participate in economic sanctions against Italy with 35 other nations as a result of Mussolini's invasion of Ethiopia.

96. The practice of using Roman numerals after the date was adopted by Italy's Fascist government following Mussolini's installation as premier in 1922. The use of this method of recognizing the number of years of Mussolini's government was used by the secretaries employed by Vancouver's Italian vice-consul. Inez Falcioni, Grace Fabri, Emma Lussin and Nellie Pitton were among those Canadian-Italian women—members of the Italian Ladies' League—who had been employed at the Italian consulate's office in the 1930s. There is also evidence that the Sons of Italy used the Roman numerals in some of its correspondence. Under the signature of the secretary (Gregorio Fuoco) and initialled by W.G. Ruocco a letter dated Aug. 29, 1936 carried "XIV" after the date.

97. Dr. G. Brancucci held the rank of lieutenant in the Italian army. Excerpts from *L'Eco Italo-Canadese*, May 26, 1937.

98. A lengthy summary of Pietro Colbertaldo's 'farewell' speech was carried in *L'Eco Italo-Canadese*, May 26, 1937. Other related reference information was taken from a news item appearing in *L'Eco Italo-Canadese*, May 15, 1937.

99. Excerpts from interviews with Mary Pettovello and Emma Maffei. Also excerpts from *L'Eco Italo-Canadese*, May 26, 1937.

100. Excerpt from an interview with Gina Sanvido Benetti. "We were in the production *Cenerentola* with Ada Trevisan playing the leading role of Cinderella. Among the others in this photograph are Teresa Stancato, [Sister] Carmella Stancato, Gloria Papini, Eleanor Canal [the witch], Rina Cimolai, Ines Giuriato, Lino Giuriato, Norma Boraman, Bruna Facchin, Ozzi Panichelli, Winnie Pavan, Elvira Quarin, Lea Faoro, Irma Zamai, Delfina Basso, Gloria Genovese, Isabella Pione. I took the part of a male dancer," recalled Gina Benetti.

Ada Trevisan was crowned Queen of Grandview by the Grandview Community Association, July 10, 1941. In the next day's edition of *The Vancouver Province*, a caption to her photo read in part, "Moments such as these remain long in the memories of young women when they are grown—things they can recount to their gentlemen friends—and mayhap [sic] some day to their grandchildren. Here you see 15-year-old Ada Trevisan being escorted to her throne during the second annual community night at Grandview Park."

101. Excerpt from *L'Eco Italo-Canadese*, May 26, 1937.

102. Ines Falcioni vacationed in Italy during part of 1936. In its April 21 issue, *L'Eco Italo-Canadese* reported that upon arriving in Italy she visited the birthplace of her employer, Pietro Colbertaldo, and was well received by the Italian consul's family there. (Translation) "In Venice she was fortunate to see our beloved *Duce* with his son Romano. *Il Duce* was in Venice for the l'Esposizione Biennale d'Arte art exposition. Falcioni was quoted as saying, (translation) "The railway service is excellent and the ferry service unsurpassable. If Canada could become as disciplined as Italy everything else would follow."

103. Excerpt from separate interviews with Lily Castricano Albo, Elmo Trasolini, and later in conversation with Phyllis Culos.

104. Excerpt from *L'Eco Italo-Canadese*, May 26, 1937.

In an interview with Dave Castricano, who stated that members of the head table shouted "Viva Mussolini, Viva il Duce," which led Castricano to leave the hall with his mother. Mr. Castricano, however, could not confirm for certain that these remarks were uttered at the Colbertaldo dinner party.

The Vancouver Sun, in its story of Oct. 13, 1934, reported that "Pietro Colbertaldo gave an address, concluding with a cheer of *Il Duce*," at a banquet sponsored by the Sons of Italy, Veneta Society and the Vancouver Italian-Canadian Society.

Chapter 15

105. Angelo Branca was not personally interested in elected political office. He feared that should he seek and attain an elected position, his law practice would suffer. The only exceptions to this rule came in 1938 when he was elected to the Vancouver Parks Board and in 1947 when he failed in a re-election bid. This interest in community affairs had been preceded by his involvement as chairman of the Hastings Community Association. It was during his tenure that the association built a community centre made possible by the fund-raising efforts of the Rotary Club. The hall, constructed on acreage across from the PNE, came under the jurisdiction of the Vancouver Parks Board.

106. Excerpt from Girardi's column in *L'Eco Italo-Canadese*, May 26, 1937.

107. As per list of contributors in issues of *L'Eco Italo-Canadese*, circa 1937.

108. An excerpt from an interview with Ines Cappon suggests that her father Luigi Giuriato lost an estimated $6,000 in the ill-fated Star Cabs share purchase.

In addition to Montalban's Star Cabs, several Italians were among those providing a taxi service in Vancouver. These included Alberto Principe (Prince Albert Taxi), Dominic Soda (Avenue Cabs), Sammy De Filippo and Cyril Battistoni (Service Taxi), Art Minichiello and Tommy Paonessa (Safeway Taxi), and Joe Philliponi (Diamond Taxi and Eagle Time Delivery). Other cab companies controlled by Italian businessmen included Venice and Columbia taxi firms. Independent cab owners included Chester Ricci, Johnny Ricci and brothers Benny and Joe Thomas.

109. In conversation with Marino Culos who stated that generally speaking, it was considered correct, if not advisable, for Italian-Canadians active with the Italian community to cooperate with officials such as the Italian vice-consul.

110. Excerpts from *L'Eco Italo-Canadese*, Aug. 7 and Sept. 4, 1937. In an interview with Herman [Erminio] Ghislieri, who had given the eulogy at Marconi's service, he suggested the black shirt was worn solely in response to a request by Brancucci. Whereas, Herman concedes that his father was proudly Italian, he stated categorically that Mario Ghislieri was never a Fascist.

An item regarding the death of Marconi appeared on the editorial page of *The Vancouver Sun* dated July 24, 1937, entitled "Power Walks, Genius Rides," stating "*Il Duce* Mussolini, whose slightest word exacts obedience from all Italy and whose slightest frown makes all Italy tremble, walked behind the carriage, yesterday, that carried the great Marconi to his grave.

"There were those who watched who may have thought that Marconi was greater lying in his coffin than the powerful leader, striding with pomp and arrogance through the streets.

"They may have thought that long after Mussolini is only a disagreeable or even absurd memory, the product of that dead brain going to its last repost [sic] would continue to serve, not only Italy, but all the world.

"It may have occurred to them that years after Mussolini is only a name wherewith to frighten children, youth will grow up through all the earth to marvel at the miracles wrought by the man whose funeral *Il Duce* deigned to honour with his presence."

111. In a conversation with Marino Culos, he stated that he had been approached by Brancucci on a number of occasions to include specific items in his column, "Sidelines", which appeared in *L'Eco Italo-Canadese*, circa 1937.

112. As per a written agreement between Marino and Boccini, circa July 1938. The Memorandum of Agreement regarding the purchase of *L'Eco Italo-Canadese* provided in

item 12 that, "Proper Books of Account shall be kept by the Partners, and entries made therein of all such matters, transactions and things that are usually written and entered in Books of Account kept by persons engaged in concerns of a similar nature, and all books, securities, letters and other things belonging to or concerning the Partnership shall be kept at the Office where the Partnership business is being carried on, and each Partner shall have free access at all times to inspect, examine and copy the same."

113. From notes in the Marino Culos's personal files.

According to a duplicate copy of a Memorandum of Agreement dated Oct. 25, 1938, Marino Culos sold his share of the newspaper, for $200, to Mario Pradolini, a contractor from Revelstoke.

114. In conversations with Marino and Phyllis Culos.

115. Copy in the front page ear-lug, *L'Eco Italo-Canadese*, Aug. 7, 1939, read as follows, "Non dimenticarti sei ITALIANO"—"Direttore: Alberto Boccini."

116. Excerpt from *La Voce Degli Italo Canadesi*, Dec. 16, 1939, page 2.

117. In addition to the Liberal Party advertisements which ran in the March 23, 1940 issue of *L'Eco Italo-Canadese*, ads were placed by the Cooperative Commonwealth Federation (CCF) and National Progressive parties. News items regularly appeared in the Italian-language publication applauding the Italian Fascist regime following Canada's entry into the Second World War. The federal government also ran advertisements in *L'Eco Italo-Canadese*. One such ad ran Jan. 13, 1940. *L'Eco Italo-Canadese* in a front page ear-lug and news item publicized the sale of Victory Bonds through authorized agents Cap. [sic] J.U. Montalban and Mr. Antonio Cianci.

118. Whereas the Venice, Montreal, and National bakeries led in bread and bun products, the finest Italian specialty products were produced by Oreste Notte, who owned and operated the Bon Ton Pastry and Confectionery at 842 Granville Street, "The only Italian pastry and cake shop in Western Canada".

Chapter 16

119.Information obtained during a conversation with Marino Culos and from documents detailing the Christopher Columbus Society socials. One major exception was in reference to the Royal Visit, May 1939, when De Paola led a committee charged with organizing the Italian community's observance of the visit to Vancouver by King George VI and Queen Elizabeth.

120. Excerpt from an interview with Edie Minichiello Harris and in conversation with Pat Minichiello Seabrook.

121. Excerpt from an interview with Lily Castricano Albo, and from society reports regarding the 1934 'Popularity Contest'.

122. Excerpts from an interview with Lily Castricano Albo and a write-up in *Souvenirs 'Ricordi'*, page 20.

123. Excerpts from an interview with Lily Castricano Albo and from a news item in *The Sunday Sun*, Feb. 17, 1934.
Teresa L. Turone's candidacy was sponsored by the Ladies' Branch of YCIAA. Her application was forwarded to the manager of the popularity contest by secretary Tosca Trasolini.

124. The author interviewed the late Betty Alvaro Mansueto for his "Commento di Culos" column which appeared in *L'Eco d'Italia* in June 1979.

125. As detailed in news items which appeared in local newspapers, circa 1934. The Italian Ladies' League representative, Carolina Tonelli, was recognized as queen and her maids of honour were Caterina Fiore, Sons of Italy, and Norma Cecarini, candidate representing the Vancouver Italian-Canadian Society. As part of the Columbus Celebration a sports day was conducted at MacLean Park. Featured were a number of individual and relay races including a four-mile marathon.

126. At Queen Corrine Bland's 1935 coronation her beautifully attired maids of honour provided a spectacular addition to a marvellous crowning ceremony. The ladies-in-waiting were Lina Morelli, Olga Grassi and Lucia Ambrosi.
The Vancouver Sun publicized the upcoming Queen Contest Oct. 3, 1936 with photos of Canal, Piccolo and Pulice. In a front page item on Oct. 13, *The Vancouver Sun* ran a photo of the three contestants, captioned, "Queen of the Vancouver Italian colony, Corrine Piccolo is seen here presiding over the banquet celebrating the 444th anniversary of the landing of Christopher Columbus on the shores of America. In the evening, Miss Piccolo was ceremoniously crowned and presided over the ball from her throne."
Excerpt from *L'Eco Italiana*, Oct. 9, 1936, the date of its first issue.
The item was also reported on page one in *L'Eco Italo-*

Canadese, Sept. 4, 1937. In Marino Culos's article of that issue, the former winners of the queen contests were featured: Clorinda Piccolo, C. Paula Bland, E. Alvaro, Carolina Tonelli and Lily Castricano.

127. Excerpts from an interview with Mary Minichiello Pettovello who recalled the recommendation made by Carlo Marega to have Marino Culos placed in charge of the Italian community's float entry.

128. In conversation with Marino and Phyllis Culos.

129. Excerpt from an interview with Emma Maffei. Also from society papers and local newspaper coverage of the events, Oct., 1936.

130. In conversation with Marino Culos and excerpts from a letter written by Marino to Father Ernest Antoniolli, dated July 7, 1936.

131. Excerpt from an article published in *L'Eco Italo-Canadese*, Oct. 16, 1937. A news item in the Italian newspaper reported, "The famous Italian prima donna, Mdme. Galli-Curci, was greeted by an official reception committee and a host of members of the Italian organizations headed by the Royal Italian vice-consul Dr. G. Brancucci, when she arrived in Vancouver on Thursday, Oct. 7. Many were the compliments paid at this lovely meeting. The noted singer was delighted when she was presented with baskets of flowers by four elegantly gowned tots: Anita Satti, Flora Culos, Florinda Durante and Anita Trevisan."

132. Excerpt from an interview with Emma Lussin Maffei and in conversation with Marino Culos. "[I enjoyed participating in the queen contest] until I think we got a rotten deal. Marino Culos was right there with me. He was the one who stopped the counting of the tickets. 'We have an error.' He was very nice, until we discovered Nellie Santamaria's tickets were in Rosina Signori's packet. What I remember most is a meeting that was called. [We were told] whoever needed more tickets should just call a meeting and more tickets would be issued to you. Everything would be fine. Everything was done correctly by Marino; very much on the ball. And that's when I discovered this error. Just by chance. We found that Rose's tickets went to supporters out of town and 25 books didn't come back. She confided in me and I said, 'You can't claim them.' That's like a lottery. She said, 'My tickets were sent north. So, I figured how could they have sold a thousand dollars worth of tickets when 25 books didn't come back. That's what I said to Marino Culos. I don't know if any tickets went to Trail. All I know they went north. Marino knows. Phyllis knows. We never thought that it could happen."

133. Excerpts from a speech entitled "The Acid Test" written by Marino Culos and read to members of the 1937 Queen Contest Committee. In his remarks, Marino stated that he had discovered that 25 books of raffle tickets of the Veneta' Society's had been given to the Vancouver Italian-Canadian Society's candidate to sell. Apparently, this was done to replace 25 books sent by the VICS to its supporters in Trail, B.C. that were never returned. Following the auditing process, Marino registered a formal complaint to Angelo Branca, the grand committee chairman, and subsequently asked that the VICS candidate be disqualified. "The chairman of the grand committee claimed that we must have faith and believe. Yet, he is the man mostly implicated in this cheap trick.

"Now, morally they [Angelo Branca, Mario Ghislieri and Enrichetta Benetti] are the cause of breaking faith amongst the [committee] members and are the parties responsible for having caused a sensational scandal; one which will not be easily erased.

"I claim that these people acted voluntarily, therefore, they knew plainly what they were doing. They have admitted their guilt but only after being forced to do so."

134. Excerpts from a Letter to the Editor entitled "Spiegazione Della Festa' [Explanation of the Festivity] written by Angelo Branca and published by *L'Eco Italo-Canadese*, Oct.16, 1937. (Translation) Branca did not dispute the fact that 25 books of sold raffle tickets from the Societa' Veneta were among the Vancouver Italian-Canadian Society candidate's receipts. He did offer, however, an accounting of the ticket sales by each society's candidate. His presentation indicated the VICS's candidate had won the queen contest. This was so, because she had turned in $18.75 more in receipts than her closest rival [the Sons of Italy candidate] before taking into account the proceeds from the sales of the 25 books in question. Regarding the alleged irregularities, he reported that the organizing committee met on Oct. 10, to set the record straight. In an attempt to exact a peaceful solution to the impasse and to preserve the good which came of the five societies' cooperative effort in celebrating the Christopher Columbus Day anniversary, Branca, as grand committee chairman, accepted responsibility [for the irregularities]. He stated that notwithstanding this attempt to put an end to the dispute, he [referring to Marino Culos] continued to be "impertinent, irrational, unreasonable and insulting."

135. News item in *The Vancouver Sun*, Oct. 12, 1937 listed the queen and maids of honour, i.e., "Reigns at Columbus Fete Tonight".

136. Excerpts from the programme, printed by *L'Eco Italo-Canadese*, for the Columbus Day celebrations in which a message from each of the presidents was included: W.G.

Ruocco, chairman of the celebrations, and president of the Sons of Italy; Mrs. Rosa Puccetti, president of the Italian Ladies' League; A.E. Branca, president of the Veneta Society; and director Mary Castricano and president Josie Battistoni representing the Giovane Italiane.

Chapter 17

137. Excerpts from the Italian School Board's records, circa 1939.

In a letter dated March 1, 1939, Angelo Branca thanked Marino Culos for his assistance and support in making the Italian school a success.

138. A *L'Eco Italo-Canadese* news item of Jan. 1, 1940 announced that Italian language classes under the direction of Cleofe Forti, assisted by Anita Ghini, would commence in New Westminster. This branch of the Patronato Scolastico Italiano was being sponsored by the New Westminster Italian Mutual Aid Society.

139. Colombo Vagnini, son of Secondo Vagnini, one of the founding members of the Sons of Italy, was physically handicapped. Born in North Vancouver in 1913, Colombo had a passion for writing. He wrote short articles on sports for the *News Herald* and regularly filed his North Vancouver report to the *L'Eco Italo-Canadese*. Also an avid reader, Colombo became an acknowledged expert on Vancouver's history.

140. Colbertaldo announced the impending arrival of Cleofe Forti, a teacher in the Royal Italian school system, in a news release reproduced in *L'Eco Italo-Canadese* Jan. 9, 1937. Her teaching experience and credentials were impressive; she worked in Greece and Egypt before being assigned to Constantinople for six years and in New Orleans for the previous two and a half years.

141. In conversation with Marino Culos and excerpts from news items in *L'Eco Italo-Canadese*. The Sons of Italy's School Committee relinquished much of its involvement when Cleofe Forti arrived on the scene. The language school expenses, including the salary and expenses of its director, were borne directly by the Italian government through the offices of Vancouver's Italian vice-consul.

142. The Italian language classes gold medal recipients for the year ended June 1939-XVII were Gina [sic] Ciccone, Angela Stancato, and Luigi Cecchini [instructress Anita Ghini] and in Cleofe Forti's classes: Rosalia Franceschini, Gina Sanvido, Lino Giuriato, Florence Scoppa, Giuseppina Celli, Ronald Hambleton, Dorothy Skitch,

Valentino Padovan, Elena Munro, Giuseppe Cianci and Rina Bidin. The North Vancouver night class recipient was Colombo Vagnini.

"My sister Marchy and I attended classes in North Vancouver. The school was located upstairs in the I.O.O.F. Hall and Anita Ghini was our teacher. She was young and pretty. She had control of her class but wasn't a slave driver. She never taught us any of the propaganda that was in the reader. She didn't believe in it, as this was Canada that we lived in, and told us what was propaganda," recalled Dorina Boscariol Honey, a silver medalist.

143. Excerpts from interviews with Elio (Al) Maddalozzo and his sister Lina Tesan.

"My brothers were cheeky in an acceptable way," stated Lina Tesan. "The boys would climb the huge folding doors which would make a rattling sound as they opened onto the classroom. The boys would come in one by one and each time call out, 'Buon giorno signorina.' Then bang goes the door. Then two seconds later Elso [Genovese] would come in. Same thing. They drove her up the wall," she smilingly recalled.

"When Ines Giuriato and I, along with another friend Albina, were in Rome in 1951, we met Miss Forti. We went into a little cafe and chatted. She remembered a lot of her former students and certainly had fond memories of having been in Vancouver," concluded Mrs. Tesan.

144. Excerpt from an interview with Jimmy Ricci during which he stated that his uncle Vincenzo [Ricci] after whom he was named, was extremely proud of his progress in learning to speak Italian.

145. In the May 15, 1937 issue of *L'Eco Italo-Canadese* a news item on the front page stated that young people between the ages of 14 and 18 had an opportunity to be guests of the Royal Italian government. Teenagers from B.C., whose fathers worked for the CPR railroad might obtain a rail pass, otherwise they would have to pay the fare to Montreal.

146. *The Vancouver Sun* ran an article with photo, Sept. 13, 1937, headed "Home From Italy." It read as follows, "Guests of *Il Duce*'s government for the past two months, the young ladies above are members of 80 Canadian-Italians who returned to Vancouver Saturday after visiting parents [sic] [relatives] in Italy." The photo pictured Rose Berardino, Edith George and Rina Bidin who arrived ahead of the three Grippo girls. "'So happy and undisturbed, that you'd never know they are on the verge of war,' said Rose.

"'It's a really modern country; I thought Vancouver was modern till I saw Rome,' Rina exclaimed.

"'But we didn't see Mussolini!' was Edith's regret." (Courtesy Pacific Press Library.)

147. Excerpts from interviews with Edith George Salfi and Mary Grippo Stroppa.

148. The references to Cleofe Forti's friendships with Emmy Ragona and Rose Puccetti are from excerpts of interviews with Emmy Ragona and Rinda Dredge. Ragona and Forti travelled together to San Francisco in 1939. Forti was a regular guest at the Puccetti household.

149. Excerpts from a front-page news item in *L'Eco Italo-Canadese*, April 3, 1937.

150. Excerpts from interviews with Jimmy Ricci, Ray Benedetti and Ines Giuriato Cappon.

"We had the cap, the blue shirt, and the dark blue or black tie. We went on—I remember this like it was yesterday—we went on a bus ride. They took us on a picnic and I think we went somewhere, possibly Strawberry Hill or Langley. We had a whole bus load and right after that the war broke out. And that's when they rounded everybody up," recalled Benedetti.

And Cappon added, "I know we had a white blouse, like a shirt, a black skirt, and we had those hats. I think we had to get our own on that—but the hats were all supplied. Like a soldier's hat."

"Our parents belonged to the Lodge [Vancouver Italian-Canadian Society] so, they thought to make the Circolo Giovanile for the younger kids. But I can remember when the war broke out, they had little caps. They had given us little caps and the little tie, and then when the war broke out, they said it was too Italian. So, my mother said, 'Burn them [the club uniform], burn them'," stated another former member.

151. Reference to Ghislieri being president in 1940 is made in *L'Eco Italo-Canadese*, Jan. 18, 1940. The page 2 article headed, "Il Mest Funerale Di Un Ex Combattente" reported on the death of Luigi Nasato, a decorated veteran of the Italian Army, at Essondale, B.C. where he had been resident for five years. His funeral had been attended by Dr. Brancucci, representatives of the Italian Veterans' Association, Canadian Legion Branch from Trail, B.C. and by members of the [Italian] Returned Soldiers' Club.

152. In its Dec. 12, 1936 edition, *L'Eco Italo-Canadese* reported that a new organization, Children of Mary, had been formed. The executive members were E. Barazzuol, president; Bruna Facchin, vice-president; G. [Ella] Ghislieri, secretary; and Dora Giardin, treasurer. A list of founding members followed: "Mary Pepe, Inez Fitzpatrick, Teresa Stancato, Dora Federico, Bertha Woloschuk, Rena Maddalozzo, Lena Maddalozzo, Mary Luporini, Viola Luporini, Violet Shumas, Monica Heath, Betty Tosi,

Eleanor Caravetta, Josephine and Marie Magnola, Mary Mancuso, Emma Pozzobon, Annie Barro, Elda Rigoletto, Emily Comparelli, Victoria Giardin, Armida Pitton, Yolanda Costanzo, Lena Orlandi, Evelyn Piovesan, Mafalda Presto, Marjorie Brady, Angelina Bianchin, Delfina Basso, Nellie Filipone."

153. Excerpts from interviews with Sammy De Filippo and Cyril Battistoni. Details of taxi fares, as printed on society hand-bills publicizing picnics.

154. A significant percentage of the community's members annually attended the three main mutual aid societies' picnics.

In his article dated Feb. 10, 1934, Edgar Brown of *The Province* stated that Vancouver's Italians numbered about 3,300. Dr. William Black, Immigration Liaison Officer with the Canada Citizen Branch estimated that 12,000 Italian immigrants came to British Columbia between 1945 and 1956. *The Sun* reported on March 17, 1962 that, "Today, the flourishing little community in our own East End is home to some 20,000 Italians, some of them Vancouver-born Canadian citizens. In B.C. there are about 70,000." In a news item dated June 17, 1967, the city's Italians were thought to number 30,000.

155. Excerpt from an interview with Armida Pitton Beasley.

Iolanda Pitton with her husband Rino operated The Italian Restaurant, 4411 Main Street. They specialized in preparing home-cooked Italian meals.

The references to Teresa Pettovello are from a conversation with Phyllis Culos and the author's own personal observations.

156. In conversation with Marino Culos. He and Tosca Trasolini had been special friends which is evidenced in part by an engraved ring she gave Marino in the early 1930s. A record of Tosca's athletic achievements is recorded in an article entitled, "La Ragazza Piu' Degna Di Pregio Negli Sports e Nell'Aviazione" in *Souvenirs 'Ricordi'*, page 26.

157. Fred Minichiello provided musical entertainment for the Sons of Italy at picnics, dances, banquets and concerts. For a period of 10 years, he was a substitute accordionist in Charlie Berrettoni's Melody Kings band. "When playing for Charlie you always wore a tux. In the thirties when we worked the Silver Slipper dances, we were paid two dollars each for the night. It was unbelievable," recalled Minichiello.

In 1958, Minichiello was a member of a five-piece band that opened Ross Philliponi's Gold Room at the Penthouse which was co-operated by brother Mickey. "It was a cabaret. We would start at one o'clock in the morning and play until five. We used to host the big names in the entertainment world. These stars would be performing at Sandy DiSantis's Palamar Supper Club or over at the Cave but once they were finished for the evening, they would come to the Gold Room on Seymour Street. Guests would bring their own bottles because serving drinks was illegal in those days. They would put their booze under the table and order soft drinks. And every once in a while the cops would come in and do a little bit of a raid which meant nothing because it was alleged that many of them were getting paid off anyway," concluded Minichiello.

158. Excerpts from interviews with Guerrino Pitton and Gloria Bowe. A photo taken by a commercial photographer of the Bowen Island picnic carries the date which includes the Roman numerals XVII. In the reproduction that is mounted on the wall in the foyer of the Italian Cultural Centre, the date has been obliterated.

159. President of the Lega, Angelina Brandalise and secretary of correspondence co-signed a letter to the Italian Ladies' League and the Italian Young Girls' Club in which members were informed that due to the war, involvement in the Christopher Columbus Day celebrations would be limited to selling raffle tickets and attending the banquet. Although not mentioned specifically, there would be no popularity queen contest that year.

160. In conversation with Phyllis Culos who kept her autographed copy of the printed programme, *Natale Di Roma*, April 1940.

161. In conversation with Phyllis Culos who recalled noticing the 'waiters' making notes and being interested in her programme which had been autographed by many of the important guests.

A local newspaper reported on Nov. 11, 1942, the arrest of Brancucci in New York. The item also made a reference to his tenure as consul in Vancouver. "Consul in this city until war broke out, Brancucci used his diplomatic office to promote a Fascist organization among Italians living in British Columbia, and was active in organizing the National Fascist Party and the Circolo Roma, an Italian Fascist front organization here. In May 1938 [sic], a reporter for the *Advocate*, former labour weekly here, attended a gathering of the Circolo Roma held in Hotel Vancouver, at which Brancucci acted as host to some 50 guests. His story, published in that paper, told of guests wearing NPF buttons, toasting Mussolini and King Victor Emanuele, greeting each other with the Fascist salute. From the gathering the Circolo Roma's banner was sent to Italy as a special gesture."

162. Excerpts from the society's minute book and Marino Culos's printed inaugural address.

163. Names and positions as noted on the committee's stationery, *Comitato Esecutivo Coloniale Italiano, pro festeggiamenti visita LL.MM. Giorgio VI ed Elisabetta d'Inghilterra*.

164. An excerpt from Marino Culos's letter to Eugenio De Paola dated May 23, 1939, the eve of the Royal Visit, read in part, (translation) "As you know, last night's executive meeting ended in a state of confusion. This situation leaves me no alternative but to withdraw my support from any decisions or responsibilities which may be taken in the name of this committee."

Marino Culos, however, did continue to be involved with the committee and attended its meetings of June 7 and 19. But according to the minutes the combativeness continued, (translation) De Paola, referring to himself, stated that he had acted like a gentleman in making decisions regarding expenditures relative to the construction of the viewing stand for the Royal visit. Moreover, he informed the meeting that he had spent some of his own money to advance the cause of the committee's objectives. He then asked those present for a motion to retrieve the committee's minutes as compiled and retained by Marino Culos, secretary of correspondence. It was so moved by F. Comparelli and B. Girardi. Culos spoke against the motion suggesting Eugenio De Paola had conducted the affairs of the committee to his own liking rather than to represent the views of the [Italian] community's appointed committee. De Paola's independent actions, Culos asserted, gave the chairman no right to demand that the minutes be turned over to him. The motion, however, was passed by a majority of the eight members in attendance following which Culos handed over the minutes to Bruno Girardi.

165. An excerpt from an interview with Elisa Martini Negrin.

The Vancouver Sun's story May 31, 1939, was headed, "Italian Colony Shows Loyalty." The copy read in part, "About 1,000 members of the Italian colony here packed a grandstand opposite the CNR depot on Main Street this afternoon and waved and cheered goodbye to the King and Queen, as the Royal procession departed for New Westminster.

"The gaily decorated grandstand was built with money subscribed by members of the colony. Children from various Catholic schools and special positions added their shrill cheers and enthusiastic flag-waving to the patriotic farewell."

166. In conversation with Emma Lussin Maffei.

167. Excerpts from interviews with Elisa Negrin and Anita Panichelli Campbell.

168. An excerpt from Marino Culos's progress report delivered to the Sons of Italy's general membership meeting and reprinted in *L'Eco Italo-Canadese*, Aug. 3, 1939.

In search of a new project, Marino began to research the feasibility of establishing an Italian credit union. In correspondence with The Institute of Industrial Arts, Gardenvale, Quebec, dated July 1939, he informed secretary M.B. Stevenson that the Vancouver Italian community likely would be favourably disposed to the establishment of an Italian Credit Union. Marino reviewed a course of study of credit unions and received information pertaining to the establishment of a credit union for the Vancouver Italian community from the Extension Department of St. Francis Xavier University. When war broke out in September, 1939, however, the idea of establishing an Italian Credit Union was shelved. In addition to Agostino Martin, other prominent *friulani* (immigrants from the Friuli region of Italy) contributed to the Fogolar organization's success, including Peter Olivieri, owner of Olivieri's Ravioli Store.

In a document dated, February 1940 and entitled "La Costituzione Del Consiglio Della Comunita' Italiana" Marino Culos outlined the rationale for establishing an Italian Community Advisory Committee. It proposed that the advisory committee serve as an umbrella organization which would coordinate the educational, cultural, sport, and social affairs of the Italian community and its youth. *Article 2 (9) proposed to create interest in the importance of organizing a Credit Union within the Italian community.*

169. A photograph featured in this publication includes the members of the Sacred Heart School Building Committee.

170. An excerpt from Marino Culos's letter to Father Ernest Antoniolli dated Aug. 17, 1939.

Chapter 18

171. Details of the programme are from the printed banquet menu. The occasion of the 35th anniversary of the Sons of Italy's incorporation was celebrated at the Hastings Auditorium, March 25, 1940.

Included in Marino's remarks at the anniversary banquet was the following reference to the city's newest Italian organization, (translation) "Perhaps the latest organization created that would be of interest to Italians is the Italian Cultural Club. We now have about 20 associations which cater to our needs (including the Circolo Lavoratori Italiani). As you can see, the Italian population of Vancouver doesn't rest. Truthfully, this is a good sign as the history of the Italian portrays him fighting for his rights."

The Italian Cultural Club, Circolo di Cultura Italiana, sponsored a "Serata Artistica" in 1940 featuring a number of performers from the Vancouver Italian community. These included Claudia Fiore, violinist, Dalton Eason, singer and Elena Fiore, pianist. Claudia's recital, as accompanied by her sister Elena, featured the classic "La Capricciosa" di Ries.

172. This document marked "secret" and dated May 29, 1940, was obtained at National Archives Canada: RG18 F3 Vol. 3563 File C11-19-23 (Vol. 1)—"Index—Minister's orders—Italians."

173. Excerpts from minutes compiled and circulated by Marino Culos of the meeting held in the office of Angelo Branca, June 4, 1940.

Angelo Branca often stated publicly that Italian immigrants' loyalty must first be to Canada, their adopted country.

Reporting on the 1936 Christopher Columbus banquet, *The Vancouver Sun* in its Oct. 13 issue quoted Branca, "Italians were the pioneers, not only of the discovery of this continent but in the opening of this province.

"While we maintain a proper pride in our country, we must never swerve in our loyalty to the land we have chosen, and that has become our own."

174. The comment regarding a free trip to Italy was provided by Alice Pasqualini D'Appolonia and her daughter Lina Iacobucci.

175. The situation regarding the RCMP's instructions to the Sons of Italy Society was explained by Marino Culos in conversation with the author. Following a voluntary lifting of the suspension on sponsoring major activities, the society held a members' banquet Dec. 6, 1942. Preparing the menu were Antonio Pitton and Antonio Culos with the assistance of Maria Pontella, Antonia Pitton, and her sister Maria Carretti.

Additional information regarding the speed with which suspected Italian Fascists were arrested is from an interview with Antonietta Marino.

176. From an interview with Nellie Pitton Cavell.

A plaster bust of Mussolini, fashioned by Carlo Marega, was left behind by the fleeing Brancucci. It now rests in the City of Vancouver's Archives offices.

177. On Nov. 11, 1942, a local newspaper reported on the arrest of G. Brancucci by the FBI. "Acting on a presidential

warrant, FBI agents have arrested G. Brancucci, former Italian consul in Vancouver, and are holding him at Ellis Island, it was learned on good authority here this week. The arrest was made at Yonkers, N.Y. last month."

178. In conversation with Marino Culos and excerpts from the Canadian Italian War Vigilance Association of Vancouver's minute book.

179. *The Vancouver Sun*, June 11, 1940, reported, "Benito Mussolini was castigated in a scathing address, the Italian action in entering the war at the side of Germany was repudiated, and allegiance was sworn to the British and Canadian governments at a mass meeting of 300 Canadian-Italians in Hastings Auditorium Monday night."

Also from information obtained during a conversation with Marino Culos.

By Nov. 15, the Canadian Italian War Vigilance Association of Vancouver had received $2,064 in contributions. In addition to $1,550 collected in Greater Vancouver, $171 came from Port Alberni, $65 from Cumshewa Inlet, and $22 from Goldbridge, B.C. During the same period donations were made to Vancouver Air Supremacy ($1,000), Canadian Red Cross ($250 plus $65 to the Cumshewa, $176 to the Port Alberni and $22 to the Goldbridge units). The Vancouver Symphony Association was sent $100 for its Barbirolli Concert for the Red Cross.

180. The list of persons* arrested and/or detained under the War Measures Act was obtained at National Archives Canada under the provisions of the Access to Information Act. Also excerpts from a diary maintained by Marino Culos and from data obtained from the society's minute book, circa June and July 1940.

*Rino Baesso, Alberto Boccini, Cirillo Braga, Guido Caldato, Carlo Casorzo, Antonio Cianci, Felice Cillis, Frank Comparelli, Leonardo D'Alfonso, Rosario De Rico, Angelo Dotto, Alemando Fabri and his son Ennio Victor Fabri, a lawyer practicing in Trail, Onorato Facchin, Secondo Faoro, Frank Federici, Gregorio Fuoco and his brother Vincenzo Fuoco, Mario Ghislieri, and sons, Fred Ghislieri, and Erminio Ghislieri, Bruno Girardi and brother Attilio Girardi, Antonio Granieri, Giuseppe Grimaldi, Aristodemo Marino, Oliver Marino and brothers Olivio and George Marino, *Cav.* Vincenzo Masi, Emilio Muzzatti, Alex Navarro, Piero Orsatti, Santo Pasqualini, Eugenio Pavan, Italo Rader, Vincenzo Ricci, Angelo Rita, W.G. Ruocco, his brothers Angelo Ruocco and Pietro Ruocco, Nino Sala, and Salvatore Valente and his brother Pasquale Valente.

181. Excerpt from an interview with Lina Pasqualini Iacobucci. "The RCMP had come into our house and had taken my dad away."

182. Excerpt from an interview with Lina Pasqualini Iacobucci.

183. A letter dated June 1942, is part of a collection of duplicate copies of correspondence initiated by Marino Culos on behalf of Santo Pasqualini to creditors and government officials. A copy of Marino's letter to Mr. E. Arpin, Comptroller to Assistant Deputy Custodian, Victoria Building, Ottawa, dated July 26, 1943, "Re File 5201, S. Pasqualini", as edited by Custodian officials, was obtained from National Archives Canada (Access to Information Act).

184. Excerpts from an interview with Herman Ghislieri.

185. The author interviewed Nino Sala, June 1979, excerpts of which were published in "Commento di Culos" in *L'Eco d'Italia*.

186. Excerpt from an interview between Antonio Cianci and newspaper contributor M. Ciavolella which appeared in the July 5, 1966 issue of *L'Eco d'Italia*.

187. An excerpt from an interview with Herman Ghislieri.

188. In a low-key letter to the Italian Ladies' League co-signed by Marino Culos, president, and Felice Cianci, secretary of correspondence and finance, the subject of W.G. Ruocco having been elected Director for Life of the Lega came into question. Mr. Ruocco, incarcerated at Kananaskis Internment Camp for the past five months, had been suspended from the Sons of Italy Society. Up to that date, the president of the men's lodge automatically served as director. This move on the part of the Lega affiliated with Sons of Italy may well have been a sincere show of support for the founding director but Marino found it an awkward situation.

The incident regarding the removal of furniture which had been stored at the Hotel Europe, Dora Ruocco's resignation as an officer of the Italian Ladies' League, and the sale of the piano to Sacred Heart Church Parish are documented in the society's minute book, Lega's minute book, and by notes in Marino Culos's file of correspondence.

189. *The Vancouver Sun* carried a news item on the death of Angelo Calori who was predeceased by his wife Teresa Jan. 12, 1934. "A pioneer of Vancouver, Angelo B. Calori, 79, builder and former operator of the Europe Hotel, Powell Street, died at his home at 1281 Barclay Street.

"Mr. Calori was born in Italy in 1860, came to Victoria in 1882 and four years later to Vancouver to commence construction of the Europe Hotel. In 1890, the success of his venture forced him to make a large addition to the hotel and a further concrete addition was made in 1908. This was the first concrete structure in Vancouver."

190. Details of Angelo Calori's will are found in a document marked "secret" (obtained under the provisions of the Access to Information Act) dated Jan. 6, 1941 written by the RCMP which show the family connection between W.G. Ruocco and Victor Fabri.

191. A copy of a letter, obtained under the Access to Information Act, was sent by Santo Pasqualini to his wife from Kananaskis Internment Camp Feb. 8, 1941. It appears to have been written by Victor Fabri.

192. From written material as supplied by Herman Ghislieri.

193. A letter from the RCMP to the Acting Minister of Justice dated 1/12/41 re Rino Baesso was obtained at National Archives Canada RG 18 F3 Vol. 3563 File C11-19-23 Vol. 5—Minister's Orders—Italians. (This and all other material obtained under the Access to Information Act was researched by Beth Brooks specifically for the author.)

194. From information sources at the National Archives in Ottawa as obtained for the author by researcher Beth Brooks.

195. Gabriele Iacobucci, a member of the Sons of Italy, lost his job the day Italy declared war.

Whereas Pietro Culos buried his double-barrel shotgun under his front porch, many other Italians surrendered their firearms. "My father had to take this very rifle to the RCMP and have it registered. After the war, he claimed it. I've kept it ever since," stated Ernie Maddalozzo.

196. The memorandum marked 'Secret' Re 'Aristodemo Marino, Vancouver, B.C.' in which references are made to Angelo E. Branca, Barrister, was obtained under the terms of the Access To Information Act by researcher Beth Brooks for the author at National Archives Canada. RG 18 F3 Vol. 3563 File C11-19-2-3 (Vol 1) Index—Minister's orders—Italians.

197. In a news item headed, "B.C. Italians Wait to Aid Countrymen," the local press quoted Marino Culos as saying, "We would welcome a decision made by the Italian people for a separate peace. We know they are tired of being governed by a type of people who have contaminated and profaned the life of the country. We have watched this movement coming for a long time.

"In Africa Italian soldiers willingly allowed themselves to be captured by the British and they will not even fight in their homeland because they have nothing to fight for.

They are closer to the British and Americans than they are to the Germans.

"We Canadians are looking forward to that time when we will be able to help our old countrymen get back to a sound national policy."

198. Excerpts from a "secret" RCMP document to the Minister of Justice and Attorney General for Canada, dated July 12, 1940, regarding, "The Release From Internment of Francesco FEDERICI, Vancouver, B.C." was obtained at National Archives Canada. RG18 F3 Vol. 3563 File C11-19-2-3 (Vol. 1) Index—Minister's orders—Italians.

199. Excerpts from a "secret" RCMP document to the Minister of Justice and Attorney General for Canada, dated July 25, 1940 regarding, "The unconditional release from internment of Pietro RUOCCO, Vancouver, B.C." was obtained at National Archives Canada. RG 18 F3 Vol. 3563 File C11-19-2-3 (Vol. 1) Index—Minister's orders—Italians. (All information obtained at the National Archives in Ottawa was researched by Beth Brooks specifically for the author.)

Chapter 19

200. Marino Culos's diary contains scores of entries related to the Sons of Italy, members interned and personal observations, especially during the years 1941–1943:

1941

August

5 Nino Sala returned from the internment camp on Aug. 5, 1941. Society refunded $6 [credit on dues paid prior to his internment] as requested by him.

29 Father Bortignon dropped in to see us [Marino and Phyllis Culos's home]. He related that the Church required $500 by October 1st to meet mortgage interest. He had asked Mrs. Trasolini to influence the Lega to hold a bingo night. She accepted. I promised to get the society to help. C.I.M.A. [Vancouver Italian-Canadian Mutual Aid Society] would also be asked.

October

4 L. D'Alfonso returned from the internment Camp (Ontario).

November

22 This morning by CPR, eight members of those interned returned home: I. Rader, A. Rita, A. Cianci, F. Comparelli, Marino, P. Orsatti, A. Fabri, M. Muzzatto [sic]. Telephoned Comparelli—was resting; A. Rita—out; Cianci—Twice—last time was resting.

December

11 [After three days following Japan's entry into the war] Blackout—lifted on Thursday Dec. 11, 1941.

15 This morning more internees came home: Charlie Braga, Angelo Ruocco, Patsy Valente, Jimmie Fuoco.

16 Other internees who arrived home from Petawawa, Ontario this morning were W.G. Ruocco, Caldato, B. Facchin, Dotto, Secondo Faoro, Cillis, Bruno Girardi. At 6 p.m. I phoned W.G. Ruocco. Mrs. Ruocco answered—to my question she answered that he was home and tired. She would tell him that I had phoned.

21 Called on Secondo Faoro. He was very reserved in his manner towards me. He received me favorably.

Understand that Ennio V. Fabri has returned from the Internment Camp, Petawawa, Ont. around Dec. 21–31, 1941.

25 Rosario [De Rico] and Attilio Girardi [returned from internment].

1942

January

24 Special meeting at Branca's re benefit plans for Sacred Heart School. Miss Corra, N. Di Tomaso, Branca, M. Culos. Mrs. Trasolini absent. Spoke to Angelo in regards to Santo Pasqualini (interned). He asked me to bring Mrs. Pasqualini to his office.

26 Made appointment with Branca—for Mrs. Pasqualini. Called—he took down the particulars in reference to Santo's case and promised to do his best to have him released.

27 Attended the meeting of the Lega—by invitation—officers installed. Much argument in reference to the director [W.G. Ruocco]. Mr. W.G. Ruocco's letter re invitation thanks everyone and states that "for the time being he was unable to take any active part." Mrs. Trasolini appointed to ask him his intentions re directorship.

March

1 F.d'I. meeting. V. Sabatini, Sec. of Fin. and A. Comparelli, Sec. of Corr. Only 10 at the meeting. Antonio Cianci accepted [as] member.

10 Sent letter to Deputy Minister of Justice, Ottawa, re Pasqualini from Richards, Akroyd & Gatt Ltd. Thornthwaite J.D. showed to Alice—pleased.

Boccini and V. Ricci released from Internment. Now in Ontario—(Toronto)?

April

13 Madam Boccini came in to the Strand Hotel to see me—informed me that she going to leave for Montreal on Tues., April 21. Asked for favor, as she had no money—[gave her a small loan].

22 Sent letters re credit of $6 [dues paid] to W.G. Ruocco, F. Comparelli, C. Casorzo. Met Piero Orsatti at Strand Hotel—Was particularly cool towards me.

27 Advisory Committee re internees. Telegram to Anderson, Ottawa to instruct Chairman to hear evidence. Answer through Chairman O.K. for Pasqualini's case at 2 p.m., April 28.

28 Hearing by Commissioner at 2 p.m.—A.E. Branca, Mrs. Pasqualini, M. Culos, J.W. McJannet, J.W. Murray, Geo. Jones, and L. Zanon. Very fair hearing.

Lega meeting—fuss about Director [W.G. Ruocco]—no more discussion.

May

20 Blackout—10 to 10:40 p.m.

26 Lega had their regular meeting at Mrs. Gazzola's. Whist Drive held with proceeds to Italian families who are in need. Friday, Mrs. Pasqualini informed us that she had received $5.50 from Lega—but through Father Leonard [Della Badia].

June

1 Called on R.W. Lane, legal dept., Compensation board, re Pasqualini—No 21909-6—assessment for 1940 prior to October—$4.57. Left for couple months or until Pasqualini is released.

3 Saw Alice [Pasqualini] re Compensation Board.

7 Meeting S.F.d'I. Only nine present—10 when Falcioni came almost at the finish. Letters to be written to parties re Cemetery. Letters to suspended members re time limit for re-admission. Pasqualini: letter and doctor's certificate to Deputy of Justice, Ottawa, airmail. Understand that Alice P. has been taken to Hospital by Dr. Ragona.

9 Phoned Father Leonard re Alice Pasqualini—she was in Ward X of Gen. Hosp. for observation. Children may be taken care of by the Children's Aid and that he was looking for some family to take care of them.

Phoned Trasolini to give whatever assistance she could [for Mrs. Pasqualini] which she promised.

14 Called special meeting of directors including Gino, Felix, and Armando.

Prepared questionnaire re Supt. of Insurance, Victoria. 90 members—35 at Annual Meeting.

Then—re members who were interned. Decided to write again and explain everything to them—time expires Aug. 5th.

They were very sad when I related to them that Mrs. Pasqualini was taken to Ward X, Gen. Hospital by Dr. Ragona.

After reviewing Constitution, little good could be done financially.

18 Arranged with Dr. Ragona to see Mrs. Pasqualini, at the Gen. Hosp. She was in bed. She was in bed—shook hands with me and asked for Santo.

28 Phyllis visited Alice—Gen Hosp. in another room—feeling much better.

29 Wrote to Santo—Petawawa.

July

5 Wrote to Supt. of Companies [re Santo's Paris Bakery affairs].

F.d'I. Meeting—good attendance. Six months—gain of $119.

8 Dr. Ragona phoned for me. Met him at his office at 12:30 p.m. He explained that Mrs. Pasqualini was not doing so well. No word had been received from Santo or the Advisory Board as to his release or detention . Sent night telegram to Ottawa—explaining her position—two children—home—release or otherwise.

12 In the afternoon, Mr. & Mrs. Minichiello took us to the General Hosp. The nurse refused to let us see Alice [Pasqualini]. This is the third time that I was not allowed to see her. Her condition is not so good.

13 Monday, July 13, 1942. Santo Pasqualini arrived at 9:10 a.m. by CPR from Petawawa Internment Camp, Ontario. He looks well—his hair is greyer. At the station to welcome him were Cecilia [Zanon], M. [Maria] Scodeller, H. Ghislieri, F. Ghislieri, Muzzatto, Santo's little boy and girl, my wife and I—also Patsy Valente. We drove to his home where he had a cup of coffee. He changed his clothes. Got in touch with Dr. Ragona who desired to be at the hospital to note Alice's reaction when she sees him.

Phyllis phoned Cecilia who on being asked, told her that Alice did not say much—she asked Santo—"How are the children and will you stay here?"

15 Took Santo to Social Service Dept., 530 Cambie, Room 6. Then unemployment office—then to Post Office for National Registration Card, Room 216. O.K. We got to the RCMP's at 12:25 p.m. and were late as they were all at lunch. Left Santo and returned [to work].

Santo came in and was very tired. He had been humiliated by those at the Unemployment Offices. They had made fun of him because he was an internee.

19 Santo came in to tell us that Alice would come out of the hospital at 2 p.m.

Phyllis made a call on them and found Alice anxious to please and in a happy mood.

26 After dinner Santo and Alice with Maria

Scodeller were in. Santo, Alice and I discussed Bakery affairs.

27 Phoned Price and Waterhouse, Marine Bldg.—re Alien Property—Santo was told to instruct that Mrs. Pasqualini was looking after affairs and that Santo could do the best he could.

August

2 S. of I. meeting—10 present. Usual affairs. No answers from suspended members. Amendment by Sabitini and seconded by G. Marino "That suspended members over 50 yrs. should be approached by a committee."—No support [motion rejected]. Those members have shown that they do not want to participate in the Society and therefore are considered as members 'morosi' [in default]. Registered letters to be mailed to each one to that effect and money to be refunded to those who had paid dues in advance.

7 Letters to Ruocco, F. Comparelli, C. Casorzo, C. Braga, R. Baesso, S. Faoro, V. Fuoco, G. Sala, E. Muzzatti, Angelo Rita, and P. Valente—have been prepared and ready to mail—registered. Mailed seven on the 10th and four on the 11th. These members because they preferred to keep silent after being advised, will lose their privileges as members and will be cancelled off our rolls.

September

1 Bordignon and I called on W.G. Ruocco. We received shares and copies of the constitution sent to the Registrar of Companies when application for incorporation was made. I asked him if he was absolutely definite as to his wish "not to be a member of the society," to which he answered that he had no choice in the matter. I asked whatever made him think so when he had received three letters from us asking him to return and including in them full details of our position. Among other things he admitted rather reluctantly that the society had done its duty by continuing to write to him and that he should have acknowledged the correspondence. He claims that the disturbing factor in his mind was that he was "convicted" of doings that he claimed he was not responsible—that he was held in "probation."

I invited him to come to the meeting of Sunday the 6th and assured him of a good reception and further that I would prove to his satisfaction that action was taken according to rules in the constitution in a large degree—further that we "convicted" him of nothing.

4 Toni Rita died today in Calgary. S.M.S.F.d'I.'s records show that he was paid to April—four months in arrears. No mortuary benefits.

5 Mr. & Mrs. F. Rita were in to find out if A. Rita,

deceased, was still a member of the S.M.S.F.d'I. He was four months in arrears and therefore out of the organization.

Rita asked if a registered letter was mailed to him. The Sec. of Fin. had not mailed thinking members who paid 25 cents a month did not fall within that rule. He seemed hurt and suggested that I tell this to someone else. I could not see his point. I challenged him. This made it worse. I explained that regardless of the letter anyone who fell two months in arrears with the society automatically lost all rights for benefits.

This, however, did not seem to satisfy him. I expressed my feelling towards him by inquiring as to what was in his mind. He said that the society must be a one-man affair. I resented this and hit back that it was putting his own approved clauses into effect and that he, Ruocco and others were alike when it came down to a showdown.

6 S.M.S.F.d'I. meeting today. Ruocco was not present but he sent a letter to the secretary. Admits that he was in wrong for failing to acknowledge the letters mailed to him. He states that we did not do the right thing by suspending him after he was interned, or at least it was not within the scope and power of constitution—he could not return as a member—at least not for the present—however, in all regards, he considered the matter entirely closed.

7 Saw Rita's body—very thin.

8 A. Rita's funeral. 9 a.m.—Armstrong's [Funeral Directors]—Franciscan Monastery—Oceanview Cemetery. Not many present.

9 Spoke to Nick [Di Tomaso] about society's problems. He tells me that he has taken a 'respite' for three months. Things did not seem so good. Discussed internees.

17 Called on A. [Armand] Comparelli, inquired re Rita. Rita boasted that in him the society has a man "who knows [how to apply the provisions of the constitution to support his case]," to contend with. He demanded that the society's books be shown to him. He asked what was considered in the matter concerning the Death Benefit which in his opinion, the society should pay. Comparelli answered that it was found that A. Rita was four months in arrears and that because of that he lost all privileges and benefits allowed to members. Rita remarked that A. Rita [his brother] was paid to July. That the society constitution calls for such a notice and because the society failed in this matter he (Rita) was going to sue the society for $1,000 (or would be liable for that amount).

October

4 F. d'I. meeting. It was rather a confusing one.

First, because the secretary had not stated in the minutes that A. Rita, before his death, had been four months in arrears with his dues. Second, P. Rita sent a registered letter to the society stating among other matters, the society should not overlook its last obligation towards its members and that the funeral allowance should be paid to him because of his brother's death Sept 4.

A committee [is struck] to hear F.P. Rita's points—Bordignon, Comparelli, Caravetta, Culos—Hastings Auditorium, Oct. 11, 1 p.m.

5 Met F.P. Rita as I was coming out of Metropolitan Ins. office. We shook hands. I told him that the society had appointed a committee to review his case—A. Rita. He was pleased to know we would consider it.

11 Met Piero Orsatti. A very interesting general discussion was enjoyed. He expressed his willingness to join the F.d'I. He further promised to allow his student Donati to sing for the benefit of the society at some future date.

14 Registered today at RCMP.

17 Got in touch with Mr. Robertson, manager of the Ogilvie Flour Mills in Van., and made arrangements to see Pasqualini. The three of us met at the Strand [Hotel] and discussed the matter of Santo giving his two trucks to the creditors in return for a clean sheet from them. Debts are $806.

21 Completed arrangements with Mr. D.C. Robertson and Pasqualini to sell cars to DeWolfe Mtrs. If it had not been for my interference [*intervention*] Santo would have sold the Chev [for less]. Hope this may be Santo's turning point—that is—be just a bit more fortunate.

24 The offer for $1,000 for Santo's two trucks blew up in our faces. We are advised that DeWolfe Motors Ltd. [600 Burrard Street] did not make the offer but that it was only an estimate. Santo left the whole matter with Jack McJannet.

26 Was told that Walter Winchell in the news broadcast from New York said that Dr. Giuseppe Mario Brancucci was arrested by the FBI as a Nazi spy. [This was] Verified on Tues.

28 Arranged meeting with Jack McJannet. Discussed plans re sale of Santo's trucks.

November

1 This morning at 10, a large number of members of the Lega and Figli d'Italia attended the Sacred Heart Church where Father Della Badia celebrated Mass especially for the deceased members of the Societies.

29 Went to see F.P. Rita—discussed—$135 funeral benefit—A. Rita. He believes this case to be unique—an exception and should be treated accordingly. I was firm in the conviction that A. Rita did not pay his

dues and was almost four months in arrears...He said I was prejudiced that it was not wise for the society to get into a lawsuit as it was considered an alien organization—that a judge may see things different and if so it would cost a lot more to the society.

December

6 S.M.S.F.d'I. meeting—among the important affairs discussed was a letter from F.P. Rita. Rita asked that the members make a motion to put the payment of the funeral benefit—A. Rita—to a vote by secret ballot. His reason for this was that this was an exceptional case and that it should be treated accordingly. He also states that there was one person among the committee who was prejudiced. The members decided to leave the matter in the hands of the Special Committee.

1943

January

1 3Just returned from the RCMP office—it was the last time I need report as an Alien. Following government orders which were published in the newspapers on Dec. 24, 1942—restrictions which had been imposed upon Italians who had not been naturalized before 1922, were then withdrawn. Constable Nuttall and Constable Rothmell had been good in every sense of the word in so far as their duty was concerned.

23 Wrote to Father Bortignon at All Souls' Rectory, 21 Barton St. W., Hamilton. [Father Bortignon had been removed from Vancouver for allegedly expressing pro-fascist views. *Author*]

February

12 I am told that M.V. Ghislieri returned home after spending nearly 33 months in the internment camp. In my opinion, he was an Italian Patriot and felt that fascism had accomplished much in Italy. He was an *ex-combattente* [Italian veteran of WWI].

28 Santo came in to tell me that he would join the F.d'I. I am very glad that he decided to come in.

April

4 S.M.S.F.d'I. meeting at 1:30. About 15 members were present. Of importance was the suspension of John Crosetti because he had been drafted in the army. Crosetti had been drafted in February and subsequently the society executive suspended his membership under the Military Service provision. However, Crosetti failed his medical and was given full discharge by the military March 8. Today, he was reinstated as a member of the society in good standing.

May

6 I am told that Gregorio Fuoco had been released from the internment camp about 10 or 15 days ago.

10 F. Cianci asked me if I had received a briefcase and envelopes from the RCMP when I got the society's property back] as Gregorio Fuoco told him that I had and I had signed (in black and white) for them. I wrote the RCMP for a copy. Left copy at Cianci's—Fuoco was wrong.

June

11 Mrs. Pasqualini was taken to the hospital.

14 Santo Pasqualini is upset because of a bill he must pay to the Custodian of Alien Property.

22 Called on Mr. Wright—Custodian of Alien Property offices in the Royal Bank Bldg. in reference to charges made to Pasqualini of $30.25 for administration in connection with investigation of the management of his business—Wrote to E. Arpin, Victoria Bldg., 7 O'Conor St., Ottawa for particulars.

26 Mrs. Pasqualini came home from the hospital where she had been for two weeks. She feels a lot better.

July

25 My [39th] birthday today. News over the radio announced that Mussolini resigned—Badoglio, Military Leader, is Premier.

August

1 United Nations Picnic. The Italian Group had a kitchen set up in the Picnic Grounds of the Confederation Park. A sign, "Anti-Fascist spaghetti" was quite conspicuous.

8 Pasqualini received settlement of her own accounts—Creditors receive 83%, Pasqualini 17%.

September

8 Italy surrendered—unconditionally—the Germans are enemies of the Italians.

October

13 Today, Premier Badoglio announced the declaration of war against its [sic] former ally—Germany. Marshall Rodolfo Graziani, war minister in Mussolini's Fascist Republican government, had arrived at Hitler's headquarters.

December

19 Vincenzo Ricci [former internee from Vancouver] arrived in the city this afternoon. Phyllis went to see him at his brother's where he is staying. He looks well and prefers Montreal to Vancouver. He

is in some sort of co-partnership with Olivio Marini [sic] [also a former internee from Vancouver].

25 Phyllis and the boys went to church—Orsatti sang Ave Maria "beautifully."

1944

January

9 Joe Politano, Centro, and Ottavio Bevilacqua formed a committee known as the 'Nuovi Membri'. Recommendations: open doors for those who were interned—compensate members who bring in new members—raise age of 'Morosi' to 45—to use [award] shield as a boost for competition.

29 We attended Santo's birthday party at his home—we all had a great time.

30 Attended a bingo and cards at Nellie's (Pitton) re fund for parcels to be sent to boys and girls in the service [Canadian Armed Forces]—sons or daughters of members of the Lega or the society.

February

14 Called on Armand Comparelli and after talking for a few moments, he asked me quietly if I knew Mario Ghislieri. Of course, I did. I went to where Ghislieri was sitting reading a newspaper and extending my hand towards him, [I] cordially asked him how he was. Without looking away from the paper he answered, "Fine, thank you." Because he did not attempt to see my hand, I asked him if he was afraid to take it to which he answered, "What?" He seemed to snub him [sic] and moving my hand, I made certain that he understood what it was there for—no dice—so I called him 'a disappointing fool.'

March

5 Mr. W.G. Ruocco came to the meeting of the F.d'I. He had been extended a written invitation by the Pres. and Directors to attend a meeting so that he could satisfy himself as regards motions made while he, with others, was interned and which placed him as a "membro in periodo di sospensione." He was not too friendly and he annoyed me when he kept on repeating that we had kicked him out. He began with—"If at the time of this incident, I were the president, I would 'probably' have acted in the same manner but...After much discussing and at times use of strong meaning words—he stated that he had been "offended" and that for his satisfaction, we should allow him to "come in" without the medical certificate. He [then] left. We decided that we could not grant his demand and wrote him to that effect. I don't expect him back.

We finally sold the Society's shares [in the Hastings Auditorium] to the Sons of Norway for $300 cash. Present were Mrs. Trasolini for the Lega and Bordignon, Caravetta and I for the Society.

201. In a written statement, Marino Culos informed the general membership regarding the rationale leading to the suspension of interned members. He stated that, (translation) "The question under examination is not whether the members interned are guilty of being a threat to the state or whether their arrest under the Canada Defence Regulations was justified. We did not know the reason then nor do we understand today the reason they suffered this humiliation. However, we have known from the beginning that we would be unable to communicate with these [interned] members [in order to obtain the answers to these questions].

"When a person is interned in a concentration camp [sic] he is considered a prisoner of war. These camps are under the jurisdiction of the military. One who is so interned does not have the freedom that a [Canadian] soldier is able to enjoy. Therefore, if we can rule that a member [of this society] who is a soldier [in the forces] cannot continue to be a member, how can we permit one who is interned to continue to receive benefits from the society? This rationale is the reason we have enforced the article [of the constitution under which suspensions are allowed].

"And because these members, estimated to be 15, are unable to defend themselves, we will in good faith permit them to be reinstated once they have been set free from the camp. I believe, therefore, that this point of clarification constitutes our legal and constitutional position and that the members in question are not being expelled from the society."

202. In conversation with Phyllis Culos and excerpts from the society's minute book.

203. The information regarding "zombies" was provided by one of the enlistees, now deceased, who stated that he was one of those prepared only to defend the shores of Canada from a possible invader.

204. The Italian Ladies' League received a thank-you note from most of the recipients of the soldiers' care packages. Not all recipients of the gift packages knew the source of the parcels. However, in the case of R.J. Bordignon— K8715—he was very aware that the gift had come from the Lega. In his letter dated March 29, 1945, he wrote in part, "You do not know how much it means for us fellows in the services to know that the lodge has not forgotten us and we appreciate it very much when we receive a parcel from you."

Another thoughtful note was sent by Pte. E.G. Coello— K15677—in March 1944. An excerpt from his letter reads,

"Although we servicemen that are in Canada at present, are not in need as those in different theatres of combat. The parcels we do receive, however, are deeply appreciated. It sure is nice to be back in Canada again after spending six months on the desolate island of Kiska, we did not encounter the 'Japs' but it was a great experience, and our little job was done without warfare or any bloodshed through battle."

The list of service personnel to whom parcels were sent include, Overseas: Jos. R. Donati, Louis E. Braga, Albert C. Braga, Ernest G. Coello, Bruno Gazzola, P. Mauro, A. (Tony) Mauro, Victor Mauro, Elmo S. Trasolini, Norman S. Trasolini, R. Pontella, D.B. Raino, C.E. Trono, Arthur N. Rita, Eugene S. Paone, Silvio Ruocco and brother Victor Ruocco [died on Active Duty]; and in Canada: Pte. Fonce Pulice, Mario Caravetta, Orlando V. Caravetta, Frank Amato, L.T. Guessie, F.J. Rita, Reno J. Marino, R.J. Bordignon, Alfonse L. Galetti, Gino V. Ciccone, A.L. Galette, L.L. Gallazin, J. Bruzezi, G.L. Tha, C.F. Mitchell, Frank Mazzocca, Charles A. Spatari, Henry Dickman, A.P. Battistoni, Leandro Battistoni, Romeo Bianco, Archie Comparelli, Robert Bevilacqua and his twin Albert Bevilacqua. Fulvia Trasolini, attached to U.S. Intelligence, was the sole female on the list.

For a majority of those stationed in Canada, the war ended before their units could be sent to the front. In the case of the Robert Bevilacqua, who was 18 years old when answering his call in 1945, he trained first for the European theatre and then for the Japanese war but missed both when the enemy surrendered.

Chapter 20

205. Excerpts from an interview with Bruno Girardi and his son Attilio.

206. Joe Politano was a very active member of the Sons of Italy. He was an executive member for decades during which time he handled the treasurer's portfolio. He set records for the number of new members he brought into the society. Marino Culos estimated that Politano signed up a total of 130 new members during his tenure on the membership committee.

207. When the Sons of Italy established a junior membership designation, several of the active members sponsored their sons as members of the society. At a banquet held in 1945 a number of these junior members were recognized.

The Vancouver Italian-Canadian Society organized a special youth group in 1937 which attracted scores of young members.

208. The author, six weeks from his ninth birthday, was the youngest person to join the society's juvenile division. Culos was inducted with his brother Victor, March 4, 1945, the day he turned 10.

209. *The Voice of Italy* ran a major take-out on the occasion of Sacred Heart Church officially becoming an Italian parish Sept. 27, 1936. An excerpt from the original article, probably submitted by Marino Culos, the New York newspaper's Vancouver representative, deals with a sensitive language issue involving Rev. William Blackburne, pastor and Mitred Abbot, Ernesto Antoniolli. "[In 1934] Rt. Rev. Abbot Antoniolli, without any pretence of compensation, that is gratuitously, assumed the burden of directing the welfare of the Italian Catholics, in cooperation with the local English-speaking pastor [at Sacred Heart Parish].

"Misunderstandings arose between the two Reverend Fathers who had the spiritual charge of the parish people. The Italians wanted their own pastor for baptisms, marriages and funerals. If this could not be done, ill feelings and disorders arose which were supported by the Abbot with taciturnity and prudence.

"After mature and serious deliberation, Abbot Antoniolli saw and was convinced that things could not proceed in a satisfactory manner and that all the good accomplished by him would be frustrated. Lacking any official or canonical authority in the matter and jurisdiction over the Italians, he called together at different times prominent persons of the Colony*, explaining to them the condition of affairs and the impossibility of proceeding in this way, and a way of escape had to be found, if the desired end was to be obtained."

The issue was resolved when Rev. Joachim Bortignon, an Italian citizen, was appointed pastor in 1936. In the process the Diocesan priests, of which Father Blackburne was a member, were replaced by the Stigmatine Fathers and the Franciscan Friars established at a new parish. Father Blackburne was "promoted to one of [Vancouver's] principal parishes" and the 71-year-old Abbot Antoniolli left for New Orleans, Louisiana before being transferred to Canon City, Colorado. The article concluded with, "The eternal question of the Italian Church [in Vancouver], which was hanging for more than 30 years was solved and everybody was satisfied, a thing which happens very rarely in this world. '*Chi si contenta gode*' (Who is satisfied, rejoices.)"

* A special meeting was held May 1, 1936 at the Sacred Heart Rectory. Marino Culos's notes are as follows: "It is clearly understood that no friction exists or has ever existed between Father Blackburne and Father Abbot Antoniolli. Though there may have existed possible misunderstandings owing to the fact that Father Abbot does not understand or speak the English language well.

"It is understood that Father Abbot has Father Blackburne's approval on any religious ceremonies such as baptising, marriages or funerals, though it is necessary to inform Father Blackburne of any such service beforehand.

"That a jurisdiction for Father Abbot over the Italian members of the Sacred Heart Parish could not be arranged as such a jurisdiction would naturally not be for the best interests.

"By granting to Father Abbot such privileges it would mean that the church services must be given in English and in Italian. This would mean a division of the services and past experiences have shown this to be very unsatisfactory and therefore conflicts with a rule supported by the churches.

"It is definitely understood that Father Blackburne has the absolute jurisdiction over all the territory confined to the Sacred Heart Parish.

"Assistantship [having the position of assistant to the pastor] was interpreted as being unfair to Father Abbot owing to his holy position as Abbot Mitrate of the St. Benedictine Order. It would not, however, give him jurisdiction as the assistant receives his instructions from the priest in charge of the parish.

"To nationalize a church (if it were possible) would mean that another church for the English-speaking peoples would be necessary in the same parish. However, in this particular case, Father Abbot, being restricted by his monastic vows, would be forced to comply with rules of the present church."

209A. Vancouver Canadian-Italians have earned special recognition among the city's superstar lacrosse players. The field of talent is led by Canadian Lacrosse Hall of Fame members John Cervi and the late Mario Crema, both of whom have their names engraved on the Mann Cup. Much of the credit for introducing the game to their Prior Street *paesani*, however, goes to Lino (Chichi) and Marino Cervi. When the family moved to North Vancouver for a three-year period in the mid-'30s, the Cervi brothers watched with fascination as the neighbourhood Native Indians displayed their skill at lacrosse. On their return to the East End, the Cervis brought their sticks with them and the rest is history. Marino excelled at the sport, demonstrating his burgeoning talent as a member of Joe Philliponi's Eagle-Time Delivery junior lacrosse team in 1948. When Eagle-Time was eliminated, Marino was picked up by South Hill which won the Minto Cup that year. In 1949, he again played for Philliponi's team but this time along with Larry Crema, a naturally talented athlete. After the play-off round, the team emerged as champions taking home the Minto Cup from Owen Sound. The junior league cup win was number two for Marino Cervi. As senior players, this dynamite duo was joined by Joe Durante the year they captured the coveted Mann Cup for the Salmonbellies. The senior league cup was number two for Marino Cervi.

210. Gino Bosa also attended English classes at Culos's house. "I can tell you, I came from San Zenone, Italy, June 29, 1949 and a week later Tony Borsato got me and my cousin Vince Aballini to join the society. Then we went to Marino Culos with about 15 others to learn a little English. He was a good man for the society," stated Bosa.

Gino, sponsored by his uncle Augusto Bosa to come to Canada, was contracted to report for work at a farm in Powell River as per a provision of his application for landed immigrant status. Although he reported briefly to the farmer in Westview, he located permanently in Vancouver where he found employment at Mrs. Willman's Bakery. During the 33 years he worked at the bakery, Gino also became an entrepreneur. In his spare time he worked at Bosa's Italian imported food store on Victoria Drive in which he and his uncle Augusto were business partners.

210A. Father Bortignon, well known for his pro-Italy activities, didn't hesitate to illustrate his animosity toward Britain during the war. "He once told me he liked using several one-cent stamps on each envelope so as to pound his fist on the king's face more than once. I was aghast," remembered Midge Santaga.

Chapter 21

211. In the Italian Immigrants Assistance Centre's constitution, circa 1954, the organization's objectives are outlined. The objectives were to assist Italian immigrants in areas of a non-political nature, i.e., morally, culturally and materially. From a central recreational facility, information was available that would be beneficial to members as they began the process of integration into the Canadian society. In addition, immigrants, who paid a membership fee, would be helped in finding employment. The centre owned a billiard table, a Ping-Pong table and a piano.

According to the I.I.A.C. records, the directors for 1959 were Mike Greco, Giuliano Angeli, Luigi Galvani, Rina Bidin, and Amelia Mainardi. In 1960, Dr. Tommaso Merler, Angelo Gatto, Michele Castiglia, Giorgio Passeri, and Marino Culos served as directors.

In its March 28, 1962 issue, *L'Eco d'Italia* reported Angelo Gatto elected president, Giorgio Passeri, secretary and Jolanda Pitton, treasurer. Gatto announced that the Centro Immigranti would sponsor an Italian film festival at the Olympia Theatre courtesy of Mr. Martinelli, the theatre's manager.

212. Fiorenzo's grandfather, Francesco Benincasa, first came to America from Calabria in 1876. As a child, he lived and played in the area near the site where the *fratelli Bandieri* had been killed in 1848, a story he often repeated

throughout his life. Antonio Benincasa, Fiorenzo's father, spent a total of 55 years in the U.S. and Canada, going home only periodically to be with his wife and family—the numbers of which increased with each visit. An illness prevented Marietta Benincasa from immigrating to Canada with her husband.

213. In a special feature dated Feb. 10, 1934, on Italy Week, *The Vancouver Province* mentioned the names of enterprising Italo-Canadians. "Ranking in importance with wine is macaroni. There are two factories in Vancouver. Not only do they employ a considerable number of workers and supply needs of the province but they have found a market for B.C. macaroni abroad. Two men have been leaders in this development. Joseph Tosi, an old-time resident, is proprietor of the Famous Foods plant and Italo Rader is manager of the Catelli Macaroni Works."

Chapter 22

214. The founding members' list is reproduced in *Memorie Preziose*, the official programme booklet of the Sons of Italy's 50th anniversary banquet. Ruocco's membership information was obtained from the society's monthly payment records, circa 1906. The information to do with the late Cesare Anderlini was obtained in an interview with his daughter Nita Tuan.

215. Names of the contributors and advertisers of the *L'Eco d'Italia* from copies of B.C.'s only Italian-language newspaper, circa 1956.

216. Larry Crema was one of the Sacred Heart's outstanding soccer players who later signed to play for the famed Columbus team along with John Cervi the brilliant lacrosse player.

Sacred Heart also fielded a number of women's and men's softball teams. In 1952, the men's team travelled to Squamish to play a double-header. Although the scores have since been forgotten, the comedy relief stories attached to this event are vividly remembered by Midge Santaga. "We travelled by boat to the Howe Sound town with our coach Father Charles [Sinesi]. It was the only way one could get to Squamish in those days as the road from Vancouver didn't go all the way. Boy, was it a hot day. As the game progressed, my brother Nini became bored with the lack of activity in right field. All of sudden he mounted a kid's horse and galloped to home plate yelling, 'Time! time! time!' The startled ump looked up and asked, 'What the hell is this?' Jumping off the horse, Nini replied, 'Christ, it's hot out there.' Before the umpire could think of the appropriate action to take, Nini was again on the horse riding back to right field to

resume his position. The good-natured umpire, cheered by the laughter and good-fellowship, allowed the incident to pass unchallenged," recalled Santaga.

"So, after we played the double-header, we boarded the bus that would take us to the boat. Soon, prankster Danny Owens switched on the ignition. 'Hey this thing runs.' And away we go! He stopped at bus stops to pick up a number of old ladies and drove them right to their doorsteps. 'What a gentleman,' one exclaimed. When we returned to the hotel, the Mounties were waiting for us. Poor Father Charles! He kept trying to convince the RCMP to let us go. 'But these guys are good boys, please believe me they are truly fine boys,' persisted the Stigmatine priest. As for Owens, he finally admitted to having been the driver. Although the police said charges would be laid nothing ever came of it," chuckled Santaga.

216A. Antonio V. Spada's work, *The Italians in Canada*, was published by Italo-Canadian Ethnic and Historical Research Centre, Montreal, Quebec. Reference to Marino Culos as president of the Comitato Attivita' Italiane appears on page 368.

217. Membership list from the Comitato files and from Marino Culos's personal papers. In 1957, Marino wrote to Angelo Branca about the Comitato Attivita' Italiane, "As previously stated the members wish you to be the Comitato's speaker [at its second annual banquet and dance] and look forward to your discourse in the English language. "The Comitato was organized in December 1956 and, in my opinion, it was your approval which clinched it after the support given by the move by Mr. [Giovanni] D'Appolonia."

218. Excerpts from a letter by Judge Branca reproduced in a souvenir booklet [co-edited by Ray Culos and Mario Caravetta] commemorating the 50th anniversary of Rev. Joseph Della-Torre as a Salesian priest, September 1983.

219. By this time, Nino Sala, co-operator of the Nino Rose Cafe, was well established as a foremost caterer in the Italian community. The author interviewed the late Nino Sala in June 1979 for an article written for *L'Eco d'Italia*. Mr. Sala, age 74, is quoted as stating, "I attribute our success to two important factors. First, it was Rosina [Mrs. Sala]. She was 90% responsible for making the business venture work and secondly to the good fortune we had in having an extremely fine person for our landlord." He was referring to Girardo Di Fonzo, who by the simple act of a hand shake, sealed an agreement to remodel the premises so as to provide space for a large dining area which the Salas were convinced held the key to their future success.

Nino was working for an Italian steamship line when he came to Vancouver in 1930. He fell in love with the city and did not report back to his ship at the end of his shore-leave. Instead he approached Achille Pini who gave him his first job in the restaurant business. In 1939, he opened Time to Eat Cafe on Robson Street. In 1943, he married Rosina Signori and together they managed the Latin Quarter Supper Club for a number of years.

220. There were other prominent *friulani* who contributed to the Fogolar's organization including Peter Olivieri, owner of Olivieri's Ravioli Store. In 1957 he began producing ravioli as his main pasta item which ultimately accounted for his major success as a pasta manufacturer from his Commercial Drive outlet.

Chapter 23

221. In his letter to Frank Iuele dated Dec. 7, 1959, Marino Culos also informed the immediate past president that only 15 members turned out for the election-of-officers meeting which returned Luigi Barone as president for a second term.

222. Marino Culos's campaign was vocal, visual and vibrant. Many people campaigned with great determination in an attempt to elect the district's first Italian candidate. Grant Lenfesty, co-owner of Handy Meat Market, and original candidate-favourite of the Liberal Party, worked tirelessly for his good friend Marino. Angelo Branca marshalled the business community and influential people from within and without the Liberal Party in support of Marino's campaign.

223. At the time, Elvira Pastorini was president and Pierino Mori, editor. The Italian newspaper was running a series of Varsity Theatre advertisements publicizing the movie *Two Women* directed by Vittorio De Sica and starring Oscar-winner Sophia Loren.

224. Branca's daughter Judge Dolores Holmes was admitted to the Bar in 1953 and conducted a general practice in her father's law firm. At that time there were very few female barristers practicing law and in this regard Dolores Holmes was a pioneer advocate. She was appointed to the Bench in 1975 and continues to administer her duties from the Provincial Court facilities in Burnaby, British Columbia.

225. Excerpts from Letters to the Editor, dated May 31, 1963, as published in *L'Eco d'Italia*. The controversy over the 'loss' of the Sala Veneta, i.e., Hastings Auditorium continued to affect the community's resolve in supporting a fund-raising effort. Filippo Branca's success in leading the Veneta Society's remarkable achievement in 1928 was

marred by the adverse economic conditions prevalent during the Depression. The net result of bad economic times was the Veneta's inability to meet its financial obligations. Thus, a run on the sale of shares in the Silver Slipper Hall (Hastings Auditorium) causing some investors within the Italian community to incur a financial loss.

The sense of insecurity which prevailed during the Depression and the poor economic climate contributed to the collapse of the Silver Slipper Hall enterprise. "You had to be there, at the time, in order to appreciate what was happening," stated Judge Holmes. "That's where my dad's problem with mortgages began. The Veneta lost the Silver Slipper because they couldn't afford the mortgage payment. And that's why, of course, he was adamant that this building [as constructed and financed through demand-loan mortgages by the Italian Cultural Centre Society] should be self-supporting," she concluded.

In the 1960s, Angelo Branca publicly stated his unwillingness to commence construction of an Italian hall facility until financing had been secured.

226. Lisa Negrin has vivid memories of the collapse of the Silver Slipper venture. "The Vancouver Italian-Canadian Ladies' League (formerly affiliated with the Societa' Veneta) had $800 in Silver Slipper shares. I don't know how they lost the money, it just fell through and we didn't know the details. No one knew any better. They just let it go. Our seniors [executive members] didn't know English. By the time we got in [Negrin, born in Vancouver, was elected president of the VICS's Lega in 1940], the crisis had blown over."

227. The realization that some of the community's wealthy Italians could not be enticed to make a pledge led to Fabris's decision to cancel the fund drive. Also, it became clear that only a minimal number of people were interested in pledging financial support towards the acquisition of an Italian hall. These two factors contributed significantly to the decision to end the campaign. Details of this item were obtained from the Comitato's minutes.

228. The Honourary Membership certificates were printed by Marino Culos on his manual printing press. He also regularly published many of the society's flyers, raffle books and banquet tickets.

229. Angelo Branca earned a reputation for being one of Vancouver's most successful criminal lawyers. As detailed by Vincent Moore, author of *Angelo Branca 'The Gladiator of the Courts'*, Branca defended 63 persons charged with murder, of whom only four were convicted.

Only two of his clients went to the gallows. He became a King's Counsel in 1952 a distinction given to lawyers who had conducted themselves with honour, decorum and integrity. Today, a Queen's Counsel is accorded specific privileges. For example, the distinction entitles the barrister to 'jump' those on the list waiting to have their cases called. In addition to having this advantage, Q.C.s are placed on a shorter list made up of lawyers in their peer group. In 1963 Judge Branca was appointed to the Supreme Court of British Columbia, Trial Division. Later he was made a judge of the Court of Appeal. "So, he was there for two years, and to be quite honest, he really liked it there. Because he liked the people and when you get to the Court of Appeal it is a rarefied atmosphere. If you look at the statistics, the greatest number of cases are in the Provincial Court. And I mean it's like 93% of all cases. Maybe a thousand go to the Court of Appeal, usually argued by lawyers. So, one doesn't see the people one is dealing with," stated Judge Holmes.

230. The Comitato existed throughout the mid-1960s to the time the old societies merged to form the Confratellanza Italo-Canadese. In the minutes of the Feb. 1, 1965 meeting, the active associations and representatives were as follows: Antonio Fabris, president (Comitato Attivita' Italiane); Cesare Tofini (Circolo Meridionale), vice-president; and Angelo Gatto, interim Italian consul. Representing the Sons of Italy were Luigi Barone, Marino Culos, Zefferino Bordignon, and John Savio. President Phyllis Culos represented the Lega affiliated with the Sons of Italy. F. Pistilli, Tony Borsato and G. Mangiardo were in attendance for the Veneta as were that society's women representatives, Enrichetta Benetti, Mrs. Borsato, and Mrs. Pistilli. The men representing the Vancouver Italian-Canadian Society were Joe Ghini, A. Trevisol and Schiavon. Their Lega reps were America Bianco, Cecilia Zanon and Mrs. Russo. Delegates Messrs. Altan and Infanti were there for Famee Furlane and Mario Brunoro and Luigi Zanatta for the Italian Bicycle Club. Prof. G. Rimanelli and Dr. Rachele Giese were the spokespersons for Societa' Dante Alighieri. The main business that evening was to conduct elections, the results of which included Fabris being re-elected president and Tofini being elected vice-president.

231. In conversation with Marino Culos it became clear that he was against Branca's "intrusion" in the affairs of the Sons of Italy. Bruno Girardi had not liked Angelo Branca since the 1940 internment crisis, a view he expressed in no uncertain terms during an interview conducted by the author.

232. Following the death of Tony Borsato, Oct. 21, 1973, Judge Angelo Branca offered the following eulogy: (transla-

tion) "About two weeks ago a terrible thing happened in the Vancouver Italian community. The community lost one of its most valued citizens, Paolo Antonio Borsato. He was exemplary as a father and husband and was a very generous Christian citizen. He was always prepared to help anybody but especially members of his family and the Confratellanza society which he loved and served so well.

"He emigrated to Canada from the province of Treviso, Italy where he was born May 23, 1897. Paolo [Tony] was 16 years old when he arrived in Canada with his brother, John, who was a year older. He had the pioneer spirit typical of Italian immigrants coming to Canada in search of a new life for themselves and their families.

"Paolo settled in Ocean Falls after which he moved to Trail in 1935. During the eight years he resided in the Kootenays, he established the 'Rossland Avenue Meat Market'. Once in Vancouver, he went to work for Crown Zellerbach Canada Ltd. where he remained employed until his retirement.

"In 1971, he and his wife, Rita, celebrated their 50th wedding anniversary.

"Paolo was a devoted and loving husband who loved his children and enjoyed his home and garden. He was a good citizen, worked hard for his church and was always very active in the Societa' Veneta. He was a dependable member of the club and always went by the society's rules. His unfortunate death was due to injuries sustained in a car accident which occurred while he was on an errand for the Confratellanza. He will be sadly missed."

In an article written by the author for L'Eco d'Italia, June 21, 1979, Nino Sala is quoted as describing Tony Borsato, "In a way, he was Mr. Veneta in those days [late 1950s] for he succeeded in bringing in more members into the [Veneta] organization than any other member of his administration."

233. Excerpt from a letter Marino Culos wrote to Gregorio Fuoco in 1966. Fuoco returned to Italy at the insistence of his wife who had been originally 'left behind' in Italy while Gregorio lived in Vancouver during the 1930s. The Second World War prevented her from immigrating to Canada until after the war.

234. Excerpts from the society's minute book and from obituaries appearing in L'Eco d'Italia.

The author was personally aware of the close friendship which existed between Santo Pasqualini and Marino Culos.

Details of Luigi Palazzini's singing prowess and his tile company were obtained during an interview with Clara Vagnini Arduini.

In an article published in The Vancouver Daily Province, circa 1930, Luigi Palazzini was identified as "Italian Tenor

Will Be Featured In Radio Concert at Station CKCD Tonight. Mr. Palazzini, who has a voice of fine quality, began studying his art in Vancouver under the late Signor d'Auria and completed his training in the Rossini Conservatory, Italy."

235. In the view of Marino Culos, Felice Cianci was one of the pillars of the Sons of Italy, a sentiment shared by most other active members of the society.

236. The following is a list of Italians who owned hotels and/or beer parlours, as supplied by Louie Valente and Johnny Alvaro:

Family Name	Hotels
Alvaro, Joe and sons Nick, Meco, John and Frank	London, Port Arms, New Burrard, Terminal, Tourist and Villa
Anderlini, Cesare	Europe
Angelotti, Peter	Savoy, Invermay
Berardino, Wm.	Grandview
Berrettoni, Charlie	Rainier
Berrettoni, Romeo	Marr
Brandolini, Jack	Empire, Premier
Brandolini, Gillie	Melbourne
Calori, Angelo	Europe
Caravetta, Ralph	Dominion
Carline, Roy	Minto, Cambie
Carrelli, Giovanni	Klondike, Lougheed
Cianci, Antonio	Louvre
Cillis, George	Broadway, St. Helen's
Culos, Antonio	Europe
Gallia, Antonio	St. Alice
Giovando, Pete	Stratford
Girone, Paul	Broadway
Iaci, Dominic and Frank	Martineque, American
Marchese, Frank	West Hotel
Marino, Aristodemo	Dodson
Minichiello, Sam	Savoy, Dodson
Minichiello, Peter & Art	Dodson
Nadalin, Joe	Columbia, Pennsylvania
Paletti, Leo	Broadway
Penway, Charlie	Anchor, Columbia
Pettovello, Louie	Dodson
Piscatelli, Frank	Carleton
Reda, Charlie	Palace
Rossi, Louis	American, Broadway, Turf, Carleton, Standard
Rossi, Michele	Strand
Rossi, Ralph	Manitoba
Ruocco, W.G.	Europe, Palace
Rusconi, Johnny	Broadway
Tha, John	Stratford
Tonelli, Jack	Pennsylvania, Carleton
Valente, Louie	Astoria

Index